WITCH
anthology

edited by

Michelle Tea

DOPAMINE
BOOKS AND PRINTED MATTER

Published by DOPAMINE
301 N. Kenwood St, Glendale, CA 91206
www.dopaminepress.org

Special thanks to Katie Fricas

Covert Art: Edgar Fabián Frías
Layout & Design: Brooke Palmieri

10 9 8 7 6 5 4 3 2 1

ISBN: 978-1-63590-245-7

Distributed by the MIT Press, Cambridge, Mass., and London, England.
Printed in the United States of America

Contents

Michelle Tea

Introduction

I believe that many people—in particular many women and femmes, queer and trans people, artists of all kinds—are quite naturally witches, whether or not they choose to do anything about it. Beyond these latent sorcerers, I think lots of folks experience, on occasion, twinges of the uncanny, waves of witchiness, the faint call of whatever lies beyond. In crafting this collection, while I absolutely did want to hear from witch-identified witches, with a practice they have learned from and grown within, I also was soliciting work from writers whose natural occult vibes may be somewhat amorphous and undefined, as well as those who simply have an affinity for such energy, and allow it to peek through within their work. The result, I hoped, was a collection that not only focused on actual traditions and lives spent honoring the mystical, but the way that magic operates as a backbeat to life, generally—if you are fortunate enough to be somewhat attuned.

*

If I were to have written this intro even a month ago, I would not have identified, personally, as a hereditary witch. But as of late, my 74-year-old mother, who I live with, shocked me by revealing that she thinks she might be a witch. She thinks she might be Pagan. She's been looking into it on her phone, and learning about it. She felt she needed some help arranging an altar in her bedroom—a small space already cluttered as an occult shop with knickknacks and photos of loved ones, as well as the cremains of three individuals no longer with us. I did my best to explain the elemental

1

tradition, as well as urge her to follow her fancy. From my office I hauled a stack of books it took two trips to bring her; she has especially loved Mya Spalter's *Enchantments*, as well as Judika Illes' *Encyclopedia of 5,000 Spells* (and low-key shamed me when I couldn't recall exactly which, if any of them, I've performed). A Scorpio, her procession into witchcraft has been mostly private, though she has joined an online coven of Facebook witches from Ireland. Particularly it may be the recovering and reclaiming of pre-Christian Irish spiritual traditions that feels most inspiring to her. With the holiday season ahead of us, I feel confident that I finally have someone to conspire some Yule observances with.

If I began my own magical practices decades before my mother initiated hers, am I still a hereditary witch? After all, I do trace the piquing of my witchy curiosity to my mother's Linda Goodman astrology books, her hushed discussions of reincarnation and the mystical possibilities of dreams. Is there a witch *gene*, one that found its full expression in me early on but took until the heartbreaking, infuriating second election of Tr*mp to kick madly into action within my mother's physiology. Finding herself desperately confounded, and consumed with such anger she knew she needed a spiritual outlet, my mom found the Church—so much of the engineer of her/our current woe—to be utterly bankrupt. Instinctively, she turned to where so many of us craving a structural outlet for our spiritual desires now turn. To the past made new, to traditions earth and life-affirming, ancient enough to connect us with an idea of place on this planet but individualistic and anarchic enough to welcome our own tweaks and re-writes. A tradition that welcomes, was formed by, the energies of women, feminists, freaks, misfits, sensitives, queers, trans folk and in betweens—in-between not just gender, but in-between worlds, in-between binary systems of all sorts. A tradition that welcomes the undoing of colonialism, a tradition that is anti-racist, a tradition whose many forms existed in all places prior to imperialism and Christianity's violence. A place haunted by ancestors, chosen and fleshly, that have been awaiting our return.

If I do feel like a hereditary witch it is also because the ancestors I feel are my chosen lineage—witchy chicks like Cookie Mueller and Vali Myers; mysterious powerhouses like Marjorie Cameron and Marie LaVeau; women compelled to follow their shadows, like the many Scarlet Women of Thelema, like Jane Mansfield and her fatal foray into the Satanic. Like from uber-crone Mother Shipton to Tituba, the enslaved folk magician of Salem. While none of them *raised* me into witchcraft the way a true hereditary witch is reared, I do see in them a familial conspiracy to keep me on a particular path, bringing into my life the others I need to conspire with, witches all, one way or another, and not the least of them, my very own mother!

And so I dedicate this book to her, Theresa Louise, a champion Scorpio in her marvelous ability to transform and transcend, like the final, eagle incarnation of the sign, rising ever higher towards truth and justice, regardless of how painful the views from such perches often are. I am proud of her, and proud to be her daughter.

Yumi Sakugawa

Witch Portal

THIS IS A PORTAL CONNECTING YOU TO ALL OTHER WITCHES, PRIESTESSES, MAGICIANS, ALCHEMISTS, WIZARDS, SHAMANS, CREATORS, DIVINE WEIRDOS WHO HAVE, WHO ARE, AND WHO WILL GAZE INTO THIS AS WELL. BREATHE IN THE POWERFUL BLESSING SOMEONE LEFT YOU IN THE PORTAL AND BREATHE OUT A POWERFUL BLESSING FOR SOMEONE ELSE. REPEAT AS OFTEN AS NEEDED. THEN WHISPER INSIDE AN AUDACIOUS VISION OF LIBERATION FOR ALL AND LET THAT BE BLESSED AS WELL. CAN YOU FEEL THE SILVER MOONLIT THREAD CONNECTING US ALL TOGETHER RIGHT THIS MOMENT? ANYTHING AND EVERYTHING IS POSSIBLE WHEN WE GATHER. REMEMBER THIS, AND REMEMBER AGAIN.

Kathe Izzo

The Sublime

I am grateful that I do not have the energy to be more exciting
The stories that have formed me are weary of waiting

Ever forward, baby steps
Ever forward we are learning how to be together
Ever forward we just do it again and again and see what happens
Love

Our nervous systems have been formed by the power over
The undercurrent, the button of the belly, the enteric plexus, the abyss
Connects us to the rot of the sublime

Practice gives us capacity
I had a date with God tonight
I picked up a passport
Gold is our thread

I'm going to be clumsy.
I'm going to get shit wrong.

This is the current state of affairs.

I teach yoga, I say something I can't remember. Someone sighs.

I think this is an accident. I focus more deeply. I say something else. They
sigh again.
I feel their forehead. Someone has to for God's sake.
I can feel the waterfall moving through them.
That means there are other free travelers from the future around.

When did the word healer starts to sound worse than the disease
I don't want to be healed
I want my mother
Mommy

You said I was Mother of the Void
I thought this was sexy
I didn't realize that this exhausting state of wonder
was the rest of my life

There is one more thing I would like to show you
This day's sigh
The fact that ghetto now means both broken and somehow blessed

Before me the palace of salt where the truck awaits
Behind me the world of ordinary clutter

All I want is a snack.
A bit of loose time.
My personal liberation front.
The state of affairs that is mine.

No, you actually don't know me.
This is the borderline.

Emilia Richeson-Valiente

Fiercely Noncompetitive Dance Aerobics Witchery

LETTER TO A PONY

Dear Emilia,

    I'm wondering if you have any tips for me to get over my own insecurity and get back into exercising. I lost my job last year because of Covid, and since then I've been so depressed and upset with my body that I haven't been able to even look at myself, let alone move. I see videos of you, and the videos you share, and everyone looks so happy and confident! I wish I could be like that again. If you have any tips on what could help me get there, I'd be so grateful.

Dear Anonymous Pony,

    Thanks so much for reaching out and sharing what's going on for you and your relationship to your body. I relate to what you wrote, and I'm glad to share things that have helped me feel more at home in my body.

    Pony Sweat's core value is having a practice that is nourishing, not punishing. I believe that our attitudes, beliefs, and behaviors change with gentleness, tenderness, and self-compassion. I also know it can feel impossible to access any of that for myself. So, I just kept practicing, exploring, and experimenting with those guiding principles.

Pony Sweat started as a ritual of being in my body in a way that felt nourishing and true to myself. Back then it was making up dance routines by myself to songs that I loved. To anyone struggling with a movement practice, I recommend approaching it with as much curiosity as you can muster and to follow your imagination and desire (both are uniquely yours! No one else's!!). Maybe you choose three songs to dance to by yourself every day or once a week. Or stretch on the floor and watch Buffy! Can you stretch and move in a way that's not prescribed or defined by someone else? Can you trust that you are doing it "right" if it helps you feel more connected to your body?

Are you wondering what "connected to your body" feels like? For me, my mental chatter slows, my breath deepens, I feel the earth underneath me, and I am more aware of my surroundings. I see more, hear more, smell more, feel more, taste more. I am more in reality (which sometimes feels painful, but never as painful as avoiding it). I have a greater sense of self-trust when I'm connected to my body. I am in less fear. This experience exists on a spectrum; sometimes the shift happens quickly and is big, and sometimes it's more subtle and slow.

Our bodies are our vessels and the longest relationships we will ever have. They want safety, pleasure, and care. It is not our fault that we might approach our bodies with punishment, harshness, and perfectionism.. We internalize so many lies and harmful beliefs from the moment we are born. It is important to remember that participating in any movement practice is simply availing yourself to a process. If we surrender to the magic of process, we can trust that change will happen.

I encourage you to practice tenderness one day or one moment at a time. Maybe put a hand on your heart and belly, breathing into these magnificent spaces which DON'T STOP working for us all day long!

Anyway, I hope some of this resonates with you and is helpful. Sending you and your body so much love.

*

Welcome to Pony Sweat, a fiercely noncompetitive dance aerobics practice! I started Pony Sweat in 2014 and coined the phrase "fiercely noncompetitive" to describe the container for an emotive, cathartic movement practice. The competitive culture most of us live in day-to-day is not supportive to liberatory, playful, and revelatory movement practices. I craved a very specific container that would allow and inspire me to connect with my body and express myself through dance and music. I suspected that if I wanted it, others did too. So, I created it with the encouragement of dear friends who helped me when I felt afraid to do the thing I wanted most. I also had assistance from my Capricorn sun, Aquarius rising, and Mars in Aquarius, plus Jupiter in Sagittarius and the Magician as my Soul Card!

We are fiercely noncompetitive with each other when we defy compare-and-despair thinking, when we see each of our authentic self-expressions as branches of interdependence, and when we allow ourselves and others to be visible in the vulnerable stages of Trying. We are fiercely noncompetitive with ourselves when we don't have to be the best at something in order to do it, and when we understand we don't even have to be doing our best in order to participate. There's nothing to win or lose in a fiercely noncompetitive container, just more of ourselves to express. It's an invitation to follow curiosity and desire and to defy the self-judgment so many of us spend our days in.

When I started Pony Sweat, I was not a dancer, athlete, teacher, writer, or an aerobics-witch. Pony Sweat initiated me into those roles. Over the last decade, I conceived and accumulated philosophies, rituals, and techniques that have led me and others to greater self-knowledge, self-expression, and belonging and connection with ourselves and others! All my life, I desperately sought a relationship with my body that was fun, playful, free, and expressive. I tried many ways to do this, including strategies to get OUT of my body, and discovered that dance aerobics offered an inspiring pathway IN, and a connection that I hadn't even imagined possible.

People tell me, "Pony Sweat changed my life." I tell them, "I know, it changed mine too!" That is the power of participating in dance ritual, in showing up and doing the things you have curiosity and desire about, and in approaching movement with a set of intentions to deepen embodiment and expand expression. That + endorphins + the time and space carved out for it = life-changing outcomes. That is alchemy, that is science, that is spellcasting, that is magic!

FUCK THE MOVES
Now that we are here, I will offer some patterns of movement to songs that I love that I hope you love too! Everything that I demonstrate is meant to be supportive and suggestive. Notice what patterns feel good in your body, feel fun/playful/hot/connective, or notice what patterns you feel curious about, what feels strange and interesting. If something feels physically painful, don't do it! If a move brings up shame or debilitating discouragement, fuck it! We are not here to achieve idealized body shapes. We are here to participate in the ancient practice of connecting to music

with our bodies in a group of people. Our souls already know how to do this! Let our bodies remember!! Fuck the Moves!

"Fuck the Moves" reminds us that nothing is mandatory and to follow what we want to do instead of what we think we SHOULD do or are supposed to do. It calls in our inherent autonomy. Our ability to Fuck the Moves is not ever-present, not always obvious or the most accessible choice for many of us. Fiercely noncompetitive dance aerobics can be a technology for Fuck the Moves. It's a site for application.

I wanted to be a dancer my whole life but I thought that to be a dancer, I had to learn how to move like my teachers. Or like the people in the front row of class. I thought that dancing had to look like in the dancing in my favorite movies. What did Jennifer Beals's character do before we met her in Flashdance to become this dance artiste? What strategy could I possibly employ that would take me to a country club with an underground, sexy dancing party AND to a desperate scenario that would make ME a hero, forcing the hottest dance teacher on the planet to take me on and mentor me à la *Dirty Dancing*? I had no idea. I didn't even know what questions to ask, and I already sensed that I didn't have the physical, mental, emotional, environmental, or financial resources to achieve what I was seeing on-screen. It never occurred to me, growing up and well into my adulthood, that dance class is a place to learn how *my* body moves, what it likes and doesn't like, or what inspires it to persevere from a place of desire instead of perfectionism.

"Fuck the Moves" is an incantation! It summons our most courageous parts to practice TRYING. It transforms a setting where a teacher stands at the front and leads with the presumption that we follow/imitate/emulate into a setting where the demonstration is merely an invitation, a suggestion, and a reveal. "This is something my body likes to do during this part of the song. Does your body want to do that too?"

In *Tarot for Change*, Jessica Dore writes of the Magician card, "When we do the opposite of what our programming tells us to do, we cross the threshold from the habitual to the magical."

Fuck the Moves is our call as we cross!

MIRROR MAGIC
I am thinking of my close friends who cannot and will not do movement in front of mirrors; maybe you, dear reader, also have that boundary. That is totally being fiercely noncompetitive with yourself, Fucking the Moves, in which you are now an expert... WAY 2 GO! Feel free to skip the

rest of this section if you choose to! AND/BUT, if you have any curiosity about mirror-play and feel that there is permission to explore it with my guidance, you can start by hanging lace or some other translucent fabric over your mirror. You can experiment with low light, candlelight (safely), or a colored lightbulb. These are gentle ways to approach your reflection.

I love the mirrors in dance studios and the one I have at home. I clean it regularly and use my finger and spit to draw a pentacle in the corner, like my witch friend, Isaac, showed me. As a big fan of Fantasy and Sci-Fi genres, I see mirrors as portals or windows to other times, realms, and dimensions. They literally *do not* reflect us as we really are, or even how others see us, so why not use them to project the music video fantasy version of ourselves? Why not practice seeing ourselves how we want to be seen, or acting as if we already embody the person we know ourselves to be deep down?

Witches teach us to use mirrors to cast spells or to scry. There are spells where you gaze into your reflection and summon how you want others to see you or incant words of affirmation you long to hear. So many of us just want to be seen for who we are! We seek others to ease our longing so much that we forget: we can ask ourselves for that witnessing instead! YOU can behold YOU. As a lonely kid who had a lot of big feelings I didn't know how to express to others, I subconsciously understood this. Dancing in front of my bedroom mirror made me feel less alone, it made me feel seen! We can continue this ritual as adults too.

It is suggested that you prepare the body for a spell, maybe by washing your face and hands or putting something on that makes you feel good, like a piece of jewelry, cologne, a leather jacket (a thrifted or vegan leather jacket, of course, my gods!) or some lipstick. You can put on a certain color to pay homage to a particular planet you want to work with. In this way, we prepare our vessels for ritual and transformation, we honor the energies and powers working with us, and we "act as if" we are already embodying this more authentic version of ourselves. What does that self wear?

As a dance aerobics instructor witch, I tell folks, "Outfits help!" I'll tell you why: it's because of magic! It's not because you need to buy more things or look like someone else. It's because the more we treat movement as ritual, the more intentionally we make it about play and pleasure, the more powerful the catharsis and subsequent transmutation of our realities! The Goddess wants us to like what we are wearing. (Maybe that's what "Cleanliness is next to godliness" is about—not as much to do with hygiene than as liking your outfit?)

How we show up for a ritual determines its impact. Wear things you LIKE, or are excited about, or an outfit that scares you a little in a good way! That might include doing aerobics in your sweatpants, in your pajamas, or in your jeans (nothing is more punk than showing up to workout in jeans, btw). Conversely, maybe allowing yourself to NOT dress up is the powerful choice and intention. I come from a long line of all-day pajama wearers and learned along the way that this may signal poor mental health. BUT/AND I would like to argue for the *pleasure* I get from staying in my pajamas. Like sure, if it's been more than a few days, perhaps there's a reason to reach out to my therapist. But, hell, ever heard of a pajama PARTY?! I'm having one right now as I write this, and you better believe I've made up countless aerobics' routines in front of my mirror, in my 'jams, witnessing myself making a choice that supports my desire.

I started Pony Sweat wearing the outfits I still wear to this day because I wanted to *be seen* as a dancer. So, I dressed up to be seen—by myself—as a dancer. Not the dancers I saw in real life, but the ones I fantasized about as a kid. The dancers in *A Chorus Line* with shimmery tights, cut-off tops, and high-cut dance briefs. I dress up for me. Maybe your dancer archetype wears a Victorian gown and corset, or a disco bodysuit, or a blackbubble-space-suit à la Missy Elliott, or full cowboi regalia. Whatever it is, whoever they are, dress as THEM. Who says what a dancer is supposed to look like? We are creating a new world to enter, and dancers look like all kinds of people. If you are doing mirror magic you wanna dress like you already are the person that you are becoming in the reality, that you are creating with your imagination, energies, breath, and sweat.

I jokingly call what I do "dancer cosplay." Very seriously though, it is Magic.

Here's how the spell worked: I embodied my childhood fantasy of being a dancer with the help of outfits and music. I danced to my favorite songs in front of my bedroom mirror and dance studio mirrors, invoking rehearsal montages from *Dirty Dancing* and *Fame*. I surrendered to my imagination and the possibility and presence of other timelines/lifetimes/multiverses across the spiral. I did this again and again and then I BECAME a dancer in this lifetime, in this reality, on this side of the mirror! MIRROR MAGIC WORKS, Y'ALL!

Sure, some might reason that I became a dancer by dancing. But I needed ritual to help me persevere through the painful self-doubt and self-consciousness, and magic to counter the rational mind that has been corrupted by capitalistic ideas that poison my true nature. My brain would tell me all the reasons I was not a dancer, that actually I was a waitress and a nanny, but my body has ALWAYS said, *I AM a dancer!* Luckily, I believed that I could create new realities by exerting my own efforts with the help of bigger/deeper/higher powers. I have always believed in magic.

When we surrender to this thought experiment and devote our bodies to practice, spending time in this new reality we create, our thinking begins to change, more easily refuting the old false stories we're told. Through the repetition of this ritual our perception shifts, we are transformed, and our lives change. Pony Sweat is life-changing because there is magic at work!

AEROBICS SPELLS TOGETHER + ALONE, ACROSS THE SPIRAL

You will need: a space to create a container, a way to play and feel music, water, an outfit or adornment, a fiercely noncompetitive attitude. Optional ingredients: mirror, candle, plant-matter to burn, party lights.

Do this with others or by yourself. It's part of the transformation and alchemy to do it both ways. Notice how it feels alone. Then see if you can summon those same brave parts that emerge when no one is watching in a room filled with other people. Remember that your courage helps the person next to you be courageous!

The format of dance aerobics is this: everything you do on one side, or in one direction, you repeat on the other side. This format is comforting, easier to learn than combinations, and you will discover a pattern and a puzzle that can be solved, learned, or adapted. Whatever pattern you did for the first verse, do again for the second and the third. You'll learn what's coming. Your body prepares to repeat, to practice, to try, or to decide to do something else entirely! So many chances to practice changing your mind!

TOGETHER

Come in come in come in! We are in a dance studio. A big open space that invites your body to stretch, to throw itself to the ground, to leap and bound, to twirl, to toss, to TRY. The air is thick with the distinctive smell of sweat-soaked floorboards. See a wall of mirrors reflecting the room and bodies, doubling the space, expanding the physical container. Hear the upbeat music playing, an anticipatory feeling as folks find the spots they wanna dance in, sit on the ground and stretch. Some people chat. Others are alone, together. There are queers here, the gender spectrum is present, ages vary. Some folks with haircuts, others in ponytails. People proudly wear their favorite band T-shirts over basketball shorts or leggings. Someone in a Yoko Ono shirt, a Dmode tour T-shirt. Grace Jones,

Madonna, Deerhoof, Bikini Kill, The Cure. These are bands that we dance to in class, then honor further by wearing their sacred merch. Band shirts are signifiers, points of connection. "I love your shirt!" "I was at that show too!" Some wear leotards, or lollies (dance briefs) over tights. It is fiercely noncompetitive, not a fashion show. People are dressed as themselves, or a part of themselves they want to express.

People dance in rows; the front row holds space for the back row because there is enough space when we share it. Some Ponies whoop and holler, some grin and chew gum. There are Ponies slinking, others bouncing, some thrash, and one shakes their hair in their face with their eyes closed. Some Ponies fuck the moves and hold court in the back corner, goth club style. One twirls and slides across the floor near the front. Another struts and flips their hair. Everyone moves differently, with moments of synchronization. Like dolphins, or birds! They're Ponies!

ALONE
When I pony at home, making mixtapes and creating routines, I light a candle and connect to the spiral, which is how I envision Space + Time. Within it exists an abundance of energies that humxns share in dance clubs, dance studios, villages, community rec spaces, punk shows, and house parties. Combined with the energy from all the Ponies who have come together in-person and online to do this practice, and we tap into this lineage with our intentions, imaginations, and deep reverence. I have pictures of my favorite musicians whose songs help me make sense of my inner-life and inspire me to create. Candles with Prince and Robert Smith on them, a ripped magazine photo of George Michael, a thrift-store framed late 80s Madonna, printed video stills of Janet Jackson and Kate Bush. A chunk of lapis lazuli, a silk rose, and a small amethyst tower. I ask my guides to help me be brave and truthful in my exploration, and I whisper the words that help us begin:

ACROSS THE SPIRAL!
We practice anti-perfectionism and avail ourselves to the messiness of discovery. We practice staying with our bodies. We take what we like and fuck the rest.

We use these words to express our deepest intentions for this practice. We invoke the supportive energies of Divine, Prince, Tina Turner, Sinead, Lux Interior, _____ + _____. Let's do this! <3

Excerpt from a Mixtape. Side A, Song 3.
"I Touch Roses" by Book of Love
Suggestion: Warming up!
Consider Science! Consider Magic!

Furl and unfurl. Curl up. Then expand. Feel into your center and blossom from there. Take your time!

When you're ready, stand in a wide stance with your feet slightly turned out. Spread your feet on the ground and notice the press of the earth into the soles of your feet. Notice your tailbone hanging out between your feet.

Slowly thrust your pelvis back and forth, feeling a pleasant stretch in your lower back and hip flexors. Knees are softly bent, and the muscles around your bellybutton support this movement.

Take some hip rolls by tracing circles on the floor with your tailbone.

Now trace infinity. Both directions! You are embodying Science AND Magic!

Shake out your legs!

Now roll your shoulders. Back and forth, together or alternating.

Lift your fingertips to your shoulders and trace some circles with your elbows.

Trace your name (the name you like or wish to be called) with your elbow on your dominant side and your nondominant side Trace it fast and slow. Imagine your name being written in the air in your favorite neon color!

Shake out your arms and shoulders.

Draw the back of your bellybutton to the back of your spine and from the support of your center, shift your ribcage to the right, then thrust forward, then left, then round your back.

Following that same path, rrrrrrrrrolll it out. Circling your torso, tracing circles from your heart space. Imagine you are clearing away the cobwebs of your sorrow.

How's that body roll? Describe it! Over the years, words Ponies have used include: creaky, croaky, fucking sad, heat-dome, hungry, and delicious. Let it be named!!

Excerpt from Mixtape. Side A, Song 6.
"Mind Your Own Business" by Delta 5
Suggestion: 32 Counts for Boundary-Setting

Delta 5's "Mind Your Own Business" asks us to examine the current state of our physical, energetic, and emotional boundaries. Sometimes I get caught up in what other people think about me. I get worried about another person's behavior and obsessively try to change it, thinking that I'm being helpful when it is just controlling. These may be signals that I need some boundary setting and to mind my own business! Sometimes people really want to help and start doing things that they think are helpful even though I didn't ask for their help, and the help they're giving is not actually helping me. That's probably a sign I might need to ask THEM to mind their own business.

It can be confusing! Let's explore with our bodies.

First, allow your feet and hips to settle into that beat and bassline. C'mon!

As you're dancing, prioritize a playful and carefree attitude in your bottom half. How ever that may express itself in your body today. Maybe it's twisty or bouncy, or droopy or sloopy. Let your tailbone decide!

With your top half, prioritize protectiveness. Strong center. Gaze is direct and you can see everything around you. Feel the space around your body widen and expand in an impenetrable bubble, how big is your bubble? Some days it might need to be bigger than other days.

Here's a little 32 count combo for the verse if you choose to!

Step-touch forward 4x

Then heel-tap back 4x – R foot steps back on 1, L heel taps in front on 2 then immediately steps back on 3, R heel taps 4 andsteps back 5, L taps 6 andsteps back 7, R heel taps on 8!

Pony! R, L, R, L!

Butt-kick (bend your knee to kick your heel back towards your butt). R, L, R, L as you extend your arms in a protective cheer/traced sigil: point your right and left arms out to the side and say, "No!" together with Delta 5 when the song says it. Then cross your forearms in front of your face on "mind." Scissor out and in to switch which forearm is in front on "your own," then reach both fists to the sky "biz-", then pull both down to punch down to the ground on either side "-ness!"

Back to the top and repeat, moving with greater confidence and stronger conviction each time.

During the bridge, alongside that clangy guitar, embody the confusion of codependent relationship dynamics with some head rolls and twirling. Recall the YUCK feelings when you've allowed someone to take you emotionally hostage AGAIN. Express that experience with a huge fake grin that morphs into a wide scream of misery and despair. Melt dramatically onto the floor or bed to illustrate the total soul drain after entangling with an energetic vampire. And then switch it! Find the moves/expressions/gestures that express when YOU'RE the one asking to lick their ice cream, interfere in their crisis, or vamp their energy! Let's be honest: bad boundaries usually go both ways.

Continue to repeat the moves through the verses and the choruses. Notice how different you feel in your body when you embody boundaries, and then embody boundarylessness! At the end of the song, join Delta 5 in the call, pointer fingers outstretched, auric field wide and protected, "MIND YOUR OWN BUSINESS!"

CATHARSIS

Catharsis follows an aerobics spell. With the right container and ingredients for a powerful aerobics ritual, a person will be changed by the end of it. So much is released through the pounding of feet, the clapping of hands, the twirling and switching directions, the swooping chassé, the hard breath, the sweat! The sheer act of getting our heart rates up creates alchemy within us that makes us perceive the world differently. The thing I was worried about before no longer seems like that big of a deal! My inner-child's outsized reaction that totally ran my whole life two hours ago? She is quelled by my devotional aerobics offerings to her.

A lot of the ritual we do together or alone may not show their effects immediately. In the last ten years of gathering people in a fiercely noncompetitive container, incanting *Fuck the Moves*, sweating and crying and singing, and dedicating ourselves to the values of this practice, the dance and fitness culture has changed. Ponies weren't the only ones dancing for these principles, but I know that our energies made an impact.

A liberatory movement ritual is not complete until you take what you received and transmit it to the collective. A Pony Sweat core value: Catharsis is a pathway to action. When we aren't hijacked by the trances of perfectionism and competition, when we allow ourselves to stay with our bodies, we feel into our interconnectedness. This is why aerobics, activism and witchcraft are such natural friends. We feel our connection to the earth, to the GODDDDDDDS, to each other, and that connection ENERGIZES us!! Instead of feeling outmatched, we feel connected to our true power.

Collective effervescence is magic. Mixtape-making is spellcraft, choreography can be sigil-magic, and leading a group of people in dance ecstasy is fucking WITCHERY.

Thank you for connecting through this practice, across the spiral of Time + Space, and availing some part of your past/present/future self to this ritual. Thank you, Body! Thank you, Bodies!

Molly Larkey

bill of rights for bodies when we are born on planet earth

to be born is to have rights, though rights isn't the right word for rights, because these rights are not granted by the state. they are boundless and unmitigated, and our right to them is beginningless and unyielding. they come from a time when there was no time, when we were animals and plants, spirits and others: a time when there was no separation.

these rights could be called writes, because in inscribing our rights, we conjure the power of these marks that form our writes. their potency is felt by your hands and in our spine and their rightness is known in our chest and by our ears. the resonance of these rights is felt in every part of our body, so they will be a part of our body of writes moving forward and backward from now.

these writes may also be called rites, because to speak them is to invoke them as rites. the magic of rites states that to speak is to pronounce, to pronounce is to enact, and to enact is to invoke. by the transitive properties of rites, we commute rights into writes, and writes into rites; even as we learn our rights, we also learn to always know and speak these rites.

we have always had these rites but they were hidden from us, hidden in us. they are us, and we only have to speak them to know them and have the power of them. they come from being born in this body that you have, and i have, and we are in—a body of earth, air, water, and fire—living on a celestial body made of earth, air, water, and fire. these elements make up our body and the earth's body. we thus contain the irrevocable right to these rites.

we are made of earth, so it is only right to be nourished by food that is clean, fragrant, and fortified by the earth. we have been told that the earth can be bought and sold, but it's not true. the earth is free and abundant, and its nature is to nourish, and all of us have the right to be nourished and strengthened by it. we emerged from the earth the same as all the others, and it is our right and our rite to return to the earth to nourish it back again.

the air is in you, and you are in the air. we move, sway, stand, ring out with the medium that is air. this is our right to air, yes, bright, unpolluted air. this is also our right to breath, to speech, to sound, to thought, to hold ourselves as part, and also apart. to making lines that are boundaries (to saying no), to making lines that are connections (to saying yes). to being both within and without, to being me and not you, you and also part of me.

my body is a body of water, so this is your rite to be as water: to flow, slip, evaporate, sparkle, shower, fill, and hydrate. it is our right to drink the water that covers the earth, yes, clean water that fills us to our depths. it is our write to all that is watery: to fluidity, to clarity, to transparency, to profundity, to reflectivity. it is your write to savor your feelings, to drink them in and know them to be as flowing water not to be dammed or damned, to know the tenderest depths of our watery feelings.

i know fire because i know urgency, the urgency of knowing a thing that wants to be transformed because it's dead, or just that it's time. you know fire because i know it. it's telling you what you need, what is needed, what needs to be said, to be done, to be vocalized loudly! out loud. this is our rite to fire, to heat, to volume and power. yes, to power. it is our right to transform, to be transformed, to tell it like it is, to know it like it is, and feel and tell the fire of it.

light is a force that runs through us, a gleam that is the spark of me, a flare that is the shine of you. close your eyes and look. know the knowing that you are light, moving out into the world and back into you. we have the inmost right to be this light: to blaze this light, to be combustible. to feed ourselves with light, to be devoured. to bathe and stretch in light, to bestow light, to be a torch, to disseminate the light that we are.

we hold this rite to never forget the sacred holding of our bodies, of sharing this body with the bodies our body chooses. the fire of my body tells you the truth, as lies are burning, crackling, falling away. the lie is that they can co-opt, steal, vilify, own, shame, criticize your body. even as they want to control your body, we will not allow it, not ever again. remember: your body cannot be measured or seized, it is an unbound body. it cannot be detoured.

it is my right to be other than us and still the same as you—ancients and babies, masculines and feminines, fragiles and strongs, and all the differents and sames, and opposites and alikes of us. it is your right to be the others of me, to be embodied as your body speaks you to be—strongfragile, femininemasculine, differentsame—to be a shapeshifter, to be all genders or none at all. to break gender in half or innumerable smaller pieces, to bust it right open, to exhibit it, to expose it, to play in the fragments of gender.

we have the right to think with the thinking of others, our own others, and others' others—stone thinking, ocean thinking, particle thinking, nothingness thinking. to know generosity to and from others. to know plants, to grow them and be grown by them. to know the wild knowing of animals' minds. to give back freely all the things given to us. this is our rite to generosity, at all times and everywhere. look around, feed it, cultivate it, the generosity is here to give from, and take to. amplify it, sprout it, spread it like sun on a brightness day.

it is our right to know the power that is the connection to all of these things and all of these things' things. to commune with, to be given, to know with, to feel mystery's mysteriousness. we have this right to power in all the words for it, especially the words that are gathering, rising from the words that have been hijacked or betrayed. for now, let's call it warp and weft, a vine vining, a branch branching, a root rooting. or call it everything because it is the beginning, middle, and end, and all the spaces in between.

this write is your rite to add to freely. to write rights of your own, and to share them with fighters for rights and writers of rites and riters of writes. to fight for and write more and rite more, for all of us, and all the others of us, moving backward and forward from now.

Ashley Molesso

I'm Not a Witch, But My Girlfriend Is

I text her from my couch and say, this might be crazy but do you want to meet me for a martini and then fuck me on your floor?

She tells me to meet her at the Hotel Kinsley bar at 8:50 pm, and if I get there past 9:00, I will be in trouble. She tells me to wear a skirt, no bra, a shirt that she can easily take off me. I tell her that I want to be good. I do everything she says, and I drive into town in the shortest tennis skirt I own, a long sleeve button up blouse that I only button up to the middle of my sternum and a lace choker with a silver bow charm hanging from it on the tightest clasp around my neck. I like the sensation of something tight on my neck.

She keeps line and tells me what she wants as well as what she needs. The communication is so clear it's as if she is inviting me directly into the manual of her heart, no password blocks, no security measures, no privacy settings.

We sit at the bar in the back of the hotel restaurant, the warm wood ceilings low and Σtella playing on the speakers. She shows up in a baggy airbrushed T-shirt and jean shorts, her hair pulled back loosely. I've never seen her not wearing the color black. I watch her walk across the street towards me as the sun starts to go down before we go inside. We are both being different people tonight. I am tired of making decisions, for myself, for others. I want her to tell me what to do.

At the bar, the girl in the airbrush T-shirt and the jean shorts who I met up with so that I could get fucked tells me a story and I cry. Usually when I cry, it's because she has her hands inside of me and it feels so good to the point that she pushes out tears. Or maybe it's that my body is trying to tell me something, maybe my body is still recovering from the person who used to fuck me like that before her. Whatever it is, I've come to like it, the release that, out of all of the people I've had sex with, only she can help bring out of me.

*

She pushes me down onto the ottoman inside the front door of her house, a butternut squash Victorian with a small window in the stairwell that might have been to throw the dead out of easily she once told me, and my back slides down the wall as she climbs on top of me and starts kissing me, pushing my shoulders back, her hands gently wrapping around my neck, her fingers slipping underneath my lace choker and then skating down the front of my body. Tendrils of long dark wavy hair fall from behind her ear and cover her face and I feel it touching my cheek as she kisses me. We melt off the ottoman and onto the floor, our shoes still on. The only light is coming from a dim lamp from the corner of the living room.

She unbuttons the rest of my shirt, slowly, until my tits are no longer covered by the neon polyester floral fabric that was brushing against my nipples earlier in the night when we were hunched over the bar, laughing, staring into each other's eyes, thinking dirty thoughts without saying them out loud. We didn't have to because we already knew what the other was thinking.

I am pinned down on her 100-year-old wood floor, between her arms that are the same size as mine, my body squirming as I feel my spine knock against the hard ground.

*

Someone tells me about Gin Tears earlier in the week. It's when some people cry as a result of drinking gin. Ever since I started getting gin in my martinis instead of vodka, I notice that I cry on almost every date with the girl in the airbrush T-shirt and the jean shorts. *Maybe you're just a highly emotional person*, the woman who tells me about Gin Tears says to me. I joke that it's not a real date with me unless I cry.

*

Her hands are the softest hands I've ever touched. They are the softest hands that have ever touched me. She has a touch that looks and can sometimes feel so delicate, but what a lot of people don't know is the amount of power she holds in those sweet and gentle doll hands of hers. Her hands have birthed babies, they have been the cause of pleasure, they have made me leak salty wet from my eyes, they have healed others in ways I can't imagine. They have begun to heal me.

*

When my partner and I opened our relationship up to other lovers, we didn't anticipate getting wrapped up in trysts with people who were going to hurt us. We didn't know what to expect at all; everything was a mysterious possibility. Anything could happen.

My first romance apart from my partner destroyed me. I wanted someone else to crack me open and show myself who I really was. The person who ended up filling that role dug their way into my heart and my brain and my body and I invited them in without caution. I laid myself bare for them, like I do for everyone. Maybe they were the unlucky one to have had me, though. They tore through me like a devastating storm, showing me the light and then swiftly breaking me down to a pile of rubble. But the thing is, I let them. And they did pull back all the layers for me that I was hiding beneath. I wonder if I did any of that for them in return. I wonder how much damage I caused them, but I don't think I'll ever know.

When I first met her, the girl who is now getting ready to fuck me until I scream, my clothes askew, my black boots still on, my back arched and thighs cold against the hard wood floor beneath us, I was in need of someone to reach a hand down and pull me out of whatever damp hole my previous lover had led me to, the one that I ultimately crawled into, myself.

When she first reached for my hand and began to pull, it was slow at first. I tried to claw my way up, dirt lodging under my fingernails, sharp tiny rocks scratching away at my knees, red mud and worms and cold wet surrounding me like it was trying to swallow me up for good. Our grips on each other kept slipping. I didn't know if she was going to be the one to fix me.

*

The first time that I cry in front of her is after she fucks me with her hands in the back of my car in the parking lot where I used to get fucked by them, the one who broke me open, and they're not even on my mind when it happens. I'm so lost in the moment with this other girl that they are not even the last thing on my mind, either. They're not present at this moment at all.

The second she's done fucking me, a tear trickles out from my eye, and then another one, and then I'm close to sobbing and don't understand why. I remember I wasn't even thinking about them, so what am I crying over?

She holds me in her arms and what I don't understand at the moment is that this is the beginning of me healing.

*

After she fucks me on her floor until I become dizzy, she hands me a thick glass of water ;the cup is an elongated version of the cups my partner and I drink out of at the Adirondacks cabin, but this one holds twice the water. I pull myself up and lean my back against the white-painted grate in the wall that I was screaming into minutes earlier, hearing my moans echoed back to me. I imagined I was breathing my own life into the veins and vents of her and her wife's house. My head is spinning, and my body is still tingling from being fucked liked that, my shirt still open and my tennis skirt pushed up past my waist still and all I can think about is did she take her magic hands and stretch the water cup to be longer? Why does everything look so different?

When I am done drinking the water, I set my glass down on the floor next to me and wrap my arms around her neck and pull her back down to the ground with me. Her head is heavy on my chest, but I feel weightless with her, like we are two balloons floating towards space. It's as if I am in the middle of a dream and I am half expecting to wake up soon.

*

Text me when you get home, she says at her back door as I'm walking to my car, parked in her wife's spot in the driveway. When I am home and lying in bed next to my partner, I search online for a photo of the Romeo and Juliet skeletons, the buried couple unearthed back in 2007. The ones that were discovered embracing one another as if they were cuddling on the floor together, not wanting to get up and drive home after a really nice fuck. I text it to her. Who took that picture of us? She responds, and I start to fall for her even more.

Dori Midnight

From the Diary of a Teenage Witch

Last year my mom cleaned out the garage and sent me a box of my high school journals.

What follows are excerpts from my diary from 1991-1993.

Dear Diary,

Today was the first day of 10th grade (kill me now) but I met someone who has changed my life forever. His name is Chris and he has a burgundy bob just like me and he was wearing jean shorts that he cut up the sides that were held together with ENORMOUS safety pins and HE WEARS NAIL POLISH. He held out his beautiful hand to me, so charming and elegant, and said, "Hi, you look like a witch. I am a priestess of Wicca. Want to be in my coven?" And then we sat and talked for all the rest of lunch period. I really wanted to cut 7th period math (because I already know it will be boring) to talk with him but it's the first day and that would probably be really bad, but we agreed to sit together every lunch from now on. I feel like I am knowing something about myself I have always known but didn't have the words for, like I thought something was wrong with me, but actually it's something really good and right rising up in me, and like I can't stop it. And even if it's scary I don't care, because it's true and ancient and makes everything make sense.

Dear Diary,

I feel like I should have a name for you. I am going to call you Moon, because that's who I feel like I am talking to when I write in you. I want to live in the moonlight, drink the moonlight, write with moonlight.

Dear Moon,

Chris and Victoria and I have a coven. We are the witches of North Hollywood. We are MAAAAAAGIC.

Dear Moon,

Doing witchcraft makes high school make even less sense. Like I already knew it was total BS but now all I want to do is run away and find an old hag in the forest who will take me in and make me sweep her floors and teach me to make potions and heal people. Chris and Victoria and I went to the Psychic Eye bookstore yesterday and I got a reading from this guy Ravyn who was at first kind of creepy, but also seemed like really really real and in the end I think he was just shy and has probably had a really hard time in life. I love people. He said that I am super psychic and should learn to hone my craft and I wanted to tell him everything about how I hear things and know things and see things, how I always feel like I can't go into cemeteries because it's so loud and everyone wants things from me. I didn't. But after I cried so hard in the parking lot with C and V and told them everything and they just held me and we smoked Parliaments. I got a book called *Natural Magic* by Doreen Valiente which has recipes for spells and which herbs do what and color and number magic. I am staying up all night reading it and I have the strangest feeling that I already knew these things. But I also have so much to learn. I want to be this witch. I want to be a weird old woman who does not age gracefully at all. I want to grow foxglove and drive a truck and make wine and make tea and make potions and make people laugh and make people cry. I want to dance, barefoot and bare bellied, with secrets inside about weather and stones. I want to live my dreams and keep changing forever.

Dear Moon,

Today we started our grimoire and we're keeping it in a secret hiding place off the trail near Coldwater Canyon. It's wild there. I mean you can still hear the freeway, but we decided to pretend it's a river. It is a river. Kind of. It feels wild enough. We are wild enough.

We're writing our own spells and recording all the rituals we do and all the things we are learning. We are calling the directions and casting circles.

I told C I wanted to put a hex on Andy P. but he said that we shouldn't because of the Rule of Three and that it's bad magic. But is it bad magic to right wrongs? Like if he is a total asshole, isn't it a gift to the universe to hex him? This is why I need a teacher.

Dear Moon,

I think I might actually be a fairy or an elf or some other kind of being. I really don't "fit in" and I don't want to. I'd be lying if I said I didn't care at all, but I also know that I know what is really important. I know something about magic and about life. I know I want to live in a way that is free and helps other people be free. Maybe I'm just a storm. It is what is inside of me.

When I die I want to be buried right in the earth—no coffin, no nothing—so I just decompose. So my body turns into flowers.

Dear Moon,

I went to Topanga Canyon today with Alexis. It was soooooo cool. We parked on the side of the road and slid down on our asses into the stream and took off our shoes and went barefoot along the big rocks, all tumbled out. I wanted to take off all my clothes. I felt so alive. You can know the story of the canyon from the pink-orange swirling walls, swept by time and wind and water. I noticed a dark hole in the rocks and was intrigued. I wanted to show the canyon I wasn't afraid, even though I was. It called to me. When I ducked inside the cave, there was confetti on the ground. As I looked closer I saw that it was littered with cigarette butts and beer cans. The terrible evidence of men. It felt like there were hands all over me and they were pulling my voice out of my body. Drunk crotch grabbing men. Earth raping men. My body is part of the earth—they want to control, they want to own, they want to destroy—because they are terrified of our power. I howled my wild voice into the cave. I kicked the cans with my bare feet till they bled. I am whistling in the dark. I try to be the shadow. I am the dark. I am raging raging raging. I am the rage. I will not keep it in. It is my magic, it is my power.

Cities will crumble, mountains will tumble, mortals all stumble, and the storm rumbles on.

Dear Moon,

I've been hanging out more with A. She's not a witch but I think she gets it and asked me about it. Today she took me to a cafe in West Hollywood which was really amazing. This weekend we're going to go wheatpasting bc stupid evil men are trying to ban abortion rights. I wish I could hex them. A is getting us fake IDs from J's older sister who has a shaved head and plays bass so we can go to her show on Sunset. She is so cool. I really wanna hang out with her. She wears a pentagram but I'm not sure if she means it or just likes it as fashion. She told A she thought it was cool I was a witch.

Dear Moon,

I think I'm bisexual.

I don't know if I can be a witch and not be a lesbian. Witches never have husbands.

kai cheng thom

only queer and trans people can be witches now

> *The moon is trans.*
> *From this moment forward, the moon is trans.*
> —Joshua Jennifer Espinoza, "The Moon Is Trans"

only queer & trans people can be witches now. my apologies
to the cis straight lady feminists
to the new agers
to the Harry Potter fans waving their wands
and to all the white straight girls in flowy linen dresses
with crystals and sage in hand.
i don't make the rules, only
report them, and the new decree
is that only queer & trans people can be witches now

in fact, i am told that there is newly unveiled evidence
in the scientific & historic record to show
that queer & trans people have always & forever
been the only real witches
no doubt these findings will be controversial to some
and for that, i do sympathize
but who am i to debate the findings of scholars?

but it does make a certain kind of common sense
if you ask me. after all
our people have always followed the call
of wanting & willfulness, the flowering of forbidden knowledge
in the garden of our blasphemous bodies.
in the fecund soil of our secret hearts. we had no choice
but to answer the call. we were initiates
in a sacred order. summoned by a power
a purpose greater than ourselves, blessed
by the sacraments of blood and transmutation

we made ourselves new bodies
out of magic & moonlight. whole worlds
we built from desire & despair
we traveled time, shifted shapes
gave birth to legions of exquisite beasts
we spun the shame you gave us into gold

so do not fear, my dear
uninitiated cisgender heterosexuals
you aren't really losing anything that was yours
to begin with. and after all
the rest of the world still belongs to you.

and as for the power? you need not worry
i have every confidence
that we queer and trans people
(the only real witches left in the world)
will wield it well.

i chose the devil as my lover

after they caught and burned
the Devil at the stake
i crept into the village square at night
and gathered up his ashes

i took them back to my home
in the woods beyond the village
and there in the shadows of the trees
i cast a resurrection spell
for the Devil

i put the ashes in a cauldron
i added herbs to the ashes
to the herbs i added water
that i had taken from the sacred spring
and to this brew i added the bones
of a freshly slaughtered lamb

and then i took my sharp knife
and slit the palms of both hands
till the blood welled up and ran down
i let my blood flow softly
into the ashes of the Devil
onto the bones of the lamb

and then i sang the secret words
till he sprang forth, naked and gleaming
as beautiful as the light of morning
as vengeful as the sea

he took me into his arms
and pressed his lips to mine
whispering his invitation
so i chose the Devil as my lover
and i kissed him again and again
until the sun came up

and i tasted blood in my mouth
later, as the villagers prepared
to burn me at the stake
they asked me why i did it
did you do it for power? i said no
did you do it for money? i said no
did you do it for revenge? i said no
then why did you do it?

i said as the flames kissed my flesh:
i did it for pleasure
i did it for freedom
i did it for the sake of living in truth
and i did it for me

promise spell

you know, femme
i've stopped believing in disasters
because every day is one
and every night
could be the night they come for us
and you know, friend
i've stopped being afraid
of the night
because the darkness
is where we found ourselves
so if this is it, sister
i need you to know
i'm never going to let go
because the greatest magic
lives in the space between our clasped hands
and i promise, love
if they build you a prison
i'll burn it down
and if they bury us
we'll rise again
and if the stars themselves
should fall from the sky
we'll just have to learn
to love each other
that much brighter

TJ Payne

Hexxus

She asks me one night, while we lay in bed together, what it felt like to be inside of me. That she wishes she could crawl into me and experience my body from within. I had recently seen the film *I Saw the TV Glow*, so naturally I envision a box cutter slicing down my chest, past my sternum, through my body hair and abdomen—one clean cut. No blood. But when I start to spread my skin apart to make room for her to climb in, there is no TV glow. Instead, it's Hexxus, the villain from the 1992 animated film *FernGully*. Hexxus is an evil entity of destruction whose ultimate goal is to destroy nature for his pleasure. He is a shape-shifting character who can transform himself into toxic clouds or a monstrous creature, cunningly voiced by Tim Curry. He is a swirling mass of toxic waste who manages to perform a sultry song titled, you guessed it, "Toxic Love." With lyrics like *Filthy brown acid rain, pouring down like egg chow mein* and *I feel good, a special kind of horny, flowers and trees depress and frankly bore me*.

I was immediately enamored with *FernGully*. Not because I ever fancied myself an environmentalist, but more so because I recognized a killer soundtrack and was often fascinated with the male leads—Zak, a handsome, buff, blonde tree-cutter who is just trying to do his job (destroy the rainforest) and Pips, some kind of shirtless fairy-hunk who has an incredible dance scene to Ini Kamoze's "Here Comes The Hotstepper." While I found these characters' bodies intriguing, their personalities did not interest me. Hexxus, on the other hand, drew me right in. He was after his, and a part of me wanted him to get it. He was a sexual cloud of filth. Whether or not the creators of the film intentionally made this character so sexy is unbeknownst to me, but it worked. Or maybe that is just the outcome of having Tim Curry do anything.

Back to my insides. Hexxus. Toxic waste. I see this leak out of my body slowly, as I pull my skin back, and then at the speed of a broken dam. I am so full of it. I try to close my chest back up but it's too late. The flood of waste starts to thin, and soon I'm left with my insides exposed through a film of black smog. She looks around hesitantly before climbing inside. Yes, step lightly, and watch your back. Your only way out is through.

The heaviness that lives inside of this body nearly knocks her to her knees as she enters. It is not from an object, like a piano or a house. It is a feeling that simply exists and has lived here for many, many years. Hexxus circles it like a shark, feeds it with his words, and receives pleasure from it. It is grief, pain, regret, remorse, guilt—it is all of them at once, swirled together around Hexxus's pinky finger. She is being engulfed by them now and I try to pull her out; this isn't what she wanted or expected, but this is what it feels like to be in this body. Hexxus reminds me of what I've done. He reminds me of the innocent lives I ended—taken from this realm in such a brutal manner. He shows me the images, so I never forget. Sometimes she asks me what I'm thinking, or if I'm okay, and I am lost in those images. My chest is closed, and I take several deep breaths, an attempt to clear the smog and release her from the weight of my emotions, a past that so painstakingly lives with me every single day.

She is holding onto a valve of my heart that beats rapidly. Nervous. Nervous about such exposure. Butterflies, for I love her so. It is a warm muscle and I feel her icy hands caress my heart. Much of the toxic waste of Hexxus has left this part of me, though sometimes a leak finds its way in. It is a magnificent heart—well taken care of, strong, young, resilient. It floats in a cloud of blood and flowers, sprouting new patches underneath her to soften her fall. The heart winces at her departure, it is tender, sensitive.

She explores—sliding down the intestines, searching my lower abdomen for more flowers but is met with Hexxus yet again. Turmoil. Anxiety. Anguish. Disappointment. Fear. Hexxus laughs at my weak belly—he takes up so much space down here. She kicks her legs and waves her arms to clear her pathway, to get through his filthy trail, but it becomes thicker. As she combats the smog within me, I am entering a public space—a bathroom, mentally running down my masculine checklist to ensure safety. Avoid eye contact. Straighten posture. Hands in pockets. Furrow my brow. Hold my breath. I am not to be engaged with. No stalls available. Anxiety and fear join forces, and Hexxus blows them further my way, as if blowing me a kiss. She is getting caught in the mix of it all, like the cow in the twister. I exit the bathroom and pivot my plans. It can wait. It's not that important. I'll make it. One day I won't be able to make it.

I check inside myself to see how she is doing and see her sitting atop my stomach. An area of great discomfort for much of my life. A body physique I have never felt happy with. Even on the outside, it began to sprout hair and acquire tattoos. Round, bulbous, in the way, distracting. She gives it a little pet for comfort and my heart tingles. Hexxus hates this and reminds me to be skeptical of love, particularly love directed toward me. It's all an illusion and can be gone at any moment, never to mean a thing. I swat him away, but he is being relentless today. He is showing off for her, to show her what a miserable sack I am. That I am doing a great job at hiding all of this toxic waste on the inside.

She crawls back up to the valves of my heart. It is the warmest and safest spot in here. Hexxus's cloud has turned completely black on the opposite side of my chest, leaving her very little space to move or to get out. He is taunting her—*Is this what you really want to live with the rest of your life, now that you've seen it for yourself?* He's not going anywhere, Hexxus. He has made his home within me, finding pleasure in all the disappointment and heaviness of my life. He is feeding off of me every day. Yet every day, the heart pushes him further aside, making more room for flowers, and brightness, and joy. This body does not feel like a temple, but more like an amusement park, with turbulent beauty. The light and shadow coexist. I take another deep breath, pull my skin apart and she steps back out. I close up. Zip zip zip.

Carolyn Pennypacker Riggs

Musical Incantations

Dear Reader,
I conceived the following verses as musical incantations. They are spells to be sung, spoken, whispered, etc. Music is my magic wand, and it's nice to have these tools in the trench coat when something comes up.
xoxo, CPR

Only Lovers Allowed
When I feel haunted, I sing this in a melody that can be described as "after school special," "early 90s sitcom," or "the theme song to Entertainment Tonight." There's tons of hidden magic to tap via acts of intentional stupidity, and as part of my magical practice I do things that others (former versions of myself) might describe as "embarrassing." I sing this spell with a John-Tesh-level confidence, blasting smoke and ringing bells:
Only lovers allowed only lovers allowed only lovers allowed

Garden Green
Okay, okay—I know abundance magic is hella eyeroll-inducing for some witches, and we all know money can't buy happiness, but it can buy you options, including-but-not-limited-to . . . mm, a dank sandwich. I want that sandwich. Would wary witches get into this flavor of magic if only it was called something different? [Dank sandwich*] magic? [*Sub in something that brings joy and costs dough.] I sing this spell as I deposit checks and also when I write checks because I am grateful I can pay bills, thank you green garden!

Green green garden green
I have every thing I need
Grow grow garden grow
All the earth delights in flow

Green green garden grow
Holding lightly, letting go
Thank you thank you for
Everything I need and more

Break That Spell

I yell this when I feel a creeping slime vibe. Imagine you just read a murky-toned email that radiates squiggly stink-lines. To dispell [sic] the mood, toots, yell these words loud enough to surprise yourself—shrill and wild like Ozzy O or monster/metal voice or Siouxsie cries or soaring Whitney, just bring the drama—and then spit on the ground. Don't forget to spit on the ground. I do it inside, too—polished wooden floor? Pristine carpet? Don't care. It feels good. *Optional/optimal hand gesture: middle fingers or devil's horns aka metal hands. (Thank you, Amanda for this hot tip.) You can also draw three Xs in the air with your index finger in the general direction of the email to neutralize it. (I adapted this from a book called *Positive Magic*.) I finish with a shoo-ing away motion—imagine swiping left with your entire arm. How do *you* swipe left with your entire arm?

Break
That
Spell

Empire Folds

Speaking of stink-lines, this is a spell song I wrote in 2017 to unseat odious powers that be. I admit, as of June 2024 it hasn't quite played out in the timeline I'd hoped for. But magic unfolds in strange ways and waves. And I am a sucker for a reveal. More will be revealed! The "d-d-dust" can be sung in an ominous tone e.g. the classique, descending "dun dun dunnnn!"

Molasses slow the empire folds
Columns topple, interleave
Amidst the dust, the dank debris
Statues, tombstones nod like common thieves

Dust to dust
D-d-dust to dust

Eyes roll in the back of my head
Screaming in Latin again
Circle will not hold
Oh! As the empire folds

Lawns we littered in the dawn
Where we wandered, where we played:
Only gravel, grapes to graves
Grains to gradient decay

Dust to dust
D-d-dust to dust

Eyes roll to the back of my head
Screaming in Latin again
"SACRILEGIUM!"
It is sacrilege.

Eyes roll to the back of my head
This is happening
Dream was wrong. Dream is dead. Awake now. Awaken.

Decomposition Dance

I once had a countertop compost bin that started out nice (porcelain! fancy!) but the goo stained the outside, and having to look at it all the time was a big time bum bum, even for this part-time slob. Like—I'd rather look at rotting food than this beautifully-formed yet muck-stained vessel. I left it on the back step of my apartment, and it was soon inundated with maggots. It sat on the step till one day it toppled over and cracked (porcelain! fancy!) and I finally tossed it. More waste, *wanh waw*. Now I collect my scraps in a clear to-go container that once held hot and sour soup. I wrote this spell as a personal motivation ballad to make myself compost, sung from the POV of the chorus of compost—microbes, worms, nematodes, protozoa, bacteria, fungi, water, heat. I hum it when I'm doing dishes/scraping plates. Big Dish Energy.

*As I ferry and dump the tub-scraps into the bigger bin, I say, "Enjoy, enjoy, enjoy!"

*Bring us your wasted
your uneaten, rotten
the refuse that will be forgotten
mmm
Bring us your wasted
your uneaten, untasted
the unused that won't be consumed
mmm*

*Give it to me and you shall see
what comes before the apple tree*

*Don't set it on the
growing heap
a stagnant seat
that cooks and creaks
and overheats*

*Bring it to us and
we shall transform
through warmth and worms, we turn, turn
turn it to life once more, more*

*Here under-earth we
fragment and churn
shatter and re-form form
form undone to be made more, more*

*Give it to me and you shall see
what comes before the apple seed*

Return Dance
Another song about compost—psychological event edition. I wrote it in 2019 but it ended up feeling v, v prescient once lockdown rocked-down, and I sang it to myself throughout. It became a reminder and a plea: We WILL return. And now it's a reminder of those panda days, and it feels

like communication with my selves across time / through song. A friend pointed out the melody is v, v reminiscent of the "star of wonder" chorus of *A Christmas Carol*, d'oh. I love "Return Dance." Good for hard times, fallow times, time-travel times.

We return changed in ways
we did not anticipate
we have touched the deepest reach
and rolled in waste

Waited while our gifts were gone
bound and rotting underground
so that we might greet them now
see them now

We surrendered for a spell
into stillness like . . . [wide open-mouthed exhale]
entropy devoured all cells and faculties
with the night

And from that primeval slough
came something strange and new
from all this dirt and trash,
garbage, scraps, and ash
a garden grew

Brigid's Song

Here is a hymn I wrote to bad beach Brigid, my fave metalworking deity who plays with fire and a patron to poets. I love that her two sisters are also named Brigid, and that she invented the whistle so nighttime people could call to one another for rendezvouses in the dark, huzzunhhh. Sing this song to call to your people, known and unknown.

[Begin with whistling]

You who knows where the fence leans low
Who slides the serpent from her sleep
You who has the flame fly high and well run deep
I bring you offerings: metal rings

43

For your reaching mind

You, who sing and cry at the same time
Call me to your side

You who knows how the high hedge grows
Who pulls the tendril from the seed
You who guards the edge of time along the lee
I bring you offerings: hooves and wings
For your reaching mind

You, who sing and cry at the same time
Call me to your side

[Whistle again]

You who know where the weirdos go
Who braid the waking with the dream
Here no line is drawn between what is and what is becoming
I bring you offerings: shining things
For your reaching mind

You, who sing and cry at the same time
Call me to your side

I Am Fire

Were you a fire teen? I tended my teenage fires on this wobbly tray filled with pyro-phernalia, balanced on polyblend blankets. I'd melt wax and plastic, going nutso huffing and puffing, not technically smoking, just burning braincells. Decades later, I recognize this affection as an early form of magic: transfiguration purely for kicks. Now I've got altars all over my studio scratching the same teen itch: it's art that is private, witnessed only by me and the spirits and the flames partying away. This song is good for lighting candles, fires, solar holidays, or when bravery is required.

I invite you to sing the FIRE refrain with the intensity of a 90s diva (my personal ref = Sinead).

I am fire
I am reaching flame

I'm a slow refrain
I am fire

As I strike the match
As I say the word
"I am fire."
I am fire

FIRE! FIIIIIRE!!

Call to me
I am energy
All that burns, BURNS
I am fire

Winter Invocation

Mmm I love WINTER. And mm Mm MMMMH do I LOVE the swagged out, high-achieving beasts of Winter-born—CAPRICORNS! Woefully my sun is not in Cap, but it *is* my rising sign, so when I feel doubt or fear re: my ability to complete a project, demand a higher day-rate, power through a crunchy family dynamic, ask for cold clarity, or clothe my bod in respectable attire, I call upon the stereotypical qualities of Capricorn to "Tap the Cap" or "Cap that Ass" depending on the context. You can sing this song on the first day of Capricorn aka Winter Solstice. Also easily adapted for: yule tidings, shadow tidings, and releasing.. Lean into the minor key. Sing with your spookiest friend or familiar.

Ghosts of the year
Come here, come here
Night yawns boundless
Lie down, lie down
Look up, look up!
The wheel winds around us, around us

Lady waiting underground
Ready to receive
Castings of the dying year:
Filled and failed prophesies

All we had
For wrong
For right
Surrendered to the night

Nobody Knows

I didn't mean to write this song as a spell, but it has become a stalwart part of my pratique magique vis-à-vis a handful of public performances, i.e. rituals, that changed my very marrow. This song is a symptom of—and chaperone to—my ongoing midlife psychological event.™ Every time I perform it, I feel a little closer to the center of the misty, mlurghy middle. This song is about feeling unknowable. But—twist—instead of emo alienation, the unknowableness is a magical power, a gift from the Otherworld. If you feel like you're cosplaying "basic," sing this song. I sing it any time I need to remember who I am: a tripper witch, a friend to demons, a hot-shit hunter.

There's a hunter on the road
There's a hunter at the door
There's a hunter on the threshold
Salivating, "More . . . "
[monster voice] *"MORE!"*

Nobody knows
Just what I do
Sometimes I sink to the bottom without you
Sometimes I find a writhing, rotting
Sometimes I find a glittering diamond ring

In the shadow of an ear
In the corner of a neck
There's a hunter in the mirror
"What did you expect?"
ONLY EVERYTHING

All my love
I can see it from a thousand miles up
And readily admit:
I've died died died several times and

46

I'm still afraid of it

There's a hunter in the eaves
There's a hunter listening (shh)
There's a hunter at the table, on your sleeve
Knows your name, knows your face
Knows everything

Nobody knows
Just what I do, I do
Sometimes I swim to the bottom without you
Sometimes I find a writhing, rotting
Sometimes I find a glittering diamond ring

Nobody knows
nobody knows everything

The Mystery

Are you an assiduous witch who calls in the elements for every spell? If so, I commend and envy thee! When I call the elements, aka corners, I feel the portal to the Otherworld creaking open. The air sizzles. God is Alive, Magic is Afoot. And despite this guaranteed bodacious sensation, I still resist calling them in. Why? Overwhelm, malaise, lackadaise? Or more grimly . . . self-sabotage? Regardless of the reason I then slink into, "If I'm not going to do it right, why bother?" and forgo the spell altogether. ["Noooooooooooo" reverberating from the bottom of a well.] I wrote this verse to make calling in the corners fun to do. Because the best part of Magic is DOING it! DO MAGIC. Nike swish just do it!

For easy magic, sing this to the four cardinal directions, then upwards and downwards.

I also repeat this song in my head to push other earworms out and as an instant balm when I'm twizzling late night death thoughts. However you choose to use, Enjoy, enjoy, enjoy!

The Wind
The Sun
The Stone and Stream
The Soil and Seed
The Mystery

47

Shelley Marlow

Isobel: A Witch's Life

A work-in-progress play from *The Wind Blew Through Like a Chorus of Ghosts*, a novel. Queer elders Pilar and gender-non-conforming Swann plan to travel from Brooklyn to the U.K. in 2013. After their flights are booked, Swann senses something terrible and consults a channeler who states, "You were a witch in a past life, who was murdered as a teen in 1619. As your trip progresses, you will find out all about that witch." Swann meets Isobel in Glastonbury.

NARRATOR	Contemporary voice who narrates scenes
ISOBEL	Spirit of witch in the UK, circa 1619, 19, femme
SWANN	Brooklyn traveler who was ISOBEL,
	52, non-binary in a past life
PILAR	SWANN's girlfriend and travel expert, 52, femme
BIANCA	Bearded Lady, Host, 33, femme
BAILY/WITCH FINDER	Witch hunters, various, masculine
ELDER	Claywoman or other elder, 100, non-binary

Coven and soldiers ensemble may be described by NARRATOR

Tor, Glastonbury, Dusk
    (PILAR and SWANN 52-year-old Brooklynites visit the UK, 2013.)

NARRATOR
Evening in Glastonbury on the Tor, a caravan arrives.

In the caravan's Tell A Vision tent, SWANN is hypnotized and meets the teen witch, ISOBEL, who tells her life story, circa 1619.

Rain stops, and thin clouds part to reveal a silver crescent moon glowing heavy and pulsing like a tuning fork. Ping ping (bell-like tuning fork).

PILAR and SWANN see dots of light snake into the campgrounds behind a grove. Fog clears to reveal horse drawn circus carriages, kitted out buses, and vans pull in.

They see a person pulling firewood from the hold and carrying the wood inside. Soon after, smoke billows from the bus's chimney.

PILAR and SWANN follow sign beyond the 2000-year-old trees: LARP CARNIVAL

NIGHTTIME

People with lanterns roam.

PILAR and SWANN get separated in the crowd.

PILAR wanders by magicians, witches, and other costumed throngs. PILAR stops to watch a play on the side of an open carriage.

SWANN wanders for a while, looking for PILAR, but stops at a COSPLAY HYPNOTHERAPY TELL A VISION TENT.

Caravan Park Behind Gog and Magog Trees, Glastonbury
    (Jeff Alexander's song "Come Wander with Me" floats in.)

NARRATOR
SWANN stumbles inside at the COSPLAY HYPNOTHERAPY TELL A VISION TENT

Bearded lady BIANCA approaches.
(BIANCA, more fairy than werewolf)

Another fairy stands next to BIANCA with combed red hair and crimson lipstick, wearing a red and pink sequined bathing suit-ish thing and French eyeliner.

The fairy laughs like a lemur and back flips, all with an impish smile.

A third fairy joins her, with stiff staccato movements, her hair black and sharp-edged like a wig, twists up like a pretzel and crab walks away.

BIANCA watches them flip themselves out of the tent.

BIANCA

I'm not going to do that!
>(Then runs her fingers ponderously through her beard.)

SWANN admires BIANCA's hot pink silk suit and wood cane.

Barn owls *hoot hoot*.

BIANCA

Are you here for the Tell A Vision workshop?

SWANN

I don't know . . . Maybe. Please tell me more. (reticent) I don't really know anything about that.

BIANCA smiles and waves a mirror with silver cherubs on the back.

BIANCA

Tell me about yourself?

SWANN

I get visions. I see dead people. I was a witch—

BIANCA
(interrupts)

You already get visions!! This will be easy then.

SWANN

Really? I don't think I can be hypnotized, though. How is it done?

BIANCA

You stare into your left eye in the mirror as I hypnotize you, and you fall into a trance. When you return from your trance, you tell your vision. A troupe of actors will perform your story. I will lead you out of the trance if you seem to be in trouble.

SWANN

Okay, I'll give it a try.

BIANCA helps SWANN onto a pallet of blankets.

BIANCA passes over the silver mirror.
BIANCA massages SWANN's temples.

BIANCA

Abracadabra . . . abracadab . . . abracad . . . abraca . . . abrac . . . abra . . . ab . . . aaa

SWANN shuts their eyes and falls into a trance.

BIANCA snaps her fingers by SWANN's ear. SWANN doesn't wake. BIANCA covers SWANN with a blanket.

SWANN stands up and dives forward as though passing through a portal, then lands on back on floor.

ISOBEL IN PITTENWEEM, SCOTLAND, 1619

ISOBEL appears out of nowhere on the table. Stage is dark otherwise.

SWANN recognizes her.

SWANN

Isobel?

ISOBEL

Hello. What?

SWANN

I have an offering from the tree grove.

ISOBEL

Yes?

SWANN hands over green and pink light from the trees to ISOBEL.

ISOBEL

Love from trees, thank you.

SWANN

You are welcome.

(Swann appears anxious, then relaxes.)

SWANN

We are cut from the same schemata. What happened? I mean, I don't want to pry. . .

ISOBEL

Pry? I do not know that word. Priory, I know. But, you are me?! Yes?

SWANN

Heee, heee. Yes. The same.

ISOBEL

So, yes, I will tell you my life . . .

(SWANN awaits, vulnerable and receptive.)

ISOBEL

In 1608, I survived the plague. I was left in the care of a monk. I helped in the fields. The monk wanted to absolve me. I laughed at him. As I grew, my home was a short amble to town. My elderly neighbors grew herbs. We observed foxes and bears eat. Iridescent butterflies flit about garden. Chickens, a cat, and a miniature goat wander. We bond over dry fish. My favorite place in town is this:

(ISOBEL waves her hand to reveal an apothecary.)

Here you see fresh herbs entwined in my long fingers to trade. I laugh at the sexual shaped flasks.

SWANN

I wanted to be a scientist with colorful beakers and test tubes when I grow up.

ISOBEL

As a teen in 1619, my monk brought clay jars of scotch for my tinctures. On my way to Wednesday Market, my feet sink into mud if I stop moving. I hide tinctures in my pockets to trade with fish wives for briny snail soups. Do you hear gulls?

Sailors rolled in. Cloth sold in West Market. If I sold to travelers, I'd be punished and fined.

On summer nights, I slip off after dusk, gather with friends. Especially on new and full moons. No leaders, a different person drew circle each time. Disembodied ancestors pour waterfalls of light through the top of our heads.

My visions of blue and white flowers in the dark reassure that we are safe. We dance in spiral around hilltop, skirts fly like Saturn's ring. Some spin the opposite direction to stir the pot. After rain, I always start a flame-y fire like no one else.

We improvise a twirl, stretch, and hop like egrets. Others lumber bearlike. On the hottest nights we dance naked except for slippers. Always merry meet.

I not afraid of death. I sit their ill who in my presence grew patient with pain. I speak of how we do not need religion.

I feed vegetables to fox, to not kill my chickens.

That last summer, a Bulgarian ululates as we work fields. We open our throats to sound that flies through our bodies then out.

A vision of a lost friend traveling by horse, who wants to find us and can not.

Wolves cry out.

We howl back.

We dance all night. Stomp feet to rise earth, someone shouts "Freedom" and we respond, "Freedom!"

We dance for justice in an unjust time.

I receive my broomstick made of ash. The ash broomstick spoke to me in pictures.

One of my friends with Jimson Weed, an elder has Henbane.

We mash these into an ointment to fly.

We take off above the hills, our silhouettes black against night dusk.
I fly above unseeing villagers, forests, and roads to sea.
Mine was a life worth living.

(Pause a few beats. ISOBEL's mood elated.)

Late August, sun golden on green leaves and snakeskin, sun still warm on skin though icy wind, aches my ears. I know all fields and woods by heart and love the return to darkness. My vision of flowers scatters, which means spies amongst us. I didn't recognize everyone in circle and panicked for a breath. How did anyone know to find us? So many paths in woods, each path to another field. That night, elders' teeth gleam. Youths from town giggle. I hear in their laughter they never lost anyone. Some wear jewelry, making them feel immune to trouble.

Our circle, dark except for sparks passed hand to hand. My breath deepens and I rest, again safe.

I find my route home with my eyes closed.

NIGHT

Early fall, a laird cornered me from behind in a dark street in town.

SWANN

Watch out, Isobel!

ISOBEL twinkles back at SWANN.

ISOBEL
(proudly)

I gather night's darkness to surround me. I turn to where he looms. My eyes glow. He lurches back, then backs up further, with eyes on mine. Once out of range, he turns and runs away. Night is my ally. My friend. My love.

(pause)

Our group gathers at a new, secret location.

We play kissing games one night. Kiss the person on your right, then kiss the person to your left. Lots of kissing. All kinds of lips, womanly, masculine, berry-like, full softness. I drop into minds of others through kiss and find that none of them betrayed our location.

DAYTIME AUTUMN

Later in the month, an elder Caochladh dies, and we hold a tearful ceremony in the rain, yellow leaves drop down wet and heavy.

Sadness abounds when I give Rue to my friend after a court official took advantage of her. He would force her to marry him if she bore a child.

The next time I see her, she winks, and we travel the village, arm in arm, my heart open and in love. I want more than the pipkin of wildflowers and cooking herbs she presents me. I respect her brokenness at the time and stay quiet on my love for her.

Villagers barter for healing. As I grow, I also get coin. Which I need to pay taxes.

The lairds and priories bleed common people.

I told villagers: We all embody the divine. We do not need the church.

(pause)

Early October, some in the circle held my head while I had a vision. The word epileptic didn't exist. I told them: One day soon you may reach hands up, and the hands on the other side will be mine.

They cry, *We don't see that.* You will remain with us for a long time, Isobel.

I pass the oldest grove.

TREE 1
(whispers to another tree)

I see it. Do you?

TREE 2

Yes. Our roots run deep underground beneath loam. We sense energy that runs counter-flow of our limb-sap. A shift towards the midday sun, lovely. A shift slightly to the right/the dark would threaten to flay our bark and tear your human veins.

TREE 3

Isobel, your time is running out. Be careful and not in harm's way.

ISOBEL

I see a reflection in my neighbor's looking glass plate: my red hair and freckled skin. My large, muscled limbs. My waist thin upon viewing from the side, wide from the front. I slip into the looking glass and see you, Swann, as you gaze back at me. Glasses, straight nose. Finally seeing you as I tell my story. Myself in the future! Warmth rushes through me and between us. I am grateful.

ISOBEL turns back around and continues to tell her story.

ISOBEL

1619 was a time of grief and introspection. Another elder disappeared and we could not locate her.

On those crisp nights, we make a bonfire.

Foxes secretly follow me through woods. I am about to run, but the look of kindness in all fox' eyes stuns me. I stand still and wait for their next move. Instead of speaking, the fox sends telepathic images, warning me of a man's face I should not trust.

ISOBEL cuddles an invisible fox, grateful.

ISOBEL'S COTTAGE

DAYTIME

ISOBEL

Soon after, a tall and thin BAILY, almost attractive except for cheese-sharp tightness in his face, is at my door. He wears a nightshirt with a griffin on the fabric under his coat.

(live action)

(ISOBEL speaks softly, illegibly to him, nervous.)

BAILY

I cannot hear you.

ISOBEL

(raises her voice but still whispers inaudibly.)

BAILY scowls.

BAILY

Why do you whisper as if you talk to a baby?

ISOBEL looks shocked.

ISOBEL
(speaks in a deeper voice)
What brings you in today?

BAILY steps closer.

BAILY
You tell me. You're the one, I am told, who knows everything.

ISOBEL steps back.

ISOBEL
I could, if you insist. But to respect your privacy it's better if you tell me.

BAILY
You do not want to test me.

ISOBEL moves closer to take his pulse.

ISOBEL
It's all going to be alright.

BAILY shakes ISOBEL's hand off his wrist.

BAILY
No, it's not going to be all right. Just because you say it will be doesn't mean it will. Airt and Pairt.

ISOBEL is shaken, steps back again, breathes, and regains composure.

ISOBEL
There's the door. Tell me what you want or just leave.

BAILY jumps forward and quickly grabs her wrists and spreads ISOBEL's arms open. BAILY pushes his chest forward and ISOBEL is pressed against the wall.

ISOBEL kicks his shins, and he drops her wrists and folds forward. ISOBEL wraps her hands under BAILY's chin then lifts up, then back. His body follows his head backwards. He gets up.

ISOBEL knees him below the belt then drags her forearm across his neck. BAILY tries to pitch forward but can't stop himself from falling backwards further. BAILY chokes, then drops to the ground.

ISOBEL stands steady.

ISOBEL

There's the door.

BAILY smirks then falls out the door.

NARRATOR

ISOBEL carries his overcoat to the door and tosses it onto the path next to some flowers. Two other Bailies from the presbytery hold three horses.

BAILY turns back to pick up his coat.

BAILY

The Lord Advocate seeks witches, and you are under suspicion for lies and witchcraft. Recognize henceforth you have been warned.

ISOBEL bolts her door shut.

ISOBEL

I call my guardians to cut ethereal cords that he attached to me.
Later that month, I am in deep meditation, gorgeous yellow leaves light against the lush blue and white afternoon sky. I hurry. Leaves fly up, in the chilled wind.

Children whoop in the distance. My body tenses and I think, relax. Children play hoops.

NARRATOR

OUTDOOR MARKET DAYTIME

ISOBEL

When I arrive at the market, my friend runs to me from behind the row of fruit and flowers stalls. I inhale her care, feel calm, safe for the first time in a while. I stare at her table full of golden pears and yellow grapes.

FRIEND
Please accept this package for the rue and pennyroyal a few weeks ago.

ISOBEL
(to the audience)
It was a honey cake. Cane sugarcane arrived that year. Some boiled and spun it into floss and sweets, all fancy for lairds. I had one bite of a cane cake, and my stomach ached for hours. We heard rumors of ships and kidnapped people from the African continent. I encouraged my neighbors to buy honey and not sugar. Mine was one small voice. Honey soothes. She knew I loved her honey cake.

NARRATOR
ISOBEL's face turns white as she notices BAILY.
ISOBEL glazes over and pretends to not see him. Her face tightens.
FRIEND gives a worried look back to her.
ISOBEL points her nose towards him. Her FRIEND sees him. He turns his back to them in the crowd.
ISOBEL and FRIEND hold hands to put up a psychic wall to block and shut BAILY out. Because he feels the wall, he intently tries to tear it down.

ISOBEL pokes a finger around her aura.

ISOBEL
I was happy a moment ago.

ISOBEL tries to relax back to that moment and lighten up.

ISOBEL eats a grape.

ISOBEL
(to her friend)
Sunlight has taken refuge in this grape, just as I take refuge in seeing you.

NARRATOR
ISOBEL feels something brush against the edges of her hair and dress.

BAILY is behind ISOBEL within the crowd. He hooks a thread of ISOBEL's aura into his.

(SWANN witnesses ISOBEL's story, wriggles on the pallet.)
ISOBEL turns and sees him as he walks away.

ISOBEL
(to the audience)

He pulled on my energy with force. It was exhausting, but I did quickly cut that new cord.

I was nervous on my way home, I see more signs of being hunted: shiny twigs and branches broken red around the edges of the forest, but not on my trails nor my animal friends.' I get home and organize my shelves to relieve tension. I juggle my chaos of salves and tinctures. The evening sky is purple, gray, and yellow like a bruise. I light candles, then continue to repair the slightest cracks in my walls and floors.

NARRATOR

Stars pierce velvet gray clouds and black night sky. An owl hoo hoos, perches on a branch at the top of a laurel tree.

ISOBEL

I fight the sudden urge to run into the woods to hide. Would that work?

NARRATOR

In the morning, yellow rose light mixes with pale blue sky.

ISOBEL

My finger bones vibrate and the rest of my body shakes. My mind keeps saying that I am safe as I go about my day. Later my dress drags and gathers dirt in the hem.
(pause)

ISOBEL

After a few days, my brain aches with worry while my body is calm. Look. My body is steady, have I moved out of danger's way?
No.
My stomach, like a clock face that was tilted to noon where one is supposed to be. I breathe into my body's tense spots.

My sack is ready to flee with sarsaparilla, mallow, and sage, for calmness; oatcakes and tea: mint and thyme to stay alert.

I meditate and remote view this:

THE PRESBYTERY

We will get rid of the dust that gathers in those corners of Water Wynd. That gathers in the fields at night, dancing like wild animals. The wytches, they are not like us!

THE NEXT DAY

ISOBEL

A soldier is at my door. He wears a griffin, too. I step out in the bright afternoon sun to deal with him.

He acts as if this was a "date," his desire killing him as if I was a cute miniature apple. A poison one!

SOLDIER

I adore you. Let's lie down and I will take you.

ISOBEL
(to the audience)

I look back at him with shock on my face.

He pretends to be enamored and wants sex in exchange for my freedom. We spend time sitting in my garden. As he speaks, he keeps changing the terms of his proposal, then finally reveals that he would visit me any time of day or night, whenever he wants.

He changes from seductive to threatening, and I question my own sanity. My brain scrambles.

ISOBEL
(I gather my clarity and finally blurt out)

One lie after another. You have no idea how your domination takes up all of the air. You hold me prisoner when you think you are kind.

His face turns red as he storms off into the dusk.

NIGHT

ISOBEL

Later I make a bonfire. I cuddle my goats and my cat. The smell of smoke mixes with the wet autumn leaves and hangs in the air. Embers rise high against the night's darkness. I stay home, while others gather in the fields to dance.

(songful . . . Melanie's "Lay Down")

ISOBEL

This is the night they approach my home on horses from all directions, the woods, the sea, and then swiftly charge at me. They attack. I felt I'd truly gone mad.

Several of them pick me up and swing me from both ends so I would split into many pieces. Woods animals hear me cry out and make their way over. The soldiers are about to throw me into the fire, when my fox and wolf friends fly towards the soldiers, nip and bloody their ankles and hands, unable to reach what is protected in chainmail and armor.

One soldier with log to hold the animals back then light up my house. The wolves jump on him and tear at his face.

The other soldiers steal me away.

I am tossed into the dark basement of The Church of Scotland.

ISOBEL

The soldiers force me out to be interrogated.

NARRATOR

A WITCH FINDER sits at a table laden with roasted hare and cake. He barely acknowledges her presence. He writes with elegant fine lines tilted towards the left, with flourishes and whorls. He hands the slip of paper of accusations to ISOBEL. His strangely elegant handwriting reveals that he believes himself to be good and right.

WITCH FINDER
(Between chomps.)

What demon do you worship?

ISOBEL

I worship no demon.

ISOBEL

Perhaps you can't imagine a leaderless situation, so you imagine a monster that doesn't exist.

63

WITCH FINDER's eyebrows arch, and his lips round. A look of confusion and uncertainty passes over his face.

WITCH FINDER
Who dances with you in the fields at night?
You are free to go if you tell me names.

ISOBEL
No one.

WITCH FINDER
(Stares at his own reflection in his glass of wine.)
Who do you worship?

ISOBEL
(interrupts his revery)
Everyone can speak to God. Everyone is divine. Remember your own divinity.

WITCH FINDER's brow drops and his eyes narrow.

WITCH FINDER
You are lying. Don't lie to me. I am your only salvation. Who are your demons?

ISOBEL looks up defiantly.

ISOBEL
The only demons are the ones in your head.

WITCH FINDER doesn't like her answer and grabs a leather dagger sheath and beats ISOBEL's legs until they bleed.

WITCH FINDER
I will stop if you say the names of who dances with you.

ISOBEL refuses.

ISOBEL

Guards throw me into the dark basement. I smell of hunger. My chest narrows. My breath strains. I have a lucid moment where I see that I will sacrifice my life. Staying alive would be like putting on a reality too small, and when I do die, I will have to climb through a thimble-sized hole in reality to get to the other side.

I limp in the dark until hitting a wall. I lean my arms out to find the other walls and corners, only to find elders, too, in that church basement.

The elders say they had heard of me. All in the dark. Some had been in another gaol a long time. Giant, soft, wide-bodied, thick thighs and waists hug me.

I return, broken bones from another interrogation. Their strong arms hold my cracked hips and wrap me in spider webs and torn cloth and pull me back together. I bleed into the cloth until it turns deep crimson then dry brown. The elders move me into the sliver of light to see my face. They keep an eye on my skin, vigilant that I do not turn green. In the next few days, an edge of my cheek is green . . . until they hold me and twist my back into alignment again. My energy links up and I lose the green edges. I sleep deeply then. Less pain. More blood moves.

NARRATOR

Small sliver of light arrives the next morning. The light shard travels all day along the floor then the wall. ISOBEL tries to grab ahold of the light but can only hold her hand in its warmth and make shadow shapes to amuse the others, grateful for their care.

Soldiers come again for ISOBEL to try to force her to speak.

ISOBEL

I could only whisper these words: Liberty. Justice.

The well-dressed officials kick me in the chest and back and legs and bones. I leave my body and watch from within the elegant lamps above. My body is returned to the cell, bent over, crooked, limping in pain, blood-soaked, dress a rag, all grit and hunger. Nowhere to sit and rest, the ground too cold, cave walls too cold. The giant soft people had been moved suddenly and I am alone. Were they ever there?

(pause)

In a dream, my friends sweep nearby while I prepare herbs. I wake up and find that the sweeping is rats scratching in the dungeon. The rats are free to come and go. In a thin veil, my cat spirit arrives and protects me from the rats.

I hold knees to chest and rock on the cold dirt floor. My knuckles bloody as I dig for roots and mushrooms to eat as my night vision kicks in.

(pause)

I lose sense of time. Near the end, I am given clean clothes that my friends left for me. They sewed pockets that were torn off. Every cake and other food was withheld.

In my clean clothes, I am hurried out of the basement and taken by horseback. A painful ride, wrists tied together in the back and strapped to the horse . . . dragged along if I don't stay balanced.

NARRATOR

ISOBEL is brought to St. Andrews before a judge.

ISOBEL

Every soul deserves liberty and justice.

NARRATOR

The judge writes notes and does not regard ISOBEL with sympathy, only believes lies.

ISOBEL

Back in the dungeon, I watch the sliver of light as it makes its way at a distance along the ground. My body thin and weak, my nostrils and ears caked with dirt.

I try to open and shut my mind at the same time. Now. Now. Now. Now. Now. Now. Now. It's gone. Gone. Gone. Gone. Gone. Gone. Gone. Gone beyond sorrow.

I grow numb to the cold. Numb as blood leaves my tender sweet flesh between cheek and jowl. I am ghostly white. Numb to the lump in my throat, even though it is still there. Numb to my shrunken gut, swollen glands, aching womb, broken shoulders. Numb to my thirst.

I watch the sun light sliver for the last time.

NARRATOR

In the Tell A Vision tent, BIANCA observes that SWANN's breath slows then stops, then resumes.

SWANN

66

ISOBEL! Like Joan of Arc or Nor-a-Nisa Inayat Khan.

ISOBEL

My sisters Joan and Nor. I know them well.

SWANN

My grandmother had shock treatment.

ISOBEL

So did Lou Reed. I see that your grandmother and Lou are making friends
in the afterlife, as you call it. Lou says your grandmother is a font of love.

NARRATOR

ISOBEL is tied and chained with other women accused of witchcraft and
then dragged along Cove Wynd in Pittenweem to the harbor. The walk,
long and impossible.

ISOBEL

I see one broke face, then all faces break, twist up, and swirl around in
orange browns olive. The icy wind does not move through my oily hair. I
am ripe of piss, and shite-orange mixed with crimson blood. I also smell
their thick broken animal smells. Their ugly, tight, self-righteous, smug
faces, surrounded by pearls and gold stolen from fairies.
Still I don't curse them.
I stay in love.
Love for myself.
Love for my friends.
Love for Freedom.

NARRATOR

Low tide, their chains are hammered into the jetty wall. The sky lights up
orange, then turquoise at twilight.
The waves ice cold and crushing. ISOBEL's lungs freeze then collapse one
last time. ISOBEL's body collapses. Her spirit rushes up and out.

ISOBEL

At dawn, my friends slam large stones to break my chains, then lift my
icy dead body above their heads. Their feet sink and dip into the low tide
mud. On the land, they wrap my body in muslin, that blackens from my

blood. My blood lights up golden—regal in the cold sun. My friends carry my body through the forest to a pond. Foxes and wolves along the path bow in respect. Some friends wail loudly while others weep silent tears. The wind blows through a chorus of ghosts. Leaves spiral up. My friends wash my body then wrap me in golden green silk. The group circles thrice, then lifts my body onto a raft in the pond. My red hair floats off the raft into the green glass water. Did they light my body on fire? I do not remember. An androgynous youth wades in and pushes the raft further into the water, even though it is late November when thin ice forms along the water's edge. Song and dance lift all spirits including mine.

NARRATOR

Swann rolls over in the Tell A Vision tent.

(Kate Bush's song "Jig of Life," "Never, never let me go.")

ISOBEL

My spirit rises up and rushes across the sky.
Love remains in my wake in gorgeous timeless sparkles.
Friends find traces of my spirit:
In the night's glimmering stars.
Floating within clouds just above the horizon.
Over the dense forests.
My spirit resting in red light in fox fur and in red waxberries.
A light in birds' feathers and in the roots and mushrooms on the forest floor.
A single ghost flower pushes through mulch on the forest floor, and my spirit glows within.
The foxes jump around the ghost flower.
Snowy white owls flock in from the north. They fly over the gathering, over the flowers. My coven looks overhead to a parliament of owls in one graceful glide.
They inhale my spirit like warm rain in spring. The community breathes with ease and walks with more confidence, missing me, but not to the point of despair. I never betray their trust. They absorb my love which prevails.

Ariel Gore

Cursebreaker

In the dark of our motel room, we declared it the year 12,067 D.E.—the Demon Era.

Was this in the past or the future?

We didn't know.

Were we just making things up? Were we high? Maybe. But wasn't the numbering of years always a cultural construction? Not like hours and days, delineated by the movement of the sun. And were we not a culture unto ourselves? We could construct reality.

It was the year 12,067 D.E.

The candlewick sizzled as we lit it.

Who was we?

"We" was me and the eight demons that live inside of me.

It could be worse. There used to be nine.

The psychic who works behind the barber shop that's behind the watch shop on Jay Street in Brooklyn brought the demons to my attention in January—and then in the cold of early February lured us out to Ozone Park in Queens and, in his upstairs apartment that smelled of onions and carpet cleaner, he exorcized one of them in great a fiery display that cost me one of my best black T-shirts, but then he squinted at me through thick glasses and said, "I'm so sorry, Mother. Do you mind if I call you Mother? It will cost ten thousand dollars to exorcize the rest of these terrible demons."

I shook my head. "Seriously?"

He had this super gay-looking poster of Jesus and Krishna holding hands on the wall behind him. He nodded solemnly, "It is a very strong curse, Mother. When I first saw you in my office on Jay Street, I said to myself, *The woman has the mark of the witch.* I said to myself, *Beware of this woman.* And yet something also called me to help you. I have asked myself again and again, *Who would put a curse on my kind mother?* Do you know who would put such a curse on you that you're filled with all these demons, Mother?"

We stood up from the floor, which isn't that easy these days, what with our back and right knee. We had a pretty good idea who'd put a curse on us. We weren't idiots. But we didn't have ten grand. We straightened our spine. "Can we pay you in tangerines?"

A snowstorm flashed in the man's eyes.

And we marched down his carpeted stairs and stepped back out into the blizzard, and we took one look at the old truck parked in his driveway and we thought about the truck of our childhood, and we opened the door and of course the psychic had left his keys in the center console.

See you later, Son.

We drove toward the smell of salt water.

*

We do love motels.

And the Villa Inn smelled like citrus and weed.

*

The whole reason I went to see the psychic behind the barber shop behind the watch shop in the first place was that we wanted to talk to our dead wife. I was with my friend Dusty, and she wanted to talk to her dead son, too. But as soon as we stepped into this guy's closet of an office, he looked up just at me, totally ignoring Dusty, and through the incense smoke he said, "Something bad happened to your husband."

You know the world's going to hell when even a psychic's going to misgender your wife, but something bad had happened. I said, "Yeah, she died a few weeks ago."

He nodded. "Your husband was sick four and a half years."

"Wiiifffeee," Dusty whisper-seethed.

But the guy just kept talking, "Because someone put a curse on him." He stared at me hard, "And you're next."

No chill ran through my body. I felt strangely like stone.

*

We picked the Villa Inn because one of the Ns on the neon sign outside burned out, so it's like we're staying at the Villain.

Where is this Villain?

Well, we can't tell you that part. We already told you when it is. And once you broadcast both where you are and when you're there, you start to lose a lot of power.

Power can always be restored, of course. We don't want you to worry if you've already lost a bunch of it. But you can make your life easier by learning not to lose so much so fast in the first place.

We do love motels.

We love a damp motel under the freeway in the rainy season.

We love a pink motel in the desert with crumbling stucco and the old sign that makes that buzzing sound, the red *No Vacancy*.

*

When I was little, in the always-traveling years when my dad was still trying to outrun the crazy feeling inside of him, I couldn't figure out for the longest time what that meant, *No Vacancy,* and I decided it meant they didn't want you to just vacate without saying goodbye. Like they were announcing a rule. *No Smoking. No Vacancy*. Don't get that vacant look. When the signs just said *Vacancy* I told myself the *No* had burned out, and wasn't that funny? Now they were inadvertently telling you it was okay to just vacate.

Did we want to stay in vacancy?

*

We love a motel that smells of cherry disinfectant and stale cigarette smoke.

We love motels to distraction.

*

After my wife died, I hired a German Gertrude Stein scholar as a grief counselor. She said, "It's interesting, every time you're released from responsibilities, you resume the nomadic life of the early childhood."

As if I'd never had that insight.

*

We also love hotels.

We love hotels in New York City, near the library where the hot butch with round glasses brings out original copies of Mary Wollstonecraft's letters so we can see the slant of her handwriting. That hotel still has the old red carpets and velvet rope stanchions that make us feel like we're in a movie theater. But then we notice the logo on the stationery and we realize this is the hotel when our Moonie friend grew up in the 1980s A.D.

We love hotels to distraction.

It's the year 12,067 D.E.

The Brooklyn psychic keeps leaving us messages. He says, "Mother? Am I not like a son to you? Don't you want this curse lifted? Mother, I can cast out the remaining eight demons for only six thousand dollars. I will pay the remaining four thousand out of my own pocket."

It felt like a word problem on a Demon Era standardized test.

Part of us just wanted to send him the money. Not ten grand or even six grand, but maybe we could spare a couple hundred.

Our dead wife sat on the edge of the motel bed.

We said, "You know, maybe he really needs the money. And we did just steal his truck."

But our dead wife rolled her eyes at our extreme codependence, so we said, "Okay, okay, we won't send him any money," and we texted him, "Listen, man, here's the thing: My husband thinks you actually might be part of the curse."

The psychic messaged right back: "Witch."

And we said, "That's right, Son," before we blocked his number.

Our dead wife shook her head. She said, "You can call me Spirit Wife."

We said that sounds really Sonoma County, 1990s A.D.

And she said, "That's not my subculture so that's not my association with it."

And we said, "Nothing wrong with Sonoma County in the 1990s, anyway."

*

Do you ever wonder what time it will be in the next hotel you check into? Do you like the ones that have all the different clocks behind the reception desk that show the time in New York and Tokyo and Milan? Do you remember when hotels and motels used to have metal keys on plastic keychains?

Do you know how to break a curse?

Can you hear the neon buzz of the *Vacancy/No Vacancy* sign outside?

To break the curse, to exorcize the demons, you'll need a motel room. A hotel room will do, in a pinch.

You'll need a sound you can savor.

Will you vacate?

Every ingredient for every spell is replaceable, but you want to be thoughtful. Tradition gives things power, and you don't want to take power lightly, but magic also favors change. What I'm saying is, don't replace an

72

ingredient just because you're too lazy to find what you need. On the other hand, improvisation is welcome.

When you vacate, will you remember to return the metal key to the front desk?

Will you turn around on the highway when you realize you've forgotten that it's right here in your pocket? Or will you just keep on driving?

*

We liked the German Gertrude Stein scholar grief counselor a lot, but she didn't know how to work the video call that well so we could only hear half of what she said, and we needed to prioritize our motel and hotel budget over any kind of counseling, anyway.

She said: "Motels (unintelligible) gift (unintelligible) return (unintelligible)."

I thought, *A motel is a motel is a motel.*

*

You'll need:

A room with a view of the dark moon

The sound of neon (birdsong will do, in a pinch).

A window that opens just enough to let the moths in.

*

The psychic's voice did kind of haunt us: "Do you know who would put such a curse on you that you're filled with all these *demons* now, Mother?" Because that's the whole thing, really, isn't it?

I'd left a long voice message, trying to relay the whole story to my friend, Ship, but I wondered if I'd buried the lead when she texted back, "Stop projecting your good qualities onto other people."

We wrote back, "What do you mean?"

And Ship said, "You're kind and loyal so you think other people are going to be kind and loyal. You wouldn't put a curse on anyone, so you think no one would put a curse on you. You wouldn't open a shop as a phony psychic, so you think that guy's not a phony psychic."

I said, "Are you saying there's a curse on me or that's he's a phony psychic?"

The other reason we picked the Villain was for its proximity to the water. We can hear the Atlantic lap on the shore. We can hear the buzz of neon. We are *No Vacancy* at the Villain in 12,067 D.E.

You'll need:

To face the window.

To make sure your feet are on the floor.

To close your eyes and imagine roots growing out of those feet and grounding you in the earth deep below your motel room.

Spirit Wife thought all of this was ridiculous, but she understood we had to do it.

When we opened our eyes, we were surprised to see the window wide open. The smell of garbage and salt.

We felt our roots anchoring us.

The sorry feeling started in our chest and spread outward, like ripples on a surface.

"Why are you sorry?" Spirit Wife asked from the bed.

We felt badly, we admitted, casting out all the demons. We wondered where they'd go. Still, we understood we had to do it.

It felt like a question of timing. Of time and place. Of windows and portals that open unexpectedly. You'll know when the time and the place and the conditions are just right. It's a moment that sounds of neon (or birdsong, in a pinch) and smells of salt and garbage.

We opened our mouth wide and said it, softly at first, "I cast you out, demons," and then more loudly, "Vacancy!" And because the conditions were right, because we had not been too lazy, those demons started to fly out of our mouth, hot like embers, searing like candle-flame, they shot through the room toward the window, one by one, and we counted them as they went.

"Vacate," we whispered as they flew out the window of the motel that is a motel that is a motel under the dark moon. They landed on the water and burned there, like oil spill.

The burning sizzled like beauty, but I still worried about how they felt, burning and drowning.

Maybe we weren't kind and loyal.

Maybe that was Ship projecting her good qualities onto us.

We snapped our mouth shut. There were still two demons left inside. We didn't want to let them go. And we realized we didn't have to.

Who would be without our demons?

Mya Spalter

ghost pipe

sometimes the lack of luster
I bring to the moonrise
feels an outrage not a season
winter roving through
years in I stopped observing
the wind for many seasons
could howl ouch endlessly
there's no upper limit on it
a spacious place is horror
the bottom-scrape feel
howl it really is
how like are you to die
appear again in spring
i refused to see a season
mistrusted love to its face
i sacrilege that way in secret
shhh i know there's no honor in it

the ritual is living a whole year
change roles like robes
and decay in fascinating twists
grow beautiful and horned
be born
look humbly at the moon

sometimes and sometimes
be spotlit by it
sabbath in mildnesses
or tortures of sick pain
account for seconds
like meticulous beans
each importantly speckled
each to be inspected
for discrete fissures
use my tongue
a lick of wax
as the tool it is

Emily Carr

Rx for With-nessing, or A Pile of Dropped Mics

A Spell-Antidote to Our Massive Cultural Dysfunction

This spell is an invitation to a radical and magical human endeavor: with-ness.

With-nessing is both bearing witness and being witnessed—feeling seen and valued, having agency, impacting the world in a positive way. With-ness creates a "new history": reconceptualizing truth not as infallible historical facts but as the inherent trueness of our individual and collective stories.

I spun this spell to help my queer baby poets/dreamers/disrupters at the New College of Florida grow resilience amidst acute crisis and unprecedented change. That's THE New College of Florida, the tiny liberal arts college that was once renowned as the first institution of higher education in Florida to pioneer an open admissions policy, committing the school to not discriminate based on "race, creed, national origin, or cultural status." Famously, it got caught in the crosshairs of Governor Ron DeSantis's culture wars crusade on January 6, 2023—because of its commitment to freethinking, and its predominantly LGBTQIA+ population.

And BOOM.

Our home became a battlefield and, for many of my students, there was no safe space.

I spun this spell because I wanted my baby poets/dreamers/disrupters to learn to have courage, curiosity, and compassion under extreme stress and duress, to keep loving each other as the most radical act. Throughout the Spring 2023 term—which was unimaginably brutal, heartbreaking, and violent, and after which half of the faculty, including myself, resigned—we used this spell to stay connected to our own courage and resilience, and to each other.

And you can, too! This spell will help you to:

- write from the deep cut,
- honor your future ancestors,
- grow a personal pleasure activism coven,
- craft an intimate relationship with a tree,
- leverage the most valuable asset you have—your curiosity, and
- learn to be self-sufficient emotionally so you, too, can do radical work—the kind that gets at the root.

You do not have to identify as an author, artist, or activist to cast this spell. How ever you identify—or not—you can use this spell to with-ness our collective and individual suffering and pivot toward the sacred, turning towards and not away from the great uncertainty of our lives.

Review the instructions that follow, mix and match, adapt to the magical materials available to you, and go with your gut. I advise initiating this four-week spell on a new moon that's special to you, but you can cast it whenever you like.

Week 1 | Activate | Ace of Pentacles | Curiosity
feat. Lidia Yuknavitch

Be curious. Reassemble reality. Write a revolutionary sentence.

The Ace of Pentacles asks you to see the work you do as your magic. The Ace of Pentacles wants you to keep a diary of questions. Ask open-ended questions and be okay with not knowing. Get curious about how power works and trauma manifests.

The Ace of Pentacles also invites you to embrace change. As visionary science fiction author Octavia Butler famously wrote in *Parable of the Sower*, "All that you touch you Change. All that you Change, Changes you. The only lasting truth is Change. God is Change."

The shadow side of this card—its challenging aspects—are frustration and impatience, feeling caged and overwhelmed—an opportunity (or narrative) that seemed golden turns out to be an illusion. This is an invitation to redefine wealth, power, and security. To generate your own worth, abundance, and security from the inside out.

†

"Everybody," experimental author Lidia Yuknavitch argues in her *Writing from the Deep Cut* lecture, "creates a series of necessary fictions about ourselves and our lives so we don't break down. So we both need those stories, and we also know they are stories. Occasionally write beyond them and see what's on the other side."

"Ask," Yuknavitch encourages, "what the wound is generative of (vs. how did the wound hurt me or how can I heal or how can I fight back)."

Helpfully, Yuknavitch lists her wounds as:

1. Personal: *My father and how he abused us and the death of my daughter.*
2. Historical: I was born during the civil rights movement and the women's movement, in the years JFK, MLK, and Malcolm X were shot, I came of age during the Nixon era, and I became a writer during the Reagan and Bush years and the culture wars and 9/11 and American-made wars in the Middle East and the cluster fuck we made in the world.
3. Ancestral: Lithuanian immigrant family story and lineage of abused women and how they don't die.

Yuknavitch explains: "My father's abuse created a fractured identity, I took that identity out into the world, I lashed out, I self-destructed and eventually I took the pieces of a self, this fractured identity and arranged them in patterns like a kaleidoscope, where the pieces could make a shape and lo and behold a story emerged and that story was The Chronology of Water and it became instantly ok for it to be in pieces, like my identity. And it didn't just become ok, it became the only way I could tell the story: in pieces. Similarly, the death of my daughter created a loss hole in my life, a cavernous grief inside my body that's still there, and yet that seemingly empty space had something in it, a girl who might yet be born on the page: endlessly. A girl who can save herself, decreate and recreate herself endlessly. So my hole was generative of girls who remake the world. And they're better at it than I am in my life. And that's good. And she is what came from the hole."

Asking "what the wound is generative of" takes courage; it's a radically brave response to trauma. It's the kind of courage that's fueled by curiosity, love, and awe. It's the kind of courage that radiates audacity—both in subject matter and form. It's the kind of courage that inspires you to live a life true to yourself, not the life others expected of you.

Hospice nurse Bronnie Ware, who interviewed hundreds of people who died in her care, asked each of them the same question: "What are regrets that you have?"

The number one regret of the dying?

"I wish I'd had the courage to live a life true to myself, not the life others expected of me."

What happens when you, too, live a life true to yourself—asking what the wound is generative of?

Writing From the Deep Cut Ritual

Invoke the five elements (water, fire, air, earth, spirit) by preparing a cauldron of salty water, lighting a birthday candle, sticking it in something sweet (like a cupcake or a donut), tuning into your breath, and listening. You might listen to the sound of your own breath, a meditation soundtrack, your favorite playlist, or the world around you. Listen in a way that helps you to be present and tune in to your own deep, inner knowing. My go-to meditation soundtrack is Alan Watts's "Listen, Dream" which is widely available on YouTube, Spotify, and other online venues. How ever you go about it, these ritual actions will cast a magical circle in which you can take creative risks and learn as much from your failures/wounds as your successes/achievements.

Set a three-minute timer and list your personal wounds. Write wildly, like a child. During these sprints it helps if you write as fast as you can, without worrying about sentences, punctuation, or fully formed thoughts. Focus on outrunning the internal editor, on fully trusting yourself in the sprint, so that you arrive at that moment where all self-doubt or worry or lack of self-confidence fall away. "This is where," poet and (soma) tic practitioner CAConrad explains, "We can cruise into the previously unimagined magical writing we had concealed from ourselves."

Repeat, listing your historical wounds.

Repeat, listing your ancestral wounds.

Combine the lists into a single, revolutionary sentence. (If you are casting this spell in a coven or writing workshop or with a best friend, I highly encourage you to SHARE these revolutionary sentences. This way, you can PUMP EACH OTHER UP, like witches and poets do.)

Rewrite the sentence in all caps in Sharpie. Stash it in your pocket, backpack, or purse.

Eat the sweet to ground yourself and thank your mind, body, and soul for showing up.

Place the cauldron somewhere where it can absorb the moonlight—outside, or on a windowsill—as you spin the rest of this spell.

Week 2 | Navigate | High Priestess | Courage
feat. Miranda July

Redefine courage. Connect with divine energy. Honor your future ancestors.

How, the High Priestess asks, can casting a spell inside of ourselves help us be more courageous, to not run, to look things in the eye and know that we have divine energy on our side?

The High Priestess is our own highest self, the part that can connect with divine energy, the source, which helps us to be courageous because we are everything, we are as important as everything. The High Priestess is about knowing yourself: casting spells inward (vs. out into the world like the Magician).

I think the High Priestess is also an invitation to shine a light on the deep, dark, ancient and hidden places of possibility within ourselves. As revolutionary Black lesbian poet Audre Lorde argued in "Poetry is Not a Luxury": "within these deep places, each one of us holds an incredible reserve of creativity and power, of unexamined and unrecorded emotion and feeling . . . This place of power within each of us is neither white nor surface; it is dark, it is ancient, and it is deep."

Shining a light on these places of power is haaaard psychic labor. And the High Priestess is a friendly reminder that you are part of a larger story, and your future ancestors are here to help! Future ancestors are people who were born to finish the work you started. In times of crisis, it helps to visualize those future ancestors, on alternate timelines, worshipping on the altar of you—right now. Because time is an illusion, and we aren't boxed in this dimension, this time-space continuum. There are other timelines in which you are already on someone's altar as their chosen ancestor. Now is the time to call on them: to sing your praises and motivate you to get to work so they have something to finish.

Start by collecting pictures, printing or drawing images, or describing your future ancestors in words. Be as specific and as detailed as possible. Then clear a special space—a windowsill, a bookshelf, the top of your refrigerator, your bedside table, etc.—and set up an altar. Place an image of yourself in the center, and your future ancestors all around you. Adorn your altar with offerings: loose change, coffee grounds, lemon peel, flowers, seeds, Tarot cards, salty water, crystals or stones, candles, chocolate, alcohol or cigarettes, etc.

Learning To Love You More Writing Ritual
Whenever you visit your altar, pause in yoga's Mountain Pose: close your eyes, extend your hands down to the Earth with your palms forward, and feel the energy radiating out from the top of your head and shooting down through your fingers and your feet.

Inhale and exhale from the bowels of your belly. How delicious is the air?

Now try ten physiological sighs: two quick inhales through the nose followed by a long exhale through the mouth. This breathing technique mimics crying, regulates the nervous system, and releases stress.

If tears come: embrace them. Tears are medicine that release emotion, connect us to ancient healing practices, and carry stress hormones out of the body.

When you are done breathing, and/or crying, sit down and imagine your future ancestors at a specific age: 12, 29, 34, 45, 52, 81. Pick an age that feels pivotal, a time when you yourself were at a crossroads, felt lost, and had to go with your gut. Set a timer for three to five minutes, and list all the pieces of advice you want to give your future ancestors—because you've been at this crossroads before, you know the path to take, where to make a hard left turn, where to detour, where to slow down for a tricky curve. Be as specific as you can and borrow/steal details from your own life.

Repeat as often as you can throughout the week, generating raw material for your next Great Poem/Story/Essay.

As Miranda July and Harrell Fletcher instruct in prompt #53 from their participatory art project, *Learning To Love You More*, "Don't just write Hold on to your heart, but instead say *Don't go out with Kevin, he will eventually cheat on you. Go out with Jake instead, he is actually cooler.* It is easy to say that everything happens for a reason, but take this opportunity to redirect yourself towards what you think might have been better. Sure everything turned out ok, but maybe you should have quit that job five years earlier, maybe you should have had children when you were 27, maybe you should have flossed, maybe you should have gone to the alternative high school, or not said that thing to your best friend. Tell yourself what to do in clear, specific language. Do not write an essay, make it in list form."

Add the lists to your altar and, at the end of the week, see what happens when you transform these lists into a poem/story/essay written in the form of an advice column—a capacious and delightfully enlivening form!

Week 3 | Connect | 10 of Cups | Compassion
feat. adrienne maree brown
Invest in big big community. Bring joy to others' lives. Write love notes.

The 10 of Cups is an invitation to, as punk musician and Tarot artist Cristy C. Road advises, "revel in the magic forces of community" and "redefine family security, wealth and community in terms that honor your individual story."

I like to think of the 10 of Cups as the Pleasure Activism card. Pleasure Activism is a politics of healing and happiness—writing new narratives in which changing the world is the most pleasurable human experience.

As social justice facilitator adrienne maree brown explains, pleasure activism is not just deserving pleasure; it's communal liberation: "It's recognizing that you want to be part of community where everyone's pleasure is attended to and accounted for, a community where everyone has access and time and resources to actually be able to pursue it. If you're a taxpayer in the US, then you are responsible for the wars that we're involved in, and the borders that are being erected in your name. You are responsible for people being separated from their children. You are responsible—right? So how can you bring as much joy and contentment and satisfaction to your life and other people's lives as possible?"

brown answers:

trust the people who move towards you and already feel like home. trust the people to let you rest.

trust the people to do everything better than you could have imagined. trust the people and they become trustworthy.

trust that the people are doing their work to trust themselves.

trust that each breach of trust can deepen trust or clarify boundaries. trust the people who revel in pleasure after hard work.

trust the people who let children teach/remind us how to emote, be still, and laugh. trust the people who see and hold your heart.

trust the people who listen to the whales.

trust the people and you will become trustworthy.

trust the people and show them your love.

trust the people.

Trust The People Writing Ritual

Get out a postcard or a Post-It, and write down the names of people (real or imaginary, living or dead, historical or fictional) who:

1. feel like home to you
2. help you to rest
3. are already doing the work, better than you could have imagined
4. are trustworthy
5. have good boundaries, and help you to clarify yours
6. exemplify what it means to work hard and revel in pleasure
7. teach you to be childlike
8. remind you how to emote, be still, laugh
9. see and hold your heart
10. listen to whales

Affix the list to your fridge/bathroom mirror/computer screen—somewhere where you will see it regularly, and it can remind you to tend to your big, big community—even and especially in moments of crisis. Whenever you gaze at the list, call to mind the relationships in your life that mean the most to you. Then consider what has brought you together and kept you connected.

Commit to writing handwritten love notes to the people on your list over a six-day period of communal celebration. On each note, recollect a moment of joy you shared that you will never forget. If possible, deliver these notes by hand, passing on the spark of remembered joy. If that's not possible, put that love note in the mail—send it off, no strings attached! As a last-ditch resort, snap a picture and deliver the love note digitally. This way, you grow shared joy as the foundation for navigating shared suffering when times get tough!

†

Writing love notes is a powerful antidote to our massive cultural dysfunction. That's right!

Writing love notes is an antidote to our massive cultural dysfunction!

As social critic bell hooks writes in *All About Love: New Visions*: "The moment we choose to love, we begin to move against domination, against oppression. The moment we choose to love we begin to move towards freedom, to act in ways that liberate ourselves and others. That action is the testimony of love as the practice of freedom . . . When we choose to love, we choose to move against fear, against alienation and separation. The choice to love is a choice to connect, to find ourselves in the other . . ."

What happens when you, too, make love an active practice and an invitation to connect?

Week 4 | Navigate | 9 of Cups | Love
feat. Granddaughter Crow
Get emotionally grounded. Co-create shared psyche. Dialogue with a tree.

The 9 of Cups is about being in control of your emotions, not holding onto grudges, and being able to let go of things and tread lightly—because you're self-sufficient emotionally.

The 9 of Cups has more of a solo vibe than the community-minded 10. It challenges you to stay present, self-reflect, look past what's obvious, ground your own emotional reality, and visualize alternate sources of happiness, optimism, excitement, expansion, and possibility. Think self-care as revolution.

The best way I know to ground my emotional reality is through ritual. It's a tool I often use to help students create moments of stability and calm in the midst of change. Through ritual, we invite the universe to with-ness us and share her wisdom. Through ritual, we experience the universe as one rhymed thing. Rain, then lake, then shade.

Ritual helpfully reminds us that we are part of a shared ecology that includes our ancestors, our children yet to be born, spiritual beings, and the multitude of self-determining plant and animal nations.

Ritual also invites us to invest in the non-human world, to grow relationships with the friendly magical beings who are all around us and who want to help!

Trees, for example, are resilient and know their place in the universe. The qualities they possess—longevity, inner strength and flexibility, the ability to regenerate and the way they link Earth and sky—make them particularly helpful allies in relieving and releasing tension and anxiety, boosting the immune system, and reducing stress.

Start by finding a tree that you feel attracted to, with whom you can have a reasonable amount of privacy as you grow a friendship.

Say hello and silently admire the way the sunlight is exciting the tree's leaves. Tune into the hum of the natural world around you and offer silent praise. Silence indicates patience, moderation, and thoughtfulness—and can provide grounding in a stressful world.

Thank the tree: for cleaning your air and giving you oxygen to breathe. Try using your words to offer gratitude to your tree so authentic it overflows. This will help remind you that words have power and so does silence.

Inhale deeply, opening yourself to receive the gift of life—oxygen. Exhale your own life-sustaining carbon dioxide. This will connect you to the living relationship you share with this tree, which, until now, only it had been conscious of. Let this new consciousness open your heart to the symbiosis that is always taking place and making it possible for you to live.

Now you are ready to release your fear, anger, and anxiety using a technique inspired by intuitive medicine woman Granddaughter Crow.

Praise Song Ritual

Granddaughter Crow tells the story of jogging on an autumn morning: "I noticed the trunks looked like the human spinal cord, and the branches were the neural pathway within the mind. The neural pathways in the mind are thinking pathways, connecting one though to another. Finally, a breeze came, and the magical tree released some leaves that danced happily down the road without a care in the world. It was as if to show me that there is a time for thoughts and ideas to bud and for them to grow, and that letting go of an idea can be easy, like the tree releasing its leaves. New thoughts will be buds soon. I suppose that I was under the impression that letting go of thoughts should be hard, but the tree taught me otherwise."

Pack up your writing notebook, something to write with, and a Sharpie.

Visit your tree in the twilight hour (morning or evening).

When you arrive, greet your tree, exchange some energy (by dancing, hugging, singing, climbing, etc.), and then sit comfortably underneath your tree.

Listen. To your breath. To the breath of the wind rustling the leaves of the tree. To the fur of the air and the other sounds of the world around you.

If it helps, play Alan Watts's "Listen, Dream" mediation, or another meditation or gentle playlist of your choosing.

When you are ready and/or when spirit moves you, dig a small hole in the earth near the tree and ask the tree to help you as you release whatever emotions you are feeling. Cry over and over into the hole in the earth as long as you need to. Feel the roots of the tree receive your tears as nourishment. Ask the tree to help you transform your negative feelings into creative energy you can share. Fill the hole back up. Tap the first back down with a gentle, loving touch.

Finally, set a three-minute timer and write about whatever issues and energies you no longer want and wish to release. Things you're ready to let go of, that no longer serve your growth. Write wildly, like a child.

When you are ready, get up and walk around, thinking about these issues and energies and collecting scattered leaves. Use the Sharpie to write down whatever you want to release on the leaves. If you prefer not to use words, you can use images or symbols.

When you're ready, stand with the wind at your back, holding your leaves. Release them one at a time, and envision a future moment, when these problems are no longer yours. When you are ready, turn and face the wind. Inhale the wind as deeply as you can, all the way down to the wings of your hipbones. Walk away without looking back.

†

Sometime later in the week flex your gratitude muscle and craft an ode or praise-song.

Gratitude, herbal witch Robin Rose Bennett explains in *Healing Magic: A Green Witch Guide to Conscious Living*, "is a highly underrated emotion. True gratitude fills the heart with a deliciously happy feeling. We tend to save up our gratitude for special occasions, hoarding it as if we don't have enough to go around. Most people are rushing around too much to remember to be grateful for an ordinary moment of life— for having a friend or relative who loves you, for having enough food to eat, for your breath flowing in and out. . . Authentic appreciation doesn't have room for feelings of indebtedness or entrapment. True gratitude is so fulfilling that is overflows."

Gratitude is an important form of follow-through; when we look at our lives through the lens of awareness and gratitude, we are sending out into the universe a powerful beacon that draws more of what we want and love our way.

Coda

In 1980, poet Audre Lorde, who died of breast cancer, famously wrote, "My work is to inhabit the silences with which I have lived and fill them with myself until they have the sounds of brightest day and loudest thunder."

Thirty years later, poet Anne Boyer, who survived breast cancer, talks about learning "to form a resistance to the often obliterating noise."

"Everyone," she explains, "who is not suffering now has suffered once or will suffer soon."

I spun this spell to inspire those who suffer—everyone, you—to come together and invent a new language for it. I spun this spell as an antidote to the silence/ideological noise dichotomy.

Because our individual success or failure—at being courageous, at fighting back, at acting in our integrity, fulfilling our true purpose—is not as important as the kinetic energy we generate with the greatest gifts and most valuable assets we have: our curiosity, courage, compassion, love, and gratitude.

Rachel Yoder

Tree

Listen, I am going to try and tell you about this tree. But I almost don't even want to begin because of my despair at the limitation of words to communicate anything real. But the tree is so important, and so real, so I will try.

This tree, and those like it, grow in upstate New York on an old estate now used for the events of the wealthy. Don't let this inspire judgment of the tree. It didn't ask for any of this, the wealth or the people or the estate. It is a moral tree, as close to God as anything can get.

But this tree . . .

You drive and drive and drive for three, four hours. The traffic is horrible. And then you're on dirt roads and nauseated from the motion of the car and finally you turn onto an improbable drive and there is a large stone house and wide-open space that was cleared hundreds of years ago and is still cleared, with a greenhouse that is bigger than the house itself and a garden and pastures where one assumes someone does or did ride horses. A creek and old rope hanging from a tree (not the tree I need to tell you about). The whole place is lonely, as lonely as you've ever seen, but not in a sad way, which is the first miracle of the trees.

So, you are lonely in this cleared space with the stone house. But hundreds of years ago, a man decided to leave some stands of pines, because he loved them and saw their potential, or at least this is what I'd like to believe. So, he leaves these stands of trees, he tells his workmen to leave them, and they are relieved because they've cleared so many other trees and are really looking forward to a bit of break, and these trees grow and grow and grow for those hundreds of years in between when they were left, unmolested, and when I emerged into their space.

They are one hundred, two hundred feet tall. Who can really say how tall a tree is? And they are the only things standing in this clear space around the stone house. There are a number of small stands of these tall pines. Their branches begin more than halfway up their trunks, where the light is. Below, they are all long-man trunk.

Of course I went to touch the trees, to embrace them. And I suppose I am writing about the one tree in particular whose lichen I stroked carefully so as not to break the minty growths, and then whose orange needles I picked from the ground to rub and smell and admire, for he had made such brilliant, soft and durable needles, and then to which I pressed my cheek and chest and groin and closed my eyes. I needed to communicate with the tree. It is the first plant I had ever felt a desire to make love with.

It told me how tall it was by sending its body through mine. I felt its height and strength in my pelvis, which twinged with life. It told me about its soul, another shadow tree that grew straight down into the ground, a mirror self that went as deep as it was tall, and about its upside-down branches, how the very lowest brushed the water of a black river deep underground. The tree did not know to where the river traveled, only that it keeps the furthest-reaching tips of its soul-needles cool. Only that it may be the source of the tree's immense power, while at the same time, a vision of the tree's great vulnerability. I want to imagine this tree will live forever. It's difficult to imagine its death, and who would want to? No one knows how long a tree can live, really. Is it even truly a plant? I guess if I were a scientist, I would find this question easy to answer, but as I'm a wanderer with a poetic sensibility, I just don't know.

Meeting this tree was a turning point in my life, though I am still so close to the moment I'm not certain which way I have turned, nor what comes next.

The entire time I spent at the estate, slow groups of people dressed in blacks and browns and whites moved toward me and the tree. They continually made entrances, like in a Fellini movie, beautiful wealthy folks silently walking through beautiful old space. What must it be like to always move through such beauty? And do they?

Did they even touch a tree?

On the plane on the way home, in the dark, for it was late, I thought about the tree and cried. I had to leave behind a very special tree in New York. It felt like the end of a love affair, and I cried in the way someone cries when they know they will never see their beloved again. And I won't see that tree again.

The tree's gift is that, if I close my eyes and concentrate very hard, I can become the tree, as tall as it and as deep as its soul, or at least I can feel the immensity of it, of both its corporeal self and its soul self, and I can even feel the water in the black river far underground. And now the tree lives inside of me, as if it pollinated me somehow, as though I were a female pinecone with her seeds, but instead of birthing a new tree one day, I will grow this same tree inside me forever—it has recreated itself inside of me, I have been sown, I am the ground now, soil itself. The tree is my father, my husband, my child, and I will have it with me even when I reach the black river and step into its cold water and follow it all the way downstream. I will not be afraid.

Kirk Read

The Boss of Sauce

Witchcraft is what happens when people hold hands.

Witchcraft is what happens when a bedroom witch closes their eyes and grasps a beloved stone. Witchcraft is what happens when someone beholds the dark rose catkins of a red alder.

I arrived at California Witchcamp late. Camp started on the same day as Gay Pride in San Francisco, and I had been coordinating volunteers for a tequila-based cocktail Pride booth benefitting St. James Infirmary, a free clinic for sex workers. This was San Francisco in 2003, a time when I regularly made casual but formative life decisions based on running into someone on the street. Before we had fallen completely into the slipstream of our social media feeds. People would just tell you to do things. *You should go see Patti Smith. You should start a Roth IRA. You should go to Witchcamp.* The word *should* has gotten a bad rap. From the right people, I welcome a good should.

I arrived at the Mendocino Woodlands in the dark. I parked and walked toward a large building from the WPA era. Down the hill there was a clearing beneath massive redwood trees. I heard drumming and singing. Around a huge bonfire, 100 people stood in a circle. *Witches*, honey, these were *witches*. These were witches, and I was underdressed. There were purple velvet capes, fur boots, and green leather vests. I felt like I had come to the Ren Faire in a T-shirt and jeans.

At the center of the firepit were tiny cathedrals of intricately arranged wood. The Fire Tenders fed wood into the fire throughout the ritual—

wood they had prayed over, branches they had selected from the forest floor with an awareness of sustainability and how it might impact each microbiome.

The ritual was well underway. Shortly after my arrival, one of the priestesses started talking about the River of Blood, how we had to cross the River of Blood. There were references to the war in Afghanistan, the destruction of the environment, and Thomas the Rhymer. Someone brought out a tub of red paint, and everyone started stripping off their clothes and painting themselves and each other with the "blood." The ritual evolved into frenetic dancing around the fire. It was primeval; by describing it I run the risk of being snarky. Sardonic humor has been my favorite defense mechanism for decades. It has allowed me to cleverly characterize people and situations to make them less threatening, to give me a sense of superiority, to avoid being subsumed into a group identity.

Even though I was a freewheeling sex worker and writer, I was also a good Methodist boy from Virginia. I was raised by a retired Army Colonel and a mother who knew how to force the blooms on a forsythia bush. I had been raised to believe that the people in front of me were heathens. Even though I had crossed the United States to soak my feet in the evil waters of San Francisco, at the end of the day I was still an eight-year-old boy at his sister's wedding, wearing a seersucker suit and a straw hat, drinking a virgin mint julep. I stepped back into the forest, sitting down on a stump and watching from a distance.

The fervor of the dancing increased. People were chanting and holding their hands toward the sky, screaming, "Too much blood! There's too much blood!" Some of the people were naked, writhing in the light of the fire. The drums took everything to a crescendo and back. I would learn that this was called "building the cone." The drumming stopped. A man stepped into the middle of the circle and said, "This is what they think we do." Everyone laughed.

My mind was spinning out with judgment and terror. Why couldn't I just strip off my clothes and dance with everyone else? Why was my impulse to lurk in the shadows, indulging in the dubious comfort of stubborn separatism? I didn't know these people, but it was obvious that they cared earnestly about activism, the earth and each other. My father worked at the Pentagon in the 1960s and conditioned me to scorn anything that smacked of counterculture. And yet, these strange hippies, these people who believed that faeries and goblins were real, these weird people in capes—these people would change my life forever.

That week I took a morning path called "Elements of Magic" taught by Jack and Rose, who had a lot of bags bursting with bits of ribbon, assorted spiritual statuary, and blunt-tipped scissors for everyone. It was kindergarten for adult witches. We made paper boats, collaged onto boxes, and learned how to call the directions. Our class took place on the ground next to a creek that ran through the forest. Every day after lunch, I was part of a small affinity group of four people. We checked in with each other about social fears, crushes, and bodily matters. Later in camp, we would make a very tender ritual together involving apples.

During the nighttime rituals, I wavered between engagement and feeling held hostage when people went on too long. Everyone seemed so delighted—what was wrong with me that I couldn't just sink into the group? Why did I have to be so obstinate? Why did it bother me so much that a lady was taking so long to invoke the ancestors?

One night after dinner we did a ceremony called The Red Dragon. We drank hibiscus tea and made toasts to people who had died of blood-borne diseases. The ceremony was started to commemorate people who had died of AIDS but had grown to include friends and ancestors who had died of cancer, hepatitis, leukemia, and others. There was controversy over this, but as HIV has become a largely treatable chronic condition in places with access to treatment, it made sense to me to share cultural traditions of the AIDS epidemic with other communities. AIDS Food Banks now serve recent immigrants; AIDS service organizations have needle exchanges and programs for women with breast cancer. I think this is the right direction.

On the final day we said our goodbyes. We held hands and did a spiral dance during the daylight. I wept as everyone's faces spiraled by. I drove to Saratoga Springs to pick up my husband, Ed, who had spent the week with the Billy Club, a group of gay and bisexual men and a few women allies. I waited inside the Heart Lodge and asked someone to go and get Ed. I could not handle being around people. My heart was dialed wide open, and I wanted to stay in my experience. As I drove Ed home, I told him about the entire week. I cried while describing the rituals, the people I'd met and the food we'd eaten.

I came home completely on fire. I started three reading and performance series the next month, and started coordinating the Witchcamp talent shows the following year. Ed was heading into his 20th anniversary of doing AIDS work. I planned a full day of rituals, revisiting the original Shanti building, making a mandala at Ocean Beach. I did a guided visualization where he encountered people he'd worked with, people he knew who had died. I gathered testimonials from many of his friends, family, and coworkers. As Ed closed his eyes on a sofa surrounded by candles, I read these love letters to him. If you didn't think the proceedings could get more earnest, I played the Natalie Merchant song "Kind & Generous" while washing the feet of Ed and his coworker Bryan in a giant, aluminum salad bowl.

Witchcraft is showing up for people with creativity and kindness. Witchcraft is having a lot of cats or at least seeming like you would have a lot of cats.

The following year Ed came to Witchcamp with me. As is the case in many communities we share, people fall deeply in love with Ed, provoking my tendency to lean into sarcasm and dark humor as a differentiating tool. I didn't click with my path that year. I couldn't sing in public. I don't remember having an affinity group. I retreated. I did enjoy getting ready for rituals. We'd brought tons of face paint and costumes. Every night, people would come to our cabin—called Queen Hill—and we would help people dress up. We especially loved the shy people for whom it was a stretch; we made sure those people got Wonder Woman capes and leopard bodysuits. We went into the Ren Faire with sequins and truck stop halter tops that said *I Got It From My Mama*. After painting two dozen faces, I wandered around the edge of the ritual, unable to sink into it. This was not Ed's fault—I just wasn't that interested in the *Catholicism* of the rituals. But there was nothing wrong with the rituals. The problem was my persistent darkness.

Halfway through the week, I stopped at the Cooks' Table on the side of the dining hall. The cooks were a projection screen for everyone in camp. To some, they were the cool kids. To others, they were mysterious artisans from another century. It takes a special kind of person to feed 120 people for a week, to understand how much salad you need and how to deliver elaborate meals on time. They were mythic creatures, a Shakesperean troupe in striped pants who emerged from the kitchen brandishing hotel pans loaded with balsamic-glazed beets, lavender scones warm from the oven.

Carin, the head chef, reeled me in and lured me out of my spooky mood. I started in on a description of the ritual I'd just bailed on; I described the way they had called the ancestors with bird noises. I assessed the fashion. Instead of being offended, the cooks were laughing. After dinner each night, I'd sit down with the cooks and tell them gross stories about testing clients for rectal gonorrhea. I'd deliver anecdotes from sex work and stray bits of gossip from the world of campers. This was verboten behavior— upon arrival, campers were required to sign a pledge that they would not engage in gossip.

Witchcraft is the ancient practice of gossip. Witchcraft is saving baby food jars to hold gifts of calendula salve.

The following year, I spent my mornings in the kitchen. Up to that point, I had only cooked using recipe books. On the occasions when I went rogue, I unwittingly abused my friends by serving barely cooked plantains or oatmeal as a savory side. I can access the shame of these well-meaning attempts easily. I made this ignorance well-known to the Witchcamp cooks, and they seemed to welcome the challenge. I didn't know how to whip cream, but I could get people to take their shirts off and make up racy songs. I could pull in volunteers to help strip cases of kale from the stem. We put spells into the food, we had spontaneous fits of dancing, we cried as we made salad dressing. I had found my place among the witches.

I had grown up eating Cap'n Crunch for breakfast. Preferably peanut butter Cap'n Crunch. The way the round nuggets flavored the milk was an end of the 70s miracle. We ate a lot of vegetables out of my father's garden, but nothing weird or foreign like quinoa. Our town had a natural food store that I never went into until high school. My parents were Republicans, and natural food stores were outposts of communism, selling flowers I'd never seen. Those places bustled with people who went barefoot in Grateful Dead parking lots, spinning around stadiums high on the LSD. It did not matter that I had moved from Virginia to San Francisco. It did not matter that I had traded in my Oxford button-down shirts for leather pants. Social conditioning is deep, and these hippies were terrifying.

During my first five minutes in the kitchen, I managed to slice into my finger with the kind of knife you see in slasher movies. Teo, a chef who managed to dial-in exquisite sauces without ever yelling at anyone, guided me toward the sink. He stood behind me, our hands intertwined under the faucet. He rocked me back and forth as cold water ran over our hands. This is how men can turn out when they live in Sebastopol and attend men's groups on the regular. He was not the least bit freaked out by my gay blood. (I would later learn that his brother had died of AIDS.) Tasha brought me lavender oil, and other cooks reassured me by showing me their kitchen wounds. Instead of this being a shameful monument to my ineptitude, the cooks turned it into a rite of passage. Carin said she once got hired for a cooking job after the head chef asked her to "show me your scars."

Teo took me back to my station. He showed me how to put a dishtowel under the cutting board to make it easier on your joints. He taught me about tucking my fingertips into a claw, how to peel and chop an onion. There is a system for this, so you get uniform pieces—I'd just thought you hacked at things until they were small. Throughout the week, I would chop and slice and dice an array of ingredients. There is no better education than spending an hour turning bell peppers into strips, a pound of mint leaves into thin ribbons. You fall into relationships, and you understand the architectural strategies of plants. You get those strategies into your hands.

Being in a communal kitchen is a witchcraft of the body. You bleed, you burn, you turn ankles, all in the project of feeding hungry witches. And not just feeding them—surprising them, sending them home with aspirations and fantasies. All week there would be moments where a chef pulled out a container of something to elevate dinner. Currants they'd wildcrafted, pickled pineapple, bread made from yeast they'd somehow captured in the redwood trees just outside the kitchen. These people traveled with gallon jars. They took pleasure in making people gasp as the meal's ingredients were announced during the dinner circle.

Ed and I went to Witchcamp together for the next eight years, Ed as a camper and me as a cook. This created more connection between those worlds, and we felt like not-so-secret double agents. As the oldest of ten kids, Ed spent his childhood gathering children into the station wagon, making sure sunscreen was packed and explaining the rules of the game so that the four-year-olds could play. Ed also loves a prank. People think they are getting Mr. Rogers and then he sneaks in Pee Wee Herman. We embarked on a camp-wide prank of having a Sacred Pie Fight, where we set out a hundred tins of freshly whipped cream (yes, we included vegan options) and let all these gentle pagans go at it. We had to get the approval of camp director Madrone, since this could have gone sideways in so many ways. Madrone was not only all-in, but had the foresight to wear goggles and wrap her blonde mane in plastic wrap. A few of the campers did not take this precaution and spent the rest of the week smelling and itching as cheese formed in their ear canals.

Witchcraft is adult children's theater. Witchcraft is the interplay of woodland adventure and wise precaution.

Ed ran the raffle to raise money to make the camp more financially accessible. People routinely bought raffle tickets and wrote other people's names on them. I organized the talent show and emceed the live auction. Auctions were usually little festivals of people swinging their money-dicks around, opening their wallet for a cause. Often a teacher or cook or a lady who sold her own tinctures for a living would start bidding and tap out at $60. People would add onto their bids so financial underdogs could win big items like a photograph by Michael Rauner or Michael Starkman. This method would involve both a scribe at an easel and a math person.

Witchcraft is knowing that, until we can dismantle capitalism altogether, we can demonstrate alternatives. Witchcraft is going into the antique white rooms of the governor's mansion and guerilla-decorating a parlor with merlot walls and a silver ceiling.

I really learned about cooking when I naively suggested doing a southern-themed luncheon, the kind we would have after church in Virginia. Carin, who for years had an email address starting with "yescarin," said "Yes, you should lead this. Send me a shopping list." I still didn't really understand the chemistry of salt or what the hell a roux was, but these people were hell-bent on sharing power. Our baker Nora made buttermilk biscuits, Teo helped me adapt my mother's corn pudding recipe. Tasha made a vegetarian version of fried chicken. We had mint lemonade and a salad with candied pecans and vegan ranch dressing. We had baked beans and sneaked half a can of Budweiser into the otherwise clean and sober camp as a homeopathic agent.

The Witchcamp talent shows were the place I felt safest to be weird. We stacked wooden benches onto tables and created a shabby-chic mini-stadium with a red curtain that inexplicably had soccer balls all over it. We crammed 120 people into one side of the dining room and lit the place up with Christmas lights. If you have a few strands of white lights and a benevolent spirit, you have theater. This is where I learned the most about how to perform and emcee. It's where I decided it would be a good idea to dip pages of the Bible into my urine and paper mâché them onto my skin. It's where I used fans and a tragic wig to imagine myself as Stevie Nicks leaving rehab. One thing is for certain about modern witchcraft: at the end of the day, the only real deity is Stevie Nicks. Just as Jesus Christ is the glue that holds together myriad Protestant tribes, Miss Stephanie Lynn Nicks is the unifying force of the pagan world. She says bring me your poor, bring me your tired, bring me your leather and lace.

Witchcraft is the seemingly impossible integration of worlds. Witchcraft is trusting a group to help you do it.

Something the cooks said a lot was, "It's bright!" One would be making the sauce for the meal, which felt to me like just too much pressure. It meant reducing a gallon of material into a pungent oil slick of elixir. The sauce would need to be strong—you had to know how much salt and garlic (always more than you think), how to balance the acids and bases, the sugars and umami. You had to stir in a bit of "What the fuck is this?" The cooks would tell you if it needed something, and the way they would express approval when a sauce had really arrived was to say "It's bright!" Tasha had an apron that said Boss of Sauce. The apron might float around, depending on who was Boss of Sauce for that meal. Nobody could be Boss of Sauce all the time, they would surely crumble under all that responsibility. It's why I am happy being a registered nurse and don't want to become a nurse practitioner. I don't want to be in charge of anyone's cancer. This is how I felt about being the Boss of Sauce.

Witchcraft is writing and writing is witchcraft. Witchcraft is helping someone with their abortion.

We gave all the dishes provocative names. We would write them down on folded index cards as food was going out, a spicy afterthought. The names would be tender, like Love Yourself Soup, or sexy, like Lick Somebody Lentils. These names embodied the cook team's temperament, an intersection of sweet, salty, and bitter. Occasionally our shadows would escape the kitchen, like the time Kenneth titled a hotel pan full of couscous, "Zionist Rice." Kenneth was no Zionist and was about as leftist Jew as you can get. He was the kind of person who wildcrafts herbs and makes tinctures right there on the side of the road. We had just finished a gnarly lunch prep, frying falafel. Kenneth had been our Fry Daddy, standing for an hour over a hot stove and getting burned by splashes of oil.

Almost as soon as we returned to the kitchen, an enraged camper named Margaret flung open the door with the offending notecard held high above her head like it was fully aflame. She helmed a delegation of stern-looking campers. She was a retired public health nurse, and as a nurse myself I can tell you that you don't want a retired one angry with you.

Kenneth got his dander up. Nobody in that moment was flexing their nonviolent communication muscles. But we talked it through and made our sincere apologies. When Margaret and her coven left the kitchen, we laughed in cook solidarity. That was bad and we knew it. But we were surrounded by a lot of rose quartz-types. We were the people of gravel. We were the people who wielded hammers, splitting open rocks to reveal geodes. We were the cooks, providing persistent access to the human shadow. Sometimes that goes wrong and ideally you apologize, and your community forgives you.

Part of the beauty of Witchcamp was that it was such a heightened environment of metaphor and mythology. You were surrounded by people who thought nothing of spilling red paint on the steps of a federal building. These were people who had been lit up by Starhawk, whose goddess-based Reclaiming tradition encompassed magic and activism. Her books *The Spiral Dance* and *The Fifth Sacred Thing* were seminal texts for many of the campers. For Ed and I, she was our next-door neighbor back in San Francisco. We parked our bikes in her basement and frequently unloaded our vehicle in her driveway since our building didn't have a garage.

Witchcraft is having a community garage. Witchcraft is sharing your costume closet. Witchcraft is finding your people and bringing them jars of plum jam.

At the end of Witchcamp, we would always do a spiral dance, in the daylight. The way a spiral dance works is, you start in a circle, and it opens up in one spot to become a long, snaking line. You end up spiraling past everyone. Their faces go by. Many of them are crying or smiling. You see someone crying, someone who doesn't seem like they would do that in public, and it sets you off. Just pushes the old weep-o-rama button. Even the crustiest cooks would be leaking tears as we sang this song by Kentucky-born witch Ravyn Stanfield:

We are the kiss between earth and heaven
We are the song between sky and ground
Sing for your life and the world we're making

Nothing is lost that can't be found

The last day of Witchcamp, Tasha came up to me and handed me a small bundle. I untied it and there it was, the Boss of Sauce apron. It was covered in oil and sweat and eyeshadow and probably chipmunk poop. It was a sacred garment, one I felt I would never earn the right to wear. Anticipating my reluctance, Tasha hugged me and said, "You are if you say you are."

Who's really a witch? Who decides who gets to be a witch? A fundamental question in this modern world, where our people don't sport pointy hats and ride broomsticks. What is the qualifier? Do you have to know the names of a certain number of plants? Is there some initiation ceremony where you are led into a glade? Do you have to pass a witch exam and be licensed to practice?

You are if you say you are. That is a good place to start.

Witchcraft is whatever you say it is. Witchcraft is dark matter and can never be destroyed. Every generation tries to burn it down and relentless morels and fire-loving flowers spring up from the blackened earth. We are People of Perpetual Resurrection. We are who we say we are.

Mia Tsang

We Are W.I.T.C.H.

It's 2004 in Walnut Creek, California, and I'm lounging. Short legs stretched straight out across scratchy gray carpet, leaning against what feels to me to be an enormous backrest–in actuality it's probably just made for an adult. Our next-door neighbor Diane, a saintly Australian teetering-on-grandmother, has set me up in front of their box TV with a bowl of popcorn and turned the channel to my favorite network for cartoons: JETIX (may she rest in peace). At the top of the hour, the screen goes black. Then, a blue shimmer: a portal splits the screen, and an Evanescence-style guitar riff splits my ears. A red-haired girl in a pink hoodie materializes in the center of the portal, a pendant glowing around her neck. A pair of eyes glower down at her as Marion Raven's voice belts over a percussive explosion:

THERE IS A PLACE WHERE DARKNESS REIGNS / WE'VE GOT THE POWER TO FIGHT BACK /

WE SAVE THE DAY, UNITED FIVE AS ONE.

My parents don't let me watch cable, and my mom has a reasonable rule of "non-violence" in my shows—I'm four-years-old, after all. But whenever they leave me at Rick and Diane's, there's an understanding that I can watch whatever I want. It's usually in line with my parents' rules. Given a choice between cable and the Watsons's vast VHS collection, which includes *The Land Before Time* and *Duck Tales*, cable always loses.

Unless *W.I.T.C.H.* is on.

The short-lived cartoon follows five 13-year-old girls who aren't technically witches,–they're just fans of an acronym. At the series' opening, they are gifted/cursed (depending how you look at it) with the ability to transform from pubescent tweens into fairylike adult women with elemental powers. They are tasked with the massive responsibility of being the youngest-ever Guardians of the Veil, a metaphysical barrier separating the evil dimension of Metamoor from the rest of the universe. The Guardians must use their powers to close the portals that keep opening in the Veil and defeat the creatures that are able to sneak through the portals to wreak havoc on Earth.

Before it becomes a show, *W.I.T.C.H.* begins as an Italian manga series that's then adapted into a children's chapter book series. For my 5th birthday, my cousin Kevin gives me a boxed set of the first eight. I devour them like I do most books set in front of me. The next few years of my life, I look for them everywhere. I comb every rest stop and airport bookstore and Borders (may she rest in PEACE) and Barnes & Noble head to toe. My parents help me look for them. My birthdays are a slam dunk. Christmas set. Eventually, I collect and absorb all 26 novels in the series, eight graphic novel adaptations of the first 16 novels, and four spinoff books. In comparison to the plot of the cartoon, the manga and books deal with darker themes and delve deeper into the personal and familial lives of the girls. *W.I.T.C.H.* becomes my first real experience with fandom—I quickly grow obsessed with everything to do with the Guardians. I write elaborate Fan Fiction about them in my head (and sometimes on paper), long before I learn there's a term for what I'm doing. I spend hours on the (now-defunct) *W.I.T.C.H.* page of Disney Dot Com, where you could send messages to the Guardian of your choice. I write novels to them about my devotion, and I'm totally crushed when they never write back (but it doesn't stop me from writing). Unlike the other first-graders, I don't possess the suspension of disbelief required to have an imaginary friend, but I want to fit in so badly. So on the playground I throw wood chips in the air and tell my friends it's Cornelia whipping a powerful tornado of earth around us; I spray them with my squeeze bottle and tell them it's Irma shooting jets of water from her hands; I leap off the swings and tell them it's Hay Lin lifting me into the air, the way she carries her flightless friends to safety in battle.

Rarely do I allow myself to imagine what it would be like to actually be a Guardian. Even in my wildest fantasies, even in the stories I tell myself when I'm trying to fall asleep, I can never seem to cast myself as more than their token powerless friend who they leave behind when they go on their missions to Metamoor. Despite what my parents tell me, I have a sneaking suspicion that I am not that special—that I am boring, that I am weak, that I could never have the power to change the world, let alone save it.

This is the consensus among my classmates as well. Chalk it up to being a scrawny, ethnically ambiguous girl, chalk it up to my subtle buzz of lesbianism despite my hyper-femininity, chalk it up to the rural, lily-white town in upstate New York we move to right before I turn six. The vibrancy of how our family looks, lives, and loves blows these people's minds, in a bad way. For the twelve long years we live there I'm never able to shake the label, or feeling, of new girl.

Neither is Will.

WILL VANDOM – ENERGY/THE HEART

Will is new to Heatherfield. She has a tumultuous relationship with her single mother, and the very girls she's thrown together with for this life-changing inheritance of power were ignoring her at school just the day before. So 13. So human. Her bright red hair and tomboy presentation render her a loner among her peers. I learn at an early age from this show that girlhood doesn't have one correct aesthetic. Each of the girls were distinct characters with their distinct styles, and they expressed their femininity very differently. Will was the first girl I'd seen on TV who *was* a girl but chose to go by a "boy's" name and dress in a hoodie and jeans. Gasp. She has cripplingly low self-esteem because she is a teenager who just switched middle schools in the middle of the academic year. So when she is given possession of the Heart, the amulet that activates all of their powers and lets them transform, she gets a sense of wholeness for the first time in her life; she thinks it must be a mistake. She thinks she doesn't deserve it. She feels she needs to prove herself, and she nearly loses everything trying. But her friends believe in her. They teach her she's worthy of the power she's been given. By the end of the series, she has come into her own as a leader, the glue that holds her friends together. I want to become this kind of girl, someone who can connect my friends and help them transform into the strongest versions of themselves. Someone essential.

IRMA LAIR – WATER

I'll admit right out of the gate that I am in love with Irma. Maybe it's because she controls water, and this is my deepest, most childlike fantasy. I am my best self beside a body of water. The balance of supreme peace and supreme terror resets my emotional barometer. I can't really swim—in an emergency, maybe I could float on my back, but I lack the core strength to tread water. I almost drowned when I was three. I've seen the tapes. My older sister puts my goggles on, and I tip forward, limbs out, into the pool behind our house. I sink, slowly. I don't even try to swim. I always want to laugh when I think about this. Zero instinct for survival, even then. If I can suddenly control the thing that would otherwise kill me, I won't need to be afraid anymore. Anyone who has the power to protect me has my heart forever. In the bathtub I put my goggles on and practice holding my breath. In the shower I hold my arms out and let the water run down my fingers and pretend the trickle off my nails is really my own power.

Plus, Irma is just so funny, and she is always getting in trouble for making jokes at inappropriate times. If that isn't me, even at the age of four. She's someone who knows not to take life too seriously. (In my head she is Latina on her birth mom's side. Her lore is deep and intricate, novel—25, Enchanted Waters, still makes me cry as a grown woman.) She's also the only one who doesn't end up with a male love interest, which instantly catches my attention: she's available. It's worth noting that out of all the Guardians, I write to Irma on the *W.I.T.C.H.* website the most. By miles. I'm flirting like the baby femme I am: I compliment her outfit and fixate on her shiny auburn hair, the way it curls up at the ends. I forget she isn't real when I demand her curl routine. *luv ur hair so much but how do you get it to stay up????* I get increasingly desperate. I prostrate myself before the digital image of her transformed—the turquoise crop top, the magenta miniskirt. *pls pls write back to me and tell me, PLEASE.* And then, suddenly, I turn eight, and I move on to a girl who actually exists. God, I yearn for the amnesia of childhood.

TARANEE COOK – FIRE

Once the new girl, now mostly ~~assimilated~~ acclimated, but perpetually aware of her recent outsider status, Taranee just wants to fit in. When she's given the power over fire, she is devastated. She and Will form close bonds over feeling undeserving of their powers, but Taranee's relationship to her ability is more antagonistic. She has always struggled with a simmering anger at always having to be the top student and the perfect daughter of a well-respected judge. She craves control over her powers, her emotions, her life. Instead, she is given the ability to shoot flames out of her hands. The metaphor is perhaps clunky, but it gets the point across: if you don't learn how and when to release the fire within, it will eventually burn you alive.

As a young child I struggle with fits of rage. Whenever an emotion overwhelms me beyond articulation, I lash out. I destroy. I cut the hair off my Barbies and fling my stuffed animals against the wall. Then I sink down among the wreckage I've made and crumble with self-loathing. I immediately regret everything I've done, which didn't glue the hair back on or tape the drawings back together, or, or, or. I cradle my stuffed animals, sobbing and shaking with guilt, rocking them in my arms as though beneath their plush they're bruised. From these incidents, I learn to turn my anger inward. For many years I'm like Taranee. I'm shy, scared, my own worst critic. This way I'll only hurt myself. But eventually, late in the book series, she boils over. She learns there is a time and place for anger. There is a time and place for razing it all to the ground. In learning how to wield and tame her flames, she grows into a confident, assertive young woman. She inspires me to teach myself how to do the same.

CORNELIA HALE – EARTH

Cornelia was my least favorite of the Guardians at first. At the beginning of the series, she convinces the others to exclude Will at school and is furious that Will is chosen as Keeper of the Heart instead of her. She's always at war with Irma, shooting down her jokes and sniping at her.So out of loyalty to my girlfriend, I decide I am at war with Cornelia. She's a prototypical early 2000s mean girl. Snobby and vain, blonde and blue-eyed, whiny in that specific cartoon prissiness. But I soon learn that Cornelia and I have one major thing in common: we're both hopeless romantics. I am always opening my heart to the wrong person at the drop of a hat, giving up too much of myself too soon in exchange for far too little. I know what it feels like to love so hard the world thinks you're crazy. I know what it feels like to love so hard you'd bend the rules of the universe to have that person by your side.

While fighting alongside the Metamoor rebels, Cornelia falls deeply in love with their leader. In the books, their romance is doomed—he falls for her when she's in her transformed state and looks much older, but when he realizes she's only 13, he ends their relationship. It's a rare example in children's media of a man doing the responsible thing and deciding not to prey on a teenage girl, no matter how strong her feelings are for him. Seeing how her friends support her through her heartbreak, how they view her vast capacity for love as a strength rather than a weakness, I start to think that maybe someday I'll find friends who will do the same for me.

HAY LIN – AIR

Every time I see Hay Lin in the title sequence, I want to burst into tears. She is the first Chinese character I've ever seen on television. She's the one who comes up with W.I.T.C.H.: an acronym of the first letter of each of their first names. Her mind runs on a different frequency. She's always drawing, making her own clothes, designing sets for the school musical. Her father reminds me of my own. In the book series his mother, Hay Lin's grandma, passes away before she can reveal the full truth about becoming Guardians. (In the cartoon, Yan Lin not only stays alive but also serves as an ally to the girls. TV shows always need to have an adult involved.) Her bond with Hay Lin is the emotional heart of the book series—in memory of her grandmother, Hay Lin dedicates herself to learning how to use her powers and the mythology behind them. Her friends follow in her footsteps out of love. They know how much it means to her, so they commit themselves, even those (Cornelia) who are less thrilled about their new abilities. I envy her liberation and admire her creativity. Asian women are often fetishized for our (expected) (demanded) subservience and fragility. There is something so empowering in watching Hay Lin literally take flight, soaring out of the grasp of anyone who tries to harm her. Watching her fight sends lightning down my spine, forcing me to sit up straight, alert, alive. The call to action has never been clearer. I want to learn to defend myself. So a year later, when my mother offers to sign me up for karate in exchange for a slice of pizza, I agree. When I get my black belt six years later, I think of Hay Lin exhaling her enemies away in hurricane breaths, and for just a second I swear I feel my feet hover an inch above the mat.

W.I.T.C.H. is about many things: forever hiding a crucial part of who you are from your family out of fear, or to protect them, or both (queercoded?); first love driving you crazy, fighting with your parents, failing math class, reinstating your friend to her rightful place on the throne of another world after defeating her evil brother in an armed uprising. Ultimately, though, *W.I.T.C.H.* is about the power of friendship between teenage girls. When the Guardians' relationships to each other become strained, their powers sputter and wane. When they can embrace each other for who they are, with all their strengths and flaws, their powers blossom. My friends are the greatest loves of my life; they know me and still love me. When I was five, six, seven, etc, watching *W.I.T.C.H.* and rereading the novels until their spines cracked and flaked off, I thought it impossible to have five close friends who all got along with each other. Now, I look at my friends dancing in their seats across the table from me at Art Bar, or eating Thai takeout next to me on their couch while Tiny Desk Concerts play on the TV in the background, and cannot believe how lucky I am. As we sit in the moment's afterglow, I often describe this feeling to them as feeling *teenager* again, *high school* without all the bullshit. Strangely innocent. Pure. It has taken a long time and a lot of work to get to this point. Two decades have passed since I watched my first episode, but I still try to live my life with Will's empathy, Irma's humor, Taranee's courage, Cornelia's heart, and Hay Lin's spirit. I try to channel my fear into rage and use it to fuel me into righteous action. There will always be a place where darkness reigns—we know exactly where, and through whom, and we do have the power to fight back, but only as a collective. Our strength springs from friendship, from love. There is no difference.

Cat Tyc

I Am Because My Little Dog Knows Me

Last summer, a woman I knew invited me and most of the people I know to an inlet of land off the Belt Parkway called Plumb Beach to count mating horseshoe crabs. The invite read:

Witness the once-a-year full moon mating ritual of the horseshoe crab in Jamaica Bay. See and touch these ancient creatures as they crawl ashore at high tide. Find your spirit animal seaside with the help of a shaman. Pace the edge of the waterline with scientific experts as the full moon rises over the ocean.

So on that day, Nick and Brock and I rode the A train for a very long time. Occasionally asking each other why we were going. Listing bullet points, but still far from answers, beside the fact that it was a beautiful Sunday. A precarious mantle. A nice thing to do on a Sunday. That thing about the shaman and spirit animals sounds like a nice thing to do on a Sunday.

Once, another evening before this one, the inviting woman told me she thought that I especially needed to meet this shaman.

That night, the conversation kept pointing back to this place. A place I used to live and now often comes up in conversation where I now live as a place people imagine to be a lot easier. This place we live in is so hard and that place would be so much easier. They imagine. When this happens, people often ask about my time in that place. They find it so fascinating that I came back to this place. This awful place.

Often, I pedal back from most conversations to cover up the dread I feel towards that place and, if I am really honest, my desire to escape that brought me there. My pat answer for this situation is usually, "I'm not really the best person to ask. Check it out for yourself but don't move there." This response never accomplishes what I want, people tend to push for more. Like this night, that is what the woman did, so I felt cornered as I explained what this place represents to me.

That place. A land of knee-jerk response and self-satisfaction. Impressions collaged together to build a cut-and-paste culture to white out anything complicated. Denying any space to say anything as if erasing the problems wasn't a more problematic position.

This woman told me that she felt a soul renewal was in order for me. As if my soul was tarnished, by myself or by this place, that part was unclear. But I wanted to clear my frustration for thinking a place would have an answer. So I was interested.

After the train, we proceeded in a car to a blip off the highway. A path to a beach. Later, my friend Amalle tells me that Plumb Beach used to be a very popular spot for gay cruising because the shore was blanketed by overgrown bushes.

Now the bushes were all cut down, and we met up with others that some of us knew and some didn't standing in a parking lot with the same expression of "What am I doing here ?" on their faces.

The only ones who seemed to know what was going on were the scientists who kept thanking us for coming and taking all our information down on clipboards.

Off to the side, I saw a woman about my age wearing a long flowing skirt scream, "HEY ! I AM THE SHAMAN."

Her hair was long and free and at closer look, she seemed about twelve. And this was the fact that shattered the illusion that many, or maybe let's just say I, had—which was that this person who took on the title *shaman* would align with studies within a culture that would deem the act as one that could be appropriate. But even that word . . . appropriate.

Here we were on a beach wedged between the city and the sky with literally no idea why we were here if we were to be questioned . . . and here I was wondering about what was appropriate ? Going forward felt flimsy, but this was all we had.

Once we were all collected, she led us onto the beach and asked us to lie down on the sand in a circle and imagine a place in nature that makes us feel safe. *Can you tell me a place in nature that makes you feel safe?*

I chose the place behind my mother's house. I saw boats. A picnic table. An abandoned theater. The shaman told us to dig a hole in that place so that we could climb down into our mind. She told us to pay attention to everything. To use our imagination. That word always connects me to the naïve, so I think this is why my first draft of an animal came out kind of cartoonish. Like a street artist drawing at a tourist attraction.

I imagined a cat of human size wearing a button-down shirt, gingham, and khaki pants. A belt and the shirt tucked in like a very old man. So, that is exactly who I meet when I finish climbing down the hole but we both know that it is not right. He is not the animal I am looking for.

He tells me, "I am only a figment of your imagination." Then looks down at himself, shrugs, and says, "Not bad." Then he leads me down a hallway where behind every corner is a dog. Every dog I ever cared for when I used to work as a dog walker. And then there is the door at the end of the corridor, and I know before I open it that I will see my dog, Thurston. But this feels too obvious.

Even when it happens. We open the door and there he sits on his hind quarters looking slightly bored. I tell myself to believe that this is when he can speak.

We are not here to be our normal selves. I have to trust that he has something to say to me. I ask him what it is. And he tells me, "You have to learn to not give yourself away. Make them love you, but don't let them have you. "

And then he scratches his face with his back leg for a second and drinks in a deep yawn. Then he continues.

"This is not the same thing as not speaking your mind. State exactly what you think, tell them what you need. But they don't have you. They can never hold you.

The objective of this game is to map the field of desire. Given that the desire is positive. *We take "positive" to mean that it exists, that it is present and not absent, and that it can be positioned. For example, many desires result in what we feel are negative outcomes. Observe a given. The given could be a situation, a feeling, a problem. Anything that can be observed is given, absolute. The given may be something that was given previously. Be careful to separate observation from evaluation. For example, if it is raining, I could whine, "It's not supposed to rain." You would hear it in my voice. But it is absolutely raining. If I feel bad, I can't say, "I shouldn't feel bad." I just feel bad. So I make that sound. To let you know. I'm not happy about the rain.* Now, position a desire.

This may be in the form of a question, command, request, or simply those things you call words. The desire may be directly related to the given, the result of cause/effect, or a subconscious trigger. For example, sometimes when I feel bad,

I pant. I would like water. I'm a little nervous. That makes me feels me kind of thirsty.

So, being that I feel bad, I desire to run in the grass. Kind of like now. To work it all out. But we are only surrounded by dirt. So I will dig a hole instead. Until I feel better. Or sufficiently dirty. Whichever comes first.

Then, he stopped to dig a hole with his front paws. His concentration was remarkable in its focus. He took his time digging until he was sufficiently calmed. Then, he shook himself free from the dirt with moderate success and continued: *The desire may be realized immediately or positioned in a now possible future.*

To map a field of desire. One treats the difference between what you have and what you want as a problem of connection. From here we can map trajectories, patterns, behaviors, intersections, alignments, making it possible for one desire trajectory to activate another desire trajectory. Developing the practice entails the establishment of a resonant frequency between the desires of two or more beings—or in individual cases, your desires and your environment—without resorting to guilt, threat, or coercion.

The structure and language allow for the greatest possibility for interpretation of desire in relation to actual environment.

It is a feedback loop that hypothesizes that one's choice of a given reality determines the possibilities and outcomes of desire. I do not know how long we lay there.

When we are asked to wake, I realize my body matches the coolness of the sand. We shake out our stopped blood. The *shaman* asks if anyone wants to share and the only person who speaks is the lead scientist.

She has something to say in regard to something that was said before we began to sink into our holes. There was a group meditation. In the *shaman's* guided message, she stated something to the effect that we should send our worries to the sea, and this was something the scientist took issue with.

She felt it was important to remind the group that we didn't have the right to throw anything to the sea. Ever. The *shaman* was threatened and did very little to hide it.

The fact that our spiritual leader and science specialist had an inability to understand each other unraveled the moment.

It unraveled the night.

These politics landed like stink bombs over the sand, and made people shift their weight and look out into the sky. Too vulnerable we are from the devastation, it accumulated in our bodies. We are not Teflon, but we could have moved on. But neither the scientist nor the shaman took the lead to hear each other, so things became awkward.

Our spiritual leader couldn't perform compassion, and the scientist seemed too comfortable on the high ground, so there we were, processing vulnerability as it mutated before our eyes into disposability. I think most of us were there for the spirit but our leader on that front wasn't as authoritative in the way most of us needed.

Before we hit the beach, the woman who brought us here felt it was important to tell me that the *shaman* was a former dominatrix and that her spiritual practice was an extension of that. At a loss by what the woman's intention was in telling me this, I chose to ignore it.

All I saw was a woman putting on a costume and performing a script to allow someone to feel like they weren't really in control. That they didn't have to have all the answers. That there was a pleasure in floating above the ground and letting go of everything. Giving the moment, their time, to someone else to manage.

Saying, "Trust me, it's yours, and I am simply a conduit, one of many, escalating within the confines of the boundary you create." The levels of restriction on the clothing differed but this *shaman* gig seemed like kind of the same thing. Connecting these dots gave me insight, empathy, but also suspicion. But some people really believed.

My friend Sabine came running up to me and told me she was a rooster.

Her wide and watery grin conveyed an enthusiasm that reminded me of that childlike quality only artists seem able to hold into adulthood.

During this time, the science crew circled up with their clipboards for a bit and then the science lady returned to explain the purpose of why we were there. The real reason.

On the night of the full moon, the horseshoe crabs meet along the Eastern Seaboard to mate, a ritual for millions of years. And she was part of an organization that counted how many came up to the shore to keep track of the population. As she explained this, suddenly, I loved her, this passion so totally hers, infectious. It made me think of things that gave me a feeling of purpose. I wanted to be as present for those things as she was to this count.

We divided into various working groups. Some held tape measures, and some were responsible for counting. One group for male crabs and one for the females. Not everyone in the group had a role in the counting.

There were way more of us than necessary and I just wanted to observe so I stepped away. Others had already petered out, the ones that had taken acid, but those still standing fell into a flow, following a counter and watching. Talking. I decided to walk with the *shaman*. The others, my friends, couldn't stop bad mouthing her. By standing with them, I wasn't sure if I was being fair. But I wasn't even sure why I was there. I felt complicit to something but I wasn't sure what.

I started the conversation by telling her how I thought my dog was the animal I came to the beach in the beginning exercise and that I had some unresolved feelings about it. She seemed disinterested. Which just made me mad at her.

Once, before this night, I had a late-night email conversation with my friend T who asked me to participate in a performance that involved a seance.

They wanted me to write in the space and have my dog, Thurston, there as the representation of a maternal connection. Thurston and I were still recovering from a trip to the emergency room that he almost didn't survive so I asked them, *Why Thurston?*

They answered back in an email, *"Because you are so connected with him. Of course you don't have to bring him. You could do something else—but it is that exact thing, that material and spiritual connection (and dare I call it companionship) that extends between worlds that made me think you two would be good for this piece.*

That and something in his eyes. But I totally understand if he's not up for it. Perhaps you can think of another simple reproductive task or action that has this feel?

I answered: *I had a feeling this is why. I am questioning because I am feeling protective. So much of Thurston & I's relationship lately has been coming to terms with the inevitability of death and what that means. Holding on and letting go is what I think about deeply when I allow myself to go there so. I see where you are going with this. I think what scares me is putting him in a space opening up to the spiritual world.*

Because I am doing everything I can to keep him in this world, to keep his heart healthy. My need for him is very much based in a maternal desire that I struggle with. I adopted him knowing he had this heart murmur and that was why he was probably abandoned. When I first fell in love with him I knew part of that was to not be like the others and see him to his end.

So in my logical mind, this all makes sense and seems very strong but in practice, this is very hard. I see the potential for catharsis though.

Is it ok to say this scares me? Not in a scary ghost kind of way but more like a facing the truth kind of way?

T: *Cat, maybe Thurston stays home and we think of something else? or something that allows the confrontation for you without the discomfort. let's chat more tomorrow after a good night's rest. P.S. just so you know, I see you and Thurston and your relationship as a spiritual force in its own right, no ritual required. seance in its etymology simply means sitting or session. there are things much deeper than art and ritual. then again, art and ritual have the power to compose healing. still, this is an experiment and perhaps it's better not to take chances.*

more later.

x, T

Once, I had a friend who was a dom for several years until she retired and decided to manage an S&M club in the East 30s. When the friend told me about the shaman's previous employment, I immediately thought of her. Wondered what she was doing now.

Sometimes she would call me in the middle of the night to come over to the dungeon and share a bottle of champagne. One night, I took her up on her offer. One of the clients liked to come by and present her with a bottle of champagne to watch her drink it. It had become their ritual.

She described this as we waited for his arrival. She made it sound so normal. And when he arrived, they greeted each other like old friends, making small talk about traffic and weather. Once his jacket was off, he went straight to the task and grabbed for the bag and the bottle.

My friend became rigid and said, "No," and then pointed over at me, smoking a cigarette and sitting on the black leather couch, observing this scene like an audience member seated at a play. "Present it to her." He immediately turned and walked towards me and then got down on his knees. "Would you like me to open it?" "Sure. But I need to ask you something."

"What is it?"

"Why do you do this?"

"I don't understand."

"Why do you enjoy this?"

He took a minute to untwist the muselet cage that held the cork into the bottle. And then he seemed to understand my question.

"When I was married, my wife and I used to fight all the time. It got to be the only way I felt connected . . . was when she was yelling at me, and now she's gone." He paused. Then said, "I just really miss her," and then he popped the cork. I guess this is why I expect more from the empathetic gesture of the *shaman* than agreeance. It's just a little more work than wearing a skirt.

Somewhere along the way in this conversation with the *shaman* on the beach, she figured out I was the one in need of a soul renewal according to our mutual friend. Then, I could see the hustle stream out of her, how she was the only one that could really see what I needed, and how I should set up a time to consult with her more about this. She had very negotiable rates.

I drifted back to my friends without saying anything else because that was the last straw, the trap back into the transactional. The counting continued but the majority of us just walked.

We kept going not because it gave us a sense of purpose, but more because there was nothing else to do, like the resolve one must take when they are stranded on the side of the road with nothing else to do but stand. We also moved because it was freezing.

The crabs slowly gathered, emphasis on slow, since the weather was stormier than expected, so it seemed like many of the ladies decided to stay in. It was easy to identify the female.

She was much larger and sank herself into the sand, waiting to be straddled. The males were considerably smaller and scurried around on the banks looking for a lady.

Like most bars, this beach was swarming with men, and much of our dialogue (the counters and walkers) was focused on that, in wishing them luck. Even going so far as to pick them up and point them in the right direction. As if to pass along some sort of interspecies karmic debt. Along the way, I reconnected with someone I used to know from that place where I used to live. We dated the same girl in that place. Now, her new girlfriend is in a band with my former best friend. The last time I saw her, she gave me a pair of noise canceling headphones. Another woman, I think it is her girlfriend, is silent from cold. We all want to go home. We try not to focus on that by making small talk. She just got back from visiting that place we used to live and she tells me that there are all these great new bars.

I say something about how that always seems to be what people focus on in that place. The drinking. Where you go to drink. She seemed confused, wondered if I was actually happy here, which felt so funny to be asked on this dark, freezing beach. So far from what you imagine when you think of life in the city. And I said, "Yes, more than anything, you know, I have to admit, I don't think of that other place. Never really have."

Our trusty science pack leader interrupts the conversation I didn't want to have by asking us if anyone wants to pick up a few of the male crabs so we can feel what is underneath their slimy shells.

We say yes and slowly graze our fingers over their wriggly, tarantula-like legs.

Natalie Lima

Witches

I wasn't sure if they were witches, but they certainly checked all the boxes. When Karma Eye, a New Age shop, opened a few blocks from my house, just across the street from my used-to-be-favorite comic book store—I decided to investigate. This was 1999 Las Vegas, and my comic book store had become overrun by Pokémon dweebs in search of shiny holographic Charizard cards, so I needed a new place to hang out. I was in 8th grade and my life had recently erupted like a ripe, inner-thigh boil. Within a few months' time my father got caught screwing the next-door neighbor at some dumpy off-strip hotel; I started eating everything deep-battered and fried and blew up to over 300 lbs.; and my best friend shaved her head, began wearing purple eyeshadow, and was suddenly crowned the coolest person in school. When I invited her over for our weekly Spice Girls sing-along one Friday, she batted her lacquered eyelashes and frowned.

The witches didn't care about any of that.

They were a pale bunch with long hair dyed ink-black, and lipstick and nails to match. Inside their shop, multicolored candles flickered and melted on tables scattered around, and translucent crystals lined the walls. There were tarot card decks and spell books. Everything fit most of the stereotypes, according to what I had seen in the movie, *The Craft*.

The first visit, when I spotted some vials behind the cash register labeled *Holy Water*, I asked, "What makes the water holy?" One witch tossed her hair back and said, "Because we blessed it with magic." And my jaw flung open like a nutcracker.

A week later, I stopped by the shop on my bike after school. The only witch present was busy, sweeping and cursing someone out on the phone, but she waved me in with the broom. I tiptoed around the store and rummaged through the inventory—essential oils, herbs, vintage jewelry made of various stones, pendulums—but I paused in front of a slim, corner bookcase stacked with faux-leather journals and flipped through them. Then I felt a hand on my shoulder. "Take one," the witch said.

I closed the journal and pulled it close to my chest. "Like, for free?"

"Yes, of course," the witch tittered. "I loved journaling when I was your age."

"Damn, for real? Thank you." I paused and looked down at my feet before looking back up at her. "Can I ask a quick question? Are you all really witches?"

She smoothed out her dress with her hands and said, "All the good women are."

I was hooked.

A month later, after I'd spent the last few weekends telling the witches about the horrors of middle school, and how my best friend didn't even look cute bald because she had an awkward-shaped head, I invited the witches to a pancake breakfast. The event was a fundraiser hosted by my LDS neighbors for their church. When the swarm of witches appeared in long, black frocks and trench coats, the sea of blue eyes darted up from their pancakes, in unison, and ogled at my guests, as if they were the first sign of the apocalypse. I laughed so hard I felt like I might float.

Two months later, the witches held a poetry night at the shop. In a room full of adults, I read some poems aloud from the journal they'd given me, the kinds of poems you might imagine a 13-year-old would write—about unrequited love and despair. And though the witches weren't a particularly animated bunch, when I finished the last line of my final poem, they leaped up into a standing ovation and cheered until my ears ached.

Five months later, when the shop had to close down because the people of Las Vegas apparently didn't appreciate the metaphysical, I hugged my friends goodbye. We stood outside in the midwinter breeze—my misfit team—and we stared eastward toward the hotel lights. There was school the next morning, so I hopped onto my bike, rubbing my hands together for warmth, and my witches all smiled at me as I waved goodbye. They were quiet but their look said it all: *Remember, you will never be alone, because we outsiders are everywhere.*

Sophia Le Fraga

why-do-birds-sing-in-the-morning.html

If you're curious how pussy tastes You can always try your own.

I cried both during and Then again after.

It was an ugly cry too.
I've been wanting to make a video

Working title: "Real Lesbians of Art School"
Sort of *Project Runway* meets *The L Word* (2004):

One dyke you're in
The next dyke, you're out.

I don't spend nearly enough time Exploring my internal "experience"

The quotidian of of-colorness The question of queerness

La lesbienne n'existe pas. There is a compelling theory

That the word "pussy"
Is short for "pusillanimous."

Who doesn't love Stein? "When you are you you are

You without the memory of you." I too want a dog named Basket.

At the beach the other day
I suddenly became the beach

The zipper wave, its pointy lip The ocean's bottom.

My chest rose and fell Like the tide.

It was raining
Beside and inside me

I could feel my face upon my face From the control room where I breathe.

The opposite of awe. The higher the femme

The closer to god. The smell one smells

In the emptiness. Dark
Like the space between stars

Like *Game of Thrones*
In its last season.

I'm not sure that there's A right way to kiss.

What I mean to say is I disintegrated into

A dizzying October
And saw myself glistening wet

Glowing full-battery green Thriving in the simulation.

You were there too
Or that is what it felt like

We were this fraction of A massive thing

Trapped in our bodies Unimpressed with the sky

The California coast Tiny underneath us.

Did I lose you for a second? Today I passed a restaurant

With a sign that read, "If you don't eat Here, we'll both starve."

Bras are so expensive It's insulting to boobs.

When I think of our life together
I'm proud of what we've accomplished

Unprecedented yadda yadda My hand in yours.

Blown-minded Bernadette One day we'll air on Bravo.

Other women kiss this way too.

Anywhere Biscuit

i seldom turn down a midnight snack of any nature.

this is why if you pull a tarot card, i'll say just grab me two.

i was looking through my old hard drive wondering about the lists i'd saved:

"tuesday, march 22" 10:00 - i can't wake up
10:30 - dishes from last night's shoot
11:15 - what is a surname? what is a given name?
11:30 - flirting with natasha
11:45 - hungry?
12:00 - what do i text eileen

the thing i'm avoiding saying out loud is that everything old
feels new again:

the children who need saving.
the britney song that makes me cry. the cups, the pentacles, the trees.

i've asked a lot of questions.
and my pot of water boils indefinitely. "untitled 68: a series of spells":
    1. to know you as the girl you were
    2. if in dance, stretched on pointe
    3. wilder risks, more at stake
    4. always friday dinnertime

i read all of simone weil without meaning to.

it was winter in lonavla.
a stray dog had found me
as i'd found simone
and we existed for weeks outside, the three of us.

we were in a marvelous jungle. fruits and flowers
i didn't even know how to name.

and you joined us later or was it before, all brown curls and moussey skin,
your breasts, my ass the wind said

"do you know that you're wildly attractive?"

i am flopping like a fish in my jesus year.

what in me
wants to perpetually build life with you, my
marmalade biscuit?
i am starting to get what it means. "untitled 18":
-manipulation in love poems
-time's inability to touch a person
-poetry's capacity to choreograph time

every day was tuesday when you called me sweetie.
i felt love and what was loving me was a red and yellow orb.

your appetite, my appetite.
i am trying to express the bigness. i was a branch
and you were the song of a sparrow resting upon me

can you understand this?

i asked about the thunder
i heard in the distance
my pot of water boiled with silence you sang:
it is the future.

and we are both still breathing under this sun

if we were back there with all we know now

what do you feel like we might see?

Adriana Rizzolo

Only Trust Gay Priests

I am an Italian witch from New Jersey.

Like many women spiraling in my 40s, I have survived multiple ego deaths, yet ironically, I've become more Jersey and more Italian each time. I've spent hundreds of thousands of countless hours in meditation, yoga, and relating to the living sacred feminine power inside called Kundalini Shakti. And yet, I can't seem to ever get over the fact that I am very Italian and from New Jersey.

A lineage of wild passionate lovers born from the sacred hills of India taught me that to ignore our sexuality is to mean rejecting death and therefore life. This is what Jesus said too when he came in me, literally, in a sex dream after years of me rejecting his presence.

Too boring, too white, too unreliable. I woke up thinking, was that him, or me? Whose cock was that? Do I have a cock? I wondered as I woke up in my friend Carla's house on the beach in Ventura. Fuck, I hope I wasn't moaning. You know how weird people get about kids and women's pleasure. It's disgusting although that is where we were all made. You know, the womb? In blood, love, the ejaculate that pours from a woman, in tears and tears.

I pilgrimaged to India 13 times before I ever stepped foot on the land where my ancestors worshiped the same Mother with a different name. They call her the Black Madonna. La Madonna Negra. She is the "other Mary," according to my elder gay priest friend Father Phil. I only trust gay priests.

The Divine Mother most know was born already liberated. A girl that lived in union with God from the start. Phil says she left the physical world because she was so merged with the spiritual, oozing with perfection and so interconnected with us there was no reason for her to be here.

The other Mary, the Black Madonna, came to be oh so very human. She worked for her freedom. For her Sacred Union.

This Mary seeks out those lost in between worlds, uplifts the ones who carry midnight sky and stars under their skin, dance in the shadows, make mistakes, know separation and ultimately, shine the brightest lights.

My body became a rosary, prostrated on cold temple floors countless times in India before returning to holding my own hand. I transformed into a nun in Calcutta, at Mother Teresa's home for the dying. The bread of Christ disintegrated on my tongue in true horny holy communion before I ever prayed in the language of my blood grandmothers.

But when I did, my body entered portals of timeless remembrance. I sang, danced, and spun for hours at the feet of Madonna de Libera. Madonna of Liberation. Her golden starry crown spinning with miracles. A whirling that carried me to other worlds while simultaneously welcoming parts long pushed away. A daughter in the Rose lineage.

In pre-Christian times, my Mediterranean ancestors worshiped the Goddess in the forest, invoking and embodying eros in orgiastic rituals, spinning like Sufis, singing, drumming and eating raw meat. Plant charmers and ghost dancers. Perhaps that's why I loved licking my fingers while helping my Grandma Josephine roll up meatballs every Sunday. That raw chop meat, garlic chunks, parmesan, Progresso breadcrumbs, and raw egg squishing through my fingers felt so damn good.

"Age, don't eat that you'll get sick!" My mother would yell from the living room as I snuck tiny pieces into my mouth behind my Grandma Josephine's back.

Jesus came in me, not to me, in a dream, and I awoke satisfied, tenderized, and fierce. Ready to make the world my bitch. No, my lover. Ready to take the cock Jesus gave me—non-consensually, may I add—but very much appreciated, and move in the world in a new way.

With a cock. A good one.

I could be present without pushing. No more overextending. Saying no when I meant it, yes when I felt that instant, sacral response. Filling the room, an argument, a sweet embrace with the most direct but wildly receptive penetration.

No more shrinking woman. No need to lose my voice so you can find yours.

I'd knock down every evil empire when hard and build our wolf dens when soft.

I am an Italian witch from New Jersey, in love with God and living in reverence for the rituals that remind us we have all the cock, balls, vagina, and ecstasy one could ever want, inside our human hearts.

We all carry the fertility of a future less bound and more loved. Call me Mary Magdalene, call me the Madonna, the Mother and whore who wants it all. Name me a successful, childless Mother of God bound to an eternal pregnancy. Call me what you will but know that I am not here to fuck around. Jesus fucked me for a good reason and that seed will stay protecting me so I can dismantle the calloused, abusive, boring, and plain old bad taste of the patriarchy until I rest my body back into the Earth. Into Her. Even when I return to the cosmos, this cure we create together will carry on.

We can learn to hold a womb full of creativity and pleasure within, one that can birth new worlds once we slow down to admit who we truly are.

The love we've always been. Portals to the unseen realms. Never too much, not enough. Always a dream inside a dream. Interconnected with intelligences that speak to us from the unseen, directly to the body.

A big messy cake—alive with mistakes, memories, and the Mother between my legs. Deliciously Divine.

Saskia Wilson-Brown

Witches: An Aromatic Meditation

Part 1. The Many Malodorous Fires of Post-Medieval Europe

Where does religion cede to magic? What is the line between good and evil? The post-medieval European witch embodied blurred boundaries: a healer, a harmer, demonic, magical, but often mundane. Above all, the post-medieval European witch was most commonly perceived as stinky, and decidedly up to no good.[1]

At the 1599 trial of Isabillon Parmentier in France, the suspected witch was accused of harming many cows and some people. Her behavior, which even some of her accusers didn't necessarily attribute to witchcraft, was rendered sinister primarily by her foul reputation. Occasionally, also, by the telltale aroma of sulphur. After disallowing her from passing through his garden, a laborer called Didier Langueville found his arms and legs paralyzed for six weeks, "during which time he smelled strangely of sulphur, and felt as if he was burning."[2]

In her first, second and third interrogations in May 1599, Isabillon denied being a witch, said that she didn't know Langueville and that moreover he was a "un meschant [sic] homme" (a mean man). No one believed her. How else to explain the suphur? In her fourth interrogation, and after the deployment of torture, she agreed that she had killed some people, had been to sabbath (but only once and she refused to name names), and was, indeed, a witch. Weeks later, she was executed.

---

1   Post medieval, in this context, roughly equates to early modernity, or the era after 1500 when the Renaissance started impacted thinking in Europe.

2   B 7326; Witch 123, Isabillon Femme Jean Parmentier, La Neufville-Devant-Nancy (1599). Poor. Prévôt of Bruyères 1599.

At a 1621 trial, Fleuratte Valdexey—widow of a man who had been burnt alive as a witch—was accused of talking to a suspicious unknown figure while "something like a wind came into barn, smelling of sulphur." The witness, Zabel, later testifies how she and Fleuratte were followed by a cart "drawn by 4 oxen and a black horse," which unexpectedly and suddenly disappeared from the road. Was it a phantom? Was it demonic? Fleuratte, in any case, asked Zabel to stay silent about the experience. In consequence, Zabel suspected that Fleuratte "might have been visited by her master," the Devil.[3] As with most accused witches, Fleuratte first denied being a witch, while providing more reasonable explanations for the accusations (jealousy, family disputes, etc.). But, again, how to explain the smell of sulphur? After being tortured and further threatened with the rack, she confessed. She had been the lover of a person dressed like a noble, had been to sabbath, and unlike Isabillon Parmentier, she named names. She was summarily executed in February, 1622.

Smell, while not the only marker of witchcraft, played an important part in these trials. Sulphur—or brimstone—was the accepted smell of Satan's domain: In Revelation 21:8, "murderers, the sexually immoral, sorcerers, idolaters, and all liars" will live in "the lake that burns with fire and sulphur."[4] Drawing from this entrenched cultural understanding, sulphur enlivened Didier Langueville and Zabel's accusations. No righteous woman could be accompanied by the smell; it was too clearly the sign of evil. The malevolent intentions of the accused were thus made indubitable through their olfactory link with Satan.[5]

Even when not visited by the devil, witches still reeked. In the context of Judaism, scholar Ana Sierka notes that "a foul odor appears as one of the most crucial features of the religious 'other'."[6] Across cultures and religions, witches, the perennial other, were repeatedly described as stinky and fetid.[7] The demonic Jewish lilioth, for instance, were attuned to the

3   B8730; Witch 309, Fleuratte Veuve Anthoine Valdexey, De Clefcy. Prévôt of Bruyères 1621.

4   "Revelation 21:8." Bible English Standard Version. Web. July 28 2024.

5   Graham, Jordan. "The Suspicious Smell of Witchcraft." *The Many-Headed Monster*. 2022. Web. June 12 2024.

6   Sierka, Anna. "The Smell of Mortal Man: When the Demonic Female Preys Upon the German Pietist." *Harvard Theological Review* 116.4 (2023): 575-98. Print.

7   Marovich, Beatrice. "Baba Yaga and the Mushrooms." Galactic Underworlds 2023. Web.

sweet scent of mortal men, which presented a stark contrast with their own fecal smell.[8] Pliny the Elder, for his part, associated witches with the unpleasant smell of burning chameleons.[9] In Shakespeare's Macbeth, the titular character notes the foulness of the day as he comes upon the Weird Sisters, playing on foul's double meaning as signifier of bad weather, and of bad smell.[10]

When not outright repugnant, witches smelled animalic. Their physical and olfactory connection to animals appears in countless descriptions. For Horace, an olfactory note is implied in a witch's hair, which was "fierce and bristling like a spiny sea urchin or like a wild-boar in the chase."[11] Scholar Jordan Graham notes that witches took the "shapes of unhealthy small animals such as toads, salamanders and rats through the use of inspissated air." And then, of course, there were goats, whose smell was associated with Satan, and sometimes extended to his witch agents.[12]

All this malodor, of course, can lead to only one logical conclusion in the Medieval European mind: Obliteration, and preferably by fire. Accordingly, these putrescent, animalic, magical, witchy bodies—when discovered—were often burnt to oblivion. Thus, the malodorous life of a medieval European witch ended in an equally malodorous death: animal stink, fetidness, and brimstone gave way to the pungent smell of charring flesh, eventually to be replaced by a more neutral pile of ash.

Part 2. Aromatic Potions, Powders, and Spells

Fleuratte Valdexey confessed to having been provided with powders by a fellow witch: A black powder to kill animals, a red one to kill people, a green one to cure. She tested them on a cat and a calf, both of which

8   Sierka, Anna. "The Smell of Mortal Man: When the Demonic Female Preys Upon the German Pietist." *Harvard Theological Review* 116.4 (2023): 575-98. Print.

9   Graham, Jordan. "The Suspicious Smell of Witchcraft." *The Many-Headed Monster.* 2022. Web. June 12 2024.

10   Shakespeare, William. "Macbeth." Folger Shakespeare Library. Web. September 28 2024

11   Horace, A. S. Kline. "Horace: The Epodes and Carmen Saeculare." *Poetry in Translation* 2005. Web. September 28 2024.

12   Graham, Jordan. "The Suspicious Smell of Witchcraft." *The Many-Headed Monster.* 2022. Web. June 12 2024.

died.[13] Another witch, confusingly also named Fleuratte, killed a girl—as she admitted tearfully in her 1615 trial—"by putting powder made from herbs the devil had shown her in wine."[14]

While post-medieval European witches most likely used mundane aromatic herbs as their magical materials of choice, writers often enjoyed imagining more recherché ingredients. Shakespeare's witches reached for "finger of birth-strangled babe ditch-delivered by a drab", "gall of goat and slips of yew", or "grease that's sweaten from the murderers' gibbet" to make their cauldron-boiled gruel.[15] More than a millennia earlier, Horace writes of a particularly savage witch called Candidia who starved a young boy to death in order to use his marrow and liver in a love potion. This and her other potions and unguents have unpleasant effects, as Horace describes in Epode XVII:

"My bones are covered now with yellowing skin,
My hair is whitened by your odorous unguents,
No respite ever frees me from your torments"[16]

While most likely these stomach-turning materials were based on literary fancy, ancient history certainly supports the use of repugnant materials in magic and witchcraft. A ritual from the Greco-Egyptian documents known as the Greek Magical Papyri, for instance, called for a piece of cloth "taken from one who has died violently," along with bones and nails from various animals. An Egyptian scribe tasked with compiling a list of materials most commonly used in magic details an astounding gallery of stink: Crocodile dung, bile, dirt, the blood of a baboon and of a spotted gecko, and many, many variations of semen. Also present are less malodorous materials like dill seed, chamomile, wormwood, cedar, and garlic.[17] It is these latter however that were most often included in the recorded potions, salves, and powders used by witches across the ages.

---

13 B8730; Witch 309, Fleuratte Veuve Anthoine Valdexey, De Clefcy. Prévôt of Bruyères 1621.

14 Fleuratte Femme Jean Maurice, Docelles. Prévôt of Bruyères 1615.

15 Shakespeare, William. "Macbeth." Folger Shakespeare Library. Web. September 28 2024.

16 Horace, A. S. Kline. "Horace: The Epodes and Carmen Saeculare." *Poetry in Translation 2005*. Web. September 28 2024.

17 "The Greek Magical Papyri." 2nd c. BCE - 5th c. CE. *The Greek Magical Papyri in Translation*. Ed. Betz, Hans Dieter. Chicago: The University of Chicago Press, 1986. Print.

They were, after all, far easier to obtain than lion semen, or, for that matter—the blood of Ares. They were also more empirically effective.

Enlivened by aroma, intention, and ritual, witchy concoctions were credited with all sorts of miraculous qualities. A balm used by the lilioth allowed them to "fly and copulate with each other as well as with beasts."[18] In Homer's Odyssey, Circe used herbs to help transform Odysseus' crew into pigs and other animals.[19] Greek witch Medea scattered aromatic herbs in the wind to entice her brother into an ambush.

These witches also, sometimes, put their concoctions to benevolent use.[20] In Medea's hands, the very same herbs she used to doom her brother also put a fearsome dragon to sleep, secured a king's capacity to sire an heir, and protected her beloved Jason.[21] As helpful as they were destructive, her aromatic tools—what Euripides called her Pharmaka—evolved over time to carry a more nuanced cultural meaning. They could harm, and they could heal. Even the ill-fated accused French witch Fleuratte Valdexey was given a green powder to cure.[22]

Through European history, the olfactory landscape of the witch has been suggestively linked to human perceptions of smell. She, herself, was stinking and evil—destined for ostracism or, at worst, the pyre. Her potions, unguents and powders are less clearly defined. While they certainly served as an extension of her power, they didn't necessarily carry the same immediate danger as the witch herself. In fact, sometimes they were useful. This is the space in which she was allowed a degree of nuanced complexity: The effects of her concoctions depended on her intention, and her intention wasn't always to hurt. Witches' tools—her functional herbs and potions—are in part the progenitors of modern pharmaceuticals, and their composed scents have evolved into luxury commodities in the form

18   Sierka, Anna. "The Smell of Mortal Man: When the Demonic Female Preys Upon the German Pietist." *Harvard Theological Review* 116.4 (2023): 575-98. Print.

19   Brown, Shelby. "Potions and Poisons: Classical Ancestors of the Wicked Witch, Part 1." 2015. Web. October 4 2024.

20   Ager, Britta. "Smells Like Witch Spirit: How the Ancient World's Scented Sorceresses Influence Ideas About Magic Today." *The Conversation* 2021. Web.

21   Brown, Shelby. "Potions and Poisons: Classical Ancestors of the Wicked Witch, Part 2." 2015. Web. October 4 2024.

22   B8730; Witch 309, Fleuratte Veuve Anthoine Valdexey, De Clefcy. Prévôt of Bruyères 1621.

of fine fragrance. As the witch lost her fearsome cultural importance, her magic ceded to science and commerce. Anyone who has taken a pill to alleviate a headache or joyfully sprayed a perfume owes the witches a debt of gratitude.

Sarah Shin

The Gate

> *The hour between dog and wolf . . . The hour in which . . .*
> *every being becomes his own shadow,*
> *and thus something other than himself.*
> —Jean Genet

The time between eclipses always felt self-contained. Since the first of the season a few nights ago, it was as if we were on a ship heading somewhere else: a journey within the bigger one. Like microcosms, consciousness made things graspable. It was strange work to make sense of what is— sorting the queerness of time and quantum reality, into this and that, inside and outside. But with each night, rhythms and echoes, sunken by the everyday, welled up, pointing to another world of digressions, things that can't be conceived of or fully understood.

The toy-like station we arrived at made the massive red *torii* across the road look even more striking under the full moon. Traveling had made us sensitive to every fresh influence, every snag and vulnerability in the fabric between ourselves and our new environments. A thin, spiky pulse had been running close to the surface, but dropped as we stepped through the gate, falling in line with the older heart of the shrine. The first gate required something to be left behind, something to be shed. Our soft edges, sacrificed, bled into night.

A pair of stone foxes, *kitsune*, stood on either side of the steps leading up to a bright vermilion and gold tower gate, the third and final one before the trail of approximately ten thousand that led up the mountain. The fox guarding the right side held a golden jewel in her mouth, while her left-hand counterpart held a scroll, or was it a sheaf of wheat? They wore red aprons—red for fertility, healing, prosperity, protection against evil. Their faces were determined. They were both messengers and manifestations of *Inari kami*, the spirit or group of spirits who resided at the main shrine beyond the third gate. Inari held power over agriculture and the rice harvest, primarily, but was also the *kami* of tea, foxes, sex workers, warriors, blacksmiths and farmers, and was petitioned for good health, abundance and all matters to do with finance and business. More often than not, the fox accompanied Inari, especially in her female aspect, but she could change gender and shape and multiply. Behind the candles, the foxes expressed eternal presence. The moon looked back from the circular mirror at the centre of the altar.

It was said that the Inari came to you as you need them, as you remember them. She was the fierce red feminine descended from demonesses. They taught you to eat flesh like dakini. To endure.

*

A few days ago, we went to visit the neighborhood temple in Tokyo where my friend S served as a monk. On the subway, my mind drifted to a piece of family lore from before my birth, when my mother's younger brother had vanished into the dense maze of the city. My grandma, my first and favorite storyteller, told it this way. She told me that she was exhausted after searching for him for days and had fallen asleep on the subway. That she had woken up with a jolt and stumbled off the train into an unknown neighborhood, still half asleep. Here, the story went, she followed her body into a pachinko parlor and to the back of the room. He stood there, with his back to her, at a machine. I recalled how she always embroidered the story with the detail of how she grabbed him "so that he couldn't get away." The punchline was that he never tried to get away—he only turned around to say, "I knew you would find me."

When we arrived, S was waiting for us. It was the week of the vernal equinox and many had come to pay their respects to their ancestors. He offered us tea on the balcony while we waited to enter the temple and told us about his sect, the Pure Land school of Buddhism. The character of Buddhism in Japan was ambient, he said, embedded in nature. "Listening mindfully to the sound of the surroundings, we learn that we are interbeing. Everything is interconnected, interdependent. I still have my own consciousness, or at least, I perceive my own consciousness. But what I learned through the spirits in this ambient Buddhism is that I'm not separated from others. In terms of time, in terms of space, I am beyond." The sliding doors to the temple opened. "My life is not limited within my birth to death. So everything in a temple should be something which reminds us of the fact that there are things which could last longer than our existence, right?" I nodded earnestly and his eyes crinkled. "You're like an owl," he smiled.

Inside, I inhaled the comforting scent of sweet incense and the woody tatami. The walls were lined with paintings in a style I had never seen before in a temple, familiar and ethereal like scenes from a dream, yet difficult to place in art history. Soft, pastels and metallics depicted a psychedelic world of life and death, a cosmic cycle of experience through the figure of the Buddha. One depicted a world mountain at the centre of a golden earth, with four faces and at least two rivers, one blue, one black, pouring down its sides. I asked S which his favorite image was and he nodded, looking up at the panel directly above us: "Satori. Enlightenment." A column of chakras floated in radiant sunset blues, pinks, yellows and oranges.

*

It was chilly for the time of year when we left for Kyoto a few days later, but we headed for the shinto shrine at night with the camera. After the first three gates, we entered the corridor of tens of thousands of *torii* that led up the mountain. The path forked. "Please go right way," read the sign above the right-hand side. Light and shadow fell through the gates, stripes washing over us as we climbed the stairs. The sounds of interbeing filled the forest: the trees breathing, the sound of water running past rocks in the stream, crows cawing high above and the scuffling of what I imagined to be wild boars in the mountain.

The tunnel of gates came to a pause at a landing where there was a small shrine. M wanted to film the bell, so I made an offering of warm tea from a nearby vending machine and wandered away. In this patch of the mountain, vigilant foxes guarded mossy stone altars and plinths. The *torii* they stood among were smaller than the ones we had walked through, but still person-sized. These gates were surrounded by, contained, and seemed to propagate many more gates of varying sizes. I was drawn into these little *torii* universes, looking into gates within gates, and tiny gates flanked by even tinier gates. There had been many seeking good fortune. It was like a strange stage set of sets, but I had no-one to make my meta references to. It was just me and the relics of human need and hope, sincere petitions to eternal spirits. But I wasn't alone: something moved, and I saw it was furry—a black cat. I moved to greet it but paused. There was something unusual: a red gap, a fleshy negative universe, where its left eye may once have been. The cat was unperturbed. I stepped back, leaving him to continue his watch among the foxes.

My grandma always said my cousin, my uncle's daughter, was a fox. In Korean fairy tales, the nine-tailed fox spirit could turn into a beautiful woman—a wily shapeshifter who would lure people into her clutches to devour their livers or hearts. But what about me, I thought. What about my animal nature? What about me sucking out people's livers?

I left the congregation of gates and returned to the shrine where M was waiting for me. As we continued our hike up the steeper part of the climb, he showed me the footage of the bell, which moved almost imperceptibly in the small screen of the camera. Only the moving flame of the candles indicated the image wasn't a photograph. "There were echoes," he said, "still sounding from the past." Soon, we came upon an unmarked path, inviting us away from the main route. We decided to follow it through its wooden, unpainted *torii* to a bamboo grove and a small structure, another shrine: to Amaterasu, the most important *kami*—the *kami* of the sun.

The quality of air changed as we walked through the last gate, like ink dropping through water. It was a colder, deeper place further away from the human world. Yet here too, human hands had given form to the ineffable in a circular act of faith. Stone dragons, spirits of water, held wishing stones in their mouths, just like the *kitsune* they stood among in the garden. The jewels suggested a net of wordless experience. The parts of us that were hidden away, that were too much, too inhuman, to bear whole —but recognized, gotten a hold of, could be mineralized and put outside of ourselves. I had the sense that death was an eternal awakening: the revelation that happens to you. Here, it wore the face of the red feminine, while earlier S had described it as the pure land. The shrine of the sun goddess was also a place of her eclipse.

*

We ran down the mountain to catch the last train, just past midnight. On the journey back to Kyoto, I read about the myth of Amaterasu. With her brothers Tsukuyomi, the moon *kami*, and Susanoo, the storm god, the sun goddess was born of Izanagi and Izanami, the creator deities of the Japanese archipelago and the last of seven generations of the gods who emerged when heaven and earth came into existence. The stories around the gods teemed with bodily metonyms of waste and viscera. One by one, the children metastasized from Izanagi's eyes and nose when he washed them. Another sibling, Ukemochi, connected with Inari, opened her mouth and spewed rice onto fields, fish and sea vegetables into the ocean, and meat into the forest. After her brother kills her for being so disgusting, Ukemochi's corpse produced grain from her anus, animals from her head and silkworms in her mouth. The chaos engine Susanoo's achievements included vomiting weapons, defecating in Amaterasu's palace, killing her maiden through her genitals and flaying and hurling whole horses. Finally, he drove Amaterasu into hiding in a cave, bringing about the eclipse that almost ended the world.

Amaterasu became revered as the celestial ancestress of the Japanese imperial line, and Susanoo, came to be identified as a god of its colony, Korea. A little brother god of shadow and disorder; hiding in a cave, hiding in a pachinko parlour. Running away from the gods and the stories we tell about them, and which they tell about us.

After Amaterasu went into the cave, taking the earth into shadow, the other *kami* devised a plan to bring her back. They built a large wooden perch in front of the cave and brought all the roosters to sit on it. The roosters crowed and crowed outside, until Amaterasu emerged out of her hiding place to see what was going on. For its role in returning the rising sun to rule the universe, the *torii* became the most important shinto symbol.

As a child, my grandmother would tell me a different story about darkness and light, sun and moon. A long time ago, when Korea was the land of tigers, there was once a poor but exceptionally resourceful woman like my grandma, who was also a tiger—as was I, according to her. "A tiger's daughter is a tiger," she would say. In the folktale, this woman would go to the market over the valley to sell her delicious rice cakes, leaving her young daughter and son at home. One day, she met a hungry tiger as she made her way out of the marketplace and over the first hill. In exchange for letting her live, the tiger first demanded her rice cakes, then her clothing. Sometimes the tiger ate her whole anyway; at other times, he ate only her limbs, leaving her to crawl home on her belly like a worm. Always, he continued to her home to feed on her children too, wearing her clothes to trick them into opening the front door. When the disguise didn't work, he covered his paws in rice flour to imitate her pale skin and succeeded in his ruse. But the children escaped the house and began climbing up the great tree, and then, when the tiger started chopping it down with an axe, prayed for a rope from the heavens. The tiger also asked for a rope, but his was rotten and he fell away while the children climbed all the way into the upper world.

Before they took their final places as the sun and the moon, they switched. The girl, originally the moon, was scared of the dark, so her brother exchanged places with her. She became the sun in the day and her brother the moon at night, reunited with their mother, who had become the stars in the sky.

Kyoto station was almost deserted. Earlier in the day, a moving sea of passengers defined the building. Now, the architecture gave space to its ambient sounds: the friction of escalators rising up and descending, although there were no passengers to use them; trains chugging in and out of the station; a recorded voice over the speakers; and the strangely pleasing tonal pinging of various signals.

When the sun rose in a few hours, the station would again become governed by human time, but the world I was coming back to was not the same as the one I had left. The shadows of the night mountain were still present with me, waiting to be brought into light, like a story that must be told. My story, picked up and carried from where others had left it and made my own—and yet, not just mine. It would have to be told in a voice I did not yet know, but would have to find: one that spoke with nature and its spirits and within the weave of our imperfect interpretations of them. All I knew was that I would see the one-eyed cat again. And I did, later on in my journey. *Did this really happen? Yes, this is all true.*

Outside, the moon reflected the light of the sun so brightly that the stars couldn't be seen. Even tigers have to die so we can shine.

Sarah Yanni

To Be Carried Is to Become Somebody

The word "amulet" is derived from an Arabic root meaning "to bear, to carry,"
hence, "amulet" is something which is carried or worn, and the name is applied
broadly to any kind of talisman or ornament to which supernatural powers are
ascribed ... which were laid upon the breast of the deceased.
—Egyptian Magic, E.A. Wallis Budge

i. The Amulet of the Scarab

the oil of creation
to desire what is new
to desire wanting, not professing a force so fertile
I become somebody

ii. The Amulet Nefer

simply music luck and beauty
who doesn't need this?
my father plays his instruments and it feels like casting spell

iii. The Amulet of the Frog

I hear the croaks at night
when we are near the mountains like white noise unceasing
you hold me
conjure a woman with amphibian head call her resurrection
please
    call her goddess

i. The Amulet of the Ladder

heaven could be clouds could be blue, white
or night sky dark as ink I'm tired of ceilings from now on
I want only floors

ii. The Amulet of the Heart

the heart is a double for the soul
nothing as ridiculous as my self in love

Veronica Gonzalez Peña

Through the Raw Meat

Why was she so affected by his death? She had never actually known him.

She could still feel the meat inside her and her stomach ached with all of it. She felt a sudden wind blow up against her face, her arms, her bare legs. She attempted to replay the feel of the initial attraction which had struck her at her center. But it began to rain and the water hit her cold. The sky to the east, beyond the thundering clouds, was red. It was a swampish Brooklyn August, early evening. She began to cry, in that park, unwashed hair, lips shivering as she tried to control them, while she stared at four soaked children rhythmically rising and falling as they shifted weight on the damp wood of the distant seesaw.

No. First person:

It was raining. It was hot. I was sitting in a seedy park. The children were, in fact, soaked, but refused to go in, even as their mothers yelled at them from open windows. And my hair was dirty. I'd begun to like it that way.

It was then that I first saw him. He appeared and somehow he wasn't soaked like the rest of us—his hair was only lightly covered in a silver veil of tiny drops. I got up off my bench and followed him as he walked through water, or rather, the rain. He proceeded with sullen eyes focused on the ground. It was almost involuntary, as if I'd been drawn up, off my bench, and made to follow him down Big Oak Street to Fragrant Pine Avenue. Past stores where cheap merchandise would have, on a sunny day, lined the street on long tables, past bakery after bookstore after bank to Quaking

Aspen Road, where he walked half a block down and into a rundown gated house with asbestos siding.

After slowly passing, I turned back and stood in the now pouring rain mutely staring at the building's streaked facade.

I'd been sitting in that park feeling sorry for myself and wondering why, in an attempt to ditch my past, I had moved to this city where I knew almost no one. That's when he'd come out of nowhere, that thin man in black clothing. He was tall and had, I think, light hair. He had green slits for eyes, and lips and a nose, and his shorts were too baggy and overly long, and he wore ugly, thick-soled shoes.

I stood in the rain, and I knew where he lived, and I'd hang out in the park—every day—until I saw him again. Then I'd run up to him and reach for his arm and stroke his thick (I think light) hair, look into his green slits for eyes and whisper my name. And that's how it would begin. It stopped raining and I walked home.

Indoors I jutted my head out the window of my third-story room and jeered at the old men who had already, post rain-shower, gathered on the stoop below. The gesture made me feel better. I was getting sick of them and the same beer-tainted questions they asked every day. Yeah, I was from California. Yeah, I didn't have a job. Yeah, I stayed indoors an awful lot, was awful quiet. Yeah, almost every time I came home, after finally venturing out, I carried with me packages full of cheap junk I didn't really want.

I pulled my head in and read the letter I reached around the fat one, who always wore a muscle T-shirt, to get. Why did they have to sit in front of the mailboxes? It was from my mother.

Another earthquake. The heat. She and my father had visited my grandmother. The psychics had predicted another, bigger quake, on the 25th. The cats were fine and so were my grandmother's eyes. The newscaster on channel nine had said the psychics were often right. There was, in fact, a fault line going right through the mountains where they'd said it would occur. And my mother, whose own mother, my father claimed, was a wannabe santera, was worried about these psychic predictions.

I felt something must be wrong for her; she was a statistician and had never believed in psychics. And I worried. But I didn't call.

Instead, I jotted a short description of the guy I had seen on a small piece of paper, which I then folded and refolded. I didn't know his name and I hoped it would work anyway. I lit a pink adoration candle and placed the piece of paper under it on a dish I'd covered with honey. I tried to remember the Hail Mary but couldn't. I wondered if menstrual blood really worked, and if so, how it was that women got men to drink the love-inducing blood? I might have to ask my grandmother.

My hair was still wet. I stood in front of the mirror and flattened it down on my head, then pulled it back hard until I felt my scalp hurt and painted my eyes black. Black eyes and a fake mole by my mouth, and I looked at myself in the mirror until I was satisfied with the altered image. There.

I walked one block down to Cock Tales where I had agreed to meet my friend Eve. I ordered a Cuba Libre and tried to eavesdrop on the two women in the next booth.

I tried but couldn't hear, so I watched them laugh and sip and smile and lick red lips. When glasses were emptied, the taller one stood and held her arms out, indignant, as her friend offered her money she wouldn't take. She fluffed her hair and strutted toward the bar, and the friend, still smiling, glanced my way. I imagined it an accusatory smile so looked away, pretending I had not been watching them. I took a large gulp of my drink and as my discomfort grew in the crowded bar, I wanted more and more to go home—so I could focus my thoughts on the guy I had followed.

But I heard Eve's voice and when I turned, I saw she was surrounded by full glasses and laughing faces.

She saw me, shimmied over, and gave me a dry peck on the cheek.

The smiler waved at Eve, "How long you been here?"

"I don't know. Not long. I don't feel too well though." I did my best to fashion a convincing grimace which might serve to indicate an undefined ailment.

Eve ignored my encoded grimace, "Well you look fine—very dramatic."

I remembered the mole and was suddenly embarrassed, "Yeah, the wonders of eyeliner. Look, I think I'm gonna go after this drink."

"What's wrong? Listen, you have to start getting out. I wanted you to meet some people."

She was clearly disappointed, maybe even a little disgusted, so I touched at my center and continued the lie, "You know. . . my weak stomach."

While I finished my drink, I asked some questions and learned some things. She'd only been in New York a couple of years but in this part of Williamsburg she knew everyone and could offer layers of information to pile onto the thinnest of descriptions: tall, thin, long (I think light) hair, green eyes, ugly brown shoes. Lives at 296 Ainslie. She'd known his brother, Jack, and told me he'd died in a fight two years prior. He, whose name she couldn't recall, was pretty strange, never went out, had no close friends.

He'd gotten weirder since his brother's death. People said he walked with rocks in his shoes, as penance for the death he felt he'd somehow caused. She asked why I asked, but of course it didn't matter because Eve loves to divulge information in an urgent uninterrupted straight line. I ignored her question, leaned slowly forward and kissed her cheek, "I'll get used to New York soon, you'll see."

She frowned at my departure and threatened to call my mother to discuss my wellbeing as I walked out the door.

I would sleep in the glow of my pink candles. And I would follow him. Follow him again.

It was by following that I learned he worked at The Butcher's. There were several on my street and he worked at the one furthest from my house, and I didn't eat meat but I started going there anyway. I would order what I heard the other ladies order, and I would give the meat to the stray cats that lived in the park. Those cats started recognizing me and would wait drooling in the early afternoon.

And then, after three weeks, he did too: he started recognizing me. And I knew that my magic had begun to work.

I'd heard his name—Edward—on my second visit to the shop. I'd written it on a piece of paper and switched it with the description I had previously placed on the honey covered plate, under the candle. I'd resurrected it, out from deep within:

Hail Mary full of grace
The Lord is with Thee.
Blessed art thou amongst women
And blessed is the fruit
of thy womb Jesus.
Holy Mary, Mother of God
pray for us sinners now
and at the hour of our death.

Amen

and I'd recite it three times whenever I lit a new candle. I scrubbed my hair clean, dried it, then re-wet it with my grandmother's violet holy water every day before I went in; and now I noticed he looked at me. Looked in a decidedly direct way while I ordered what I heard other ladies order.

And the next day it was the same look. And the next day it was the same look. And that look, in combination with the smell and the long wait in the overly crowded shop, made me dizzy. He handed me the white papered package and I gave him the money in exchange for the meat and those now noticeably penetrating stares—and my cheeks became red with the heat.

I loved him. At least I felt pretty sure I loved him. And all the way home I thought about our words:

"Half a pound of flank steak . . . please."

"Is this piece alright?"

"Yes . . . please."

I manipulated the memory, replaying it again and again. And as I walked, I brought him forward: Edward in his blood-stained apron surrounded by slabs of this beast and that, and huge tongues and ripped-out hearts. And I smelled his meat-soaked skin, and I saw him chopping and cleaving with huge knives. And I saw his fingers, always tinged with red, wrapped around the whiteness of my package as he handed me what I'd been waiting for; and I felt pretty sure.

I didn't stop for the cats. I got the flank steak home, unpacked it, and sliced it into tiny strips which I fried on the highest flame. The meat worms crinkled and sizzled and their vapor settled in my pores. I went to my bed and sat with the steaming hot plate on my lap and ate them slowly, counting as I went. And though my stomach began aching at number 33, I kept eating and counting, and I knew that the cats would be angry, mewling and pacing.

And then I dreamt. For three days I dreamt awake. And in my daydream I'd see Edward in his shop, exactly as in wakefulness, flanked by those large dirtied posters of Saint Luke and Saint Bartholomew, the patron saints of butchers. And as in life, he rarely said a word, only occasionally lifting his beautiful green eyes, catching mine, then letting them drop to continue his chopping. And in my dream I realized it was this that drew me to him: his aloneness—his silent somber solitude. And then, in the dream, I would take control; I would stand firm, the ladies falling back and forming a horseshoe around me, me in a white crinoline robe, and whisper to him:

With the aching in my heart
as I wait until tomorrow
When I spy on your large hands
make their way through the raw meat

With the mocking in my ears

of the ones who saw my
stares at smooth
Severance; the cleave,
As instructed by your saints

With the pain I felt inside
As you tore my things away:
my eyes and ears
and throat and heart
They were yours—to you I gave

                   And I settled for the knowledge
that you didn't know a thing
as I waited for a breath
of an air that held your scent.
                   Amen

And then he'd look at me. One of those noticeably long looks. Then, finally, he'd smile. He'd reach over with long strong arms, and he'd tear my things away, and feed them to me slowly—slowly. And I would know I loved him. Then he'd float, up toward the ceiling, and his feet, freed of the thick-soled shoes, would drip blood from the wounds inflicted by the rocks. And I'd catch those small drops in my mouth where they tasted of wine, intoxicating with the thought of his liquid inside me. For three days I saw these images, over and over again—circular so that the end became the beginning—and each time I became more convinced.

When, after three days, I rose from my bed, I'd decided. I lit my candles and washed my hair. I re-wet it with holy violet water, then walked the twelve blocks to The Butcher's—counting the tiny strips of meat inside me as I went.

Today I will stop, I told myself. Today I will blow out the candles. Today I will stop believing in Saint Antony who as a child I'd used to find things, "Go get a sock. Tie a knot in it. You're tying Saint Antony of Padua's balls together. He'll be in so much pain he'll help find what you've lost." I would obediently bind his balls, as my grandmother with the bad eyes gave me power over the world. Today I will stop using the sickly sweet violet holy water she'd given me as a gift to take to New York. To keep me safe, she'd said. Today I will call my overly analytical mother whom I've been worried about for a month. Today I will go meet Eve and her beautiful friends at Cock Tales. Today I will put an end to my own self-lacerating silence; and today, I told myself, Edward will be mine.

When I got there the shop was closed. My shop was closed. There was a sign in the window saying it would remain closed all the following week. How could they? When I had decided that: today. I must have stood there rereading for much too long because that nosey old bat with the black wig and white powdered face walked up behind me and started in on me with that running voice of hers.

"They're closed, you know. For a whole week they're closed."

"Yes, I see . . . "

"On account of Eddie. I see you in here every day, didn't you know? It's been closed since yesterday. You should've known. So much suffering in that poor family. Horrible."

"What?"

"Right off the Williamsburg Bridge. They found traces of blood on his shirt, under his nails and on his feet, and they thought he'd been involved in something bad, some kind of crime. But, of course, they soon found out he was just the butcher. It was mentioned on channel five two days ago, didn't you see? His uncle is furious . . . about the TV; his idiot cousin is a reporter and put it out there for eve ryone to see. He thought it only right to close for a while. Respectful. Eddie was his favorite."

"What?" I wanted her to stop, to shut up, but instead I asked to be tortured, to have it drawn out. I realized she had probably been standing there waiting, waiting for just such an opportunity—someone she could tell it to—and instead of asking her to stop, I begged her to go on, "What's that?"

"The church bells? Afternoon mass."

"No, I mean . . . "

"Oh. Yeah. Of course. His favorite nephew. Nice boy, that Eddie, pretty strange though, so quiet. His brother was killed while breaking up a fight between Ed and another boy a year ago. Really it was the other boy, not Eddie who started it. Now this. Their poor mother, all the tragedy has her wrinkled."

I walked away as she began to hum.

I thought about how he'd come to me in a vision, allowing me to drink from his wounds before leaving for good. I imagined the silver veil that had covered his hair the first time I saw him now lining the inside of his lungs, and nausea inched through my insides. I slowly walked home and looked right past the old men on the stoop who somehow knew not to ask questions. I went upstairs and put out the pink candles and lit a pure white one; and then I took out a black sock and tied Saint Antony's balls in a huge knot—and still haven't set him free.

Third person again. She is a fool. Eddie is alive as I write this. But you must understand, she was in a disturbed romantic way when she told you her version. And besides, she wants your sympathy.

She arrived at The Butcher's in a state. She humiliated herself that day.

She ran into the meat shop wearing nothing but the cheap crinoline lining of a tacky dress her grandmother had picked out for her years earlier. She rushed in with the words on her lips, and she couldn't control them, though in all fairness to her I should point out that a part of her tried. They were already shooting looks at her as she pushed her way through the crowded shop. She was a strange sight: unbathed and mad-eyed in the sloppily torn white lining of her grandmother's dress. She smelled bad too, the combination of the overly sweet floral perfume and a body in need of washing. And she was pushing people this way and that, almost knocked over the old lady with the white pancake makeup and matted black wig. The old lady screamed, then scowled at the girl's back.

And then, when she was right in front of him, she did it. She opened her mouth; a little too loudly exclaimed, "Edward!" and already she had gone too far, for how was it, he must have wondered, that this mad woman knew his name. He looked up from his meat and met her red eyes, "Edward! I love you." She whispered the last part, but everyone heard. Poor Edward quickly dropped his eyes, and his uncle had to come from behind the register and ask her to leave. She wouldn't move at first, just kept staring at Ed, so the uncle gently shoved at her a little, to get her feet going. Twenty-two eyes followed her out, and the old lady in the black wig elbowed her in the ribs as she moved slowly past. She stood outside of the shop, to the side of the entrance, for almost two hours, not moving at all, only occasionally blinking, and not uttering a sound. When it began to drizzle, she absent-mindedly walked to the park where she sat on the bench and, surrounded by fifteen stray cats, cried in the light August rain.

Lily Burana

My Immortal: Remembering La Strega Diviana Ingravallo

The seemingly never-ending COVID epidemic feels like loss upon loss upon loss. While the numbing collective grief over the million-plus Americans taken by the virus has blunted some of the personal devastation, the August 2021 death of Los Angeles-based artist Diviana Ingravallo hit me with the severity of a gut punch.

Diviana, a fierce Italian glamour-queer artist and activist from Mola Di Bari, Italy, emerged as an artist in San Francisco in the early 1990s, just as the city's LGBT community was forging its rage and anguish over the AIDS crisis into a potent political and cultural force. A performance artist, author, and playwright, her work was ruled be Eros and Aphrodite—anger, lust, transgression, power, and beauty were recurrent themes. She staged her shows in alternative art spaces like Theater Rhinoceros in San Francisco and Highways in Los Angeles, venues that showcased the work of a burgeoning alternative queer community and managed to bring together activists, drag queens, sex workers, club kids, and underground creatives working in every genre.

I'd had the pleasure of performing in her theater productions several times, I edited and published her short fiction, and palled around with her often. As a presence, she had all the fire of a Leo goddess: Beauty mark. Red lips. Her hair endless box-dyed onyx waves. In anger, her upper lip curled in a snarl. In joy, her laugh was frequent and unhinged. Fury and beauty were her propulsive forces, with a dash of irresistible madness.

Through her plays like *Naked Women* and *Criminal Lovers*, she chronicled the femme firewalk and its maddening contradictions: as feminine-presenting queers, we could easily command attention but not respect; we could be granted the power of desirability but not the gravitas of intellectual credibility. We were often milked for inspiration and titillation but then summarily discarded, left to rinse from ourselves the bitterness of the realization that the misogyny that chased so many of us from the straight world still followed us around our queer sanctuary, the filmy residue from the cheap trick of it all. Female archetypes dotted her narratives, particularly the women of the Bible. Her relationship to the Catholicism of her youth was fraught. She bridled against Christianity's patriarchal structure and homophobia, yet the iconography of the faith—the Madonna, the pieta, the flaming sacred heart—seeped into her work in words and images. In that way, we were the same.

Diviana did not die of COVID, but I count her among the countless oblique COVID casualties. In lockdown, she couldn't perform her day job as a highly sought-after massage therapist, and even if she could have, her body would no have let her. A recent back surgery caused incapacitating pain in her arms and neck. Income dried up. Medical care became less accessible, mental health care even less so. A once-prolific artist who had performed around the world, she hadn't produced art in years. Long struggling in a country that gives precisely zero fucks about supporting its creative class in times of strain, when Diviana was found in her bed, dead from an overdose, the letters *DNR* (Do Not Resuscitate) were spray-painted in silver on her bedroom door. She had recently turned 60.

With COVID shutting down all but necessary travel, and social gatherings put off, many funerals and memorials have been either seriously truncated, postponed indefinitely, or <u>reimagined</u>. I knew my Christian mourning standbys: in the absence of a funeral or memorial for Diviana, I could pray. I could journal. I could go to church and hit my knees. But as the days grew shorter and the air crackled with the familiar chill of autumn, I thought of Diviana, who had the *strega bellissima* magnetism of Lydia Lunch crossed with Anna Magnani, and I found myself yearning to honor her with something witchier.

Let this fiery woman be remembered by fire itself.

"Better to light a candle than to curse the darkness," goes the old saying, attributed to everyone from Confucius to Eleanor Roosevelt. At Ritualist, an inclusive, woman-owned magic shop in New Paltz, New York, I examined the spell candles. Slender beeswax tapers. Oil and herb-infused pillars. My friend Reverend Jes Kast, a pastor at Faith United Church of Christ in State College walked me through it. "Grief delayed is hard," she said. "So candles are a way to begin that process even if we can't gather in person yet." The owner, Dana Cooper, bright and elegant like her carefully curated store, approved my selections of a white beeswax spell candle and four autumn-toned smaller candles, called "chimes," meant for single use. I wondered if I belonged in this dedicated Wiccan space, but Dana assured me that candle work really isn't tied to any specific religion or spiritual practice, and that one needn't rise to some eldritch bar to use the tools. Could a Christian believer—even a wayward soul like me—do a candle ritual? I thought of Catholic churches, with their rows of glowing votives lit with balsam sticks, then remembered what Jes wrote to me conspiratorially via DM: "Honey, I need some stuff witchier than just Jesus, too."

At home, I read from *The Wicca Book of Candle Spells: The Ultimate Guide to Practicing Wiccan Candle Magic with Spells.* "All you need is a candle if you want to cast a spell. It is similar to how one would wish something while blowing out the candles on their birthday cake. The only main difference is that while you hope for something when you are blowing out your birthday cake candles, you need to assert a declaring authority whilst casting a candle spell."

What spell did I wish to cast? I didn't want to summon her; a visitation wasn't the goal. What I wanted was for my friend to know how much she is loved. How much she is missed. And maybe, if it wasn't too much trouble, to have her give me just the teensiest little sign that she's out there somewhere. A feather. The sound of footsteps. Whatever. Nothing fancy.

I realized that what I wanted to send was perhaps not a spell but a humble prayer for a God shot. "In recovery communities," explains writer Jonathan Danielle, "a God shot refers to an unexpected favor or a sign. The phrase attributes to a profound happening that cannot be explained, but not quite as remarkable as a miracle."

Tales of God shots abound in my life. Whenever my friend Anthony was about to narrowly miss danger riding his motorcycle, he'd smell his deceased grandfather's cigar smoke. My own mother swore she could hear my father's voice after he passed away, and that when she petitioned him to help find lost items, she'd find them. While mourning a broken engagement myself, I met my future husband at the gate of Green-Wood Cemetery.

American history brims with mourning ritual, from the craft of hairwork—jewelry and art fashioned from the hair of the deceased,

Victorian memorial portraiture of the dead—to the more recent trend of roadside *descansos*, to reality TV mediums who claim to converse with the departed. I was ready to reach back in time beyond that, to Pagan days, and build a prayer altar. A portable last rites kit purchased at a flea market with a chalk statue of the pieta. A photo of Divi that I took at our friend's wedding. Acorns and pinecones for fecundity, and an apple, for Eve and all the knowledge she dared acquire. There was genuine comfort in the gathering and assembly. I tucked in a statue of the Virgin Mary that I bought at a thrift store in East Nashville, and a hunk of smoky quartz, said to have properties of protection and deflecting bad energy, just in case. I flipped a random tarot card from my deck: Death. Number 13—a perfect bit of otherworldly showmanship for a Leo like my friend. Wary of white-girl spiritual dabbling, I wondered if this was appropriate, or in any way good enough. "There is a reason why Jesus took ordinary things like bread and wine, why wouldn't our spices or acorns or leaves be blessed, too?" said Reverend Kast.

I ground some autumn spices with my mortar and pestle, which, given to me by a downsizing friend, is Le Creuset (bring out the "Basic Witch" jokes. I can take it.). Soon the room filled with the aroma of cinnamon and clove. I lit all the candles, then sat and stared at the golden flames while "My Immortal" by Evanescence played, the wailing guitar solo opening my heart to tears that wouldn't come. I felt alternately sad and fraudulent. I didn't lack seriousness and reverence; rather, in the empty-tank reality that is desperate sorrow, I did my best to honor someone I'd lost, and it felt insufficient. Though Diviana didn't have HIV or COVID, there's a cruel irony to her emergence as an artist during the one pandemic, and dying in the other. The community's grief was a callback to an earlier time when we were reminded just how disposable we were (and still are), our pain and desperation lost in a sea of indifference, if not outright hostility. The searing memory of swarms of people who believed our suffering was a form of justice. Her work, and the work of other artists that flourished against the backdrop of the AIDS crisis, gave us a language when we had no words to evoke our complicated lives. A new aesthetic and vocabulary were emerging and she was there, to lend shape. And now her death underscored the ways we betray the artistic class, the self-employed—how we give them no hand up when they're down. The conditions of her demise are their own damning artist's statement.

I couldn't cry because I was angry. As the song played on and candle wax ran in runnels to the tabletop like the tracks of tears I could not call forth, I gave myself permission to grieve imperfectly.

Though Diviana was a contemporary of queer femme/female artists galvanized during the ACT-UP/AIDS activism years, like Annie Sprinkle, Julie Tolentino, and Catherine Opie, news of her passing slipped by, as if mainstream media decided that, like so many female artists, she wasn't notable enough to memorialize. Sexism and misogyny follow us into the grave, as exhibited by the paucity of obituaries about women. "Over the entire 167-year history of *The New York Times*," said the newspaper, "between 15 and 20% of our obituary subjects have been women—a frustratingly imprecise number that also fails to fully reflect huge changes over the decades in the obituary form itself." Queer women are represented even less, shoring up institutional hierarchies by reminding us, in absentia, who is—and isn't—worth remembering, writ large.

So memorialization falls to us. My ritual for her contained the solemnity of this awareness, because I knew that with her death we not only lost our friend and whatever art she might have produced, we also experienced a secondary AIDS crisis loss: so many of our friends and loved ones passed on in shocking speed and numbers back then, and now we're losing our witnesses who held the story of the specific horror of that time.

Diviana was preceded in death by her great love, Tim, a faunlike gay man who succumbed to complications from AIDS in the 90s. Queer kids understood the fungibility of the concept of "family" and the fluid boundaries of love—some of us weren't here to slot ourselves into the LBGT categories so much as redraw them entirely. The gatekeeping and internecine bitching in the queer community made Diviana increasingly furious. If nothing else, Diviana was an agitator for expansion, for liberation over political rigidity. She was, as they say, a bright light.

Photographer and community organizer Susan Forrest filmed her walk through Diviana's Hollywood apartment building—the Villa Elaine, where Man Ray once lived—and as she walked the long hallway to Diviana's front door, still sealed with the coroner's sticker, golden orbs of light bobbed in the screen, though the angle of the California sun wasn't such that the glowing dots could be attributed to lens flare. When I saw them, I thought, "Maybe Divi is that light." The idea seemed corny, improbable, yet also very true.

I looked out at the small fountain in my backyard one afternoon and saw a male and female cardinal jockeying in the plume of water. They batted each other playfully, shook the droplets from their feathers, then alighted together, never to be seen again. It is said that cardinals—their song and their presence—represent the visitation of a loved one from beyond the grave.

If I were to believe my prayer for a God shot was answered, it was in the sight of the orbs and the two joyful, quarrelsome lovebirds acting up before my eyes. We look for signs not so much because we are certain such inter-dimensional communication is possible. We look for signs because it's all we have.

In the face of uncertainty, it behooves us to make a friend of mystery, as–paradoxically—it is the possibilities contained in the unknowable that help us make sense of reality of loss. Does a glimpse of birds connect you to the person on the other side? Possibly. Does the sight of candle glow connect you to the meaning of their life, and yours, on this Earth? Certainly. Episcopal priest Liz Edman, author of *Queer Virtue: What LGBTQ People Know About Life and Love and How It Can Revitalize Christianity* says, "It matters to be aware that our relationships with folks who have died is part of a larger web of relationship. So sending them energy, remembering them, holding them in your heart, striking a match and kindling a small flame—it's a way of touching that energetic space where they live, 'a great cloud of witnesses,' who are connected with us, and connected with the transcendent."

We do what we're able to honor those who have left us and hold space for the anguish of those left behind. We hear redemption in a keening guitar. We sense protection in a whiff of smoke and find comfort in a dash of cinnamon. We can make visions of the mundane. Is the mystical significance of such things real? At all? I'm inclined to say yes, but I say so knowing that even confirmation bias can be a form of comfort. What I'm certain of is that grief is real. It deserves our attention, our tending, and our respect.

Better to light a candle than to curse the darkness. In Diviana's honor, I will do both.

May the flame of sacred remembrance burn its rage in our souls.

Brooke Palmieri

Free Style Esbat

As the sun rose and I boarded a train headed for a place I'd never been, it struck me that the dead witch I was trailing had actually found me first. This was a saving grace; until that time, my childhood attraction to necromancy, ghosts, and graveyards had been almost completely corrupted by my education. It was time to recommit to my real priorities—channeling my training as a historian (over a decade spent handling centuries-old books and papers) into ritual engagement, conjuration, spiritual fulfillment. Wanting to look at old magic books had *brought* me, salivating, into those places in the first place, but in order to stay there, I'd slowly ripped myself in half: a meticulous, Saturnian scholar inside the walls of whatever fancy library or exclusive archive; a raging pre-op transsexual baby dyke crone-worshipper outside. It was time to subject my disciplined side to my wildness, to take what I could and run, put what I'd learned to the service of building stranger altars, invoking the gods more precisely, fucking my brains out and calling it sex magick, living by my stars.

Through a series of fated encounters in the occult bookshop I worked at, a dead, gay witch had found me. His name came up again and again, alongside words and images that prompted me to remember my spiritual vocation—my ability to move between the worlds of the dead and the living to heighten the experiences of myself and those around me. The ability to collapse ten, twenty, fifty, a hundred, a thousand years into a moment of clarity and pure cosmic connection. The dead, gay witch said: Anchor yourself. *The first step toward heaven on earth is: Anchor yourself. As above, so below; as below, so above.*

The witch was named Leo Louis Martello. Like had called to like: we were Italian-American blue-collar gay witches raised as Catholics who

156

knew that total liberation must be spiritual and eternal as well as fleshly and temporal. Somehow, Martello had found me living in London, far away from his hometown in Dudley, Massachusetts, far from New York City, where he spent most of his adult life. I guess he found me because a lot of what he'd been up to creatively and magically gelled with what I was getting up to. My body and my activism—and all the passive activisms that my body was pressed into at any given moment—were acknowledgements of and offerings to the divine essence that existed in all things. Our resonance was more powerful than space or time. Reading him gave me a language to better understand my interests, the bigger picture I was part of, a family tree in the forest of my magical inheritance.

Martello first contacted me through a series of British men who were straight—which caught me off guard—but then, given that *aspirationally* white/straight/cis/British men basically invented and continued to define the modern discipline of History, it's typical to encounter these people before moving into the great beyond. Sometimes they give you what you want, sometimes you have to wrestle it out of their clutches; with Martello, things came loose pretty easily.

The first man was an encyclopedic secondhand bookseller who brought very careful selections of rare occult books from the 60s and 70s to resell at our bookshop. Part of my job was dealing with his monthly visitations. One day he presented me with *The Weird Ways of Witchcraft*, first hardback edition, 1972 (the first pulp paperback edition had been published earlier, in 1969). The dust jacket was striking: large, black lettering surrounding a devil with glowing green eyes, big red horns, and a long, pointed, red tongue. Martello himself smirked up at me from his author's photo, wearing robes in a style reminiscent of a Roman Catholic priest, with a white clerical collar and a huge chain with a heraldic shield bearing a lion.

I thought: *Look at this queen in his Catholic drag!* Sure enough, in the last chapter of the book, "The Borderline Bi-sexuality of Many Mystics," Martello took a stand on homosexual desire and gender non-conformity as not only natural but desirable states of being. Sexual dissidence and genderfuckery were sacred states, conduits to making magic, facilitating direct access to the spirit world and divine wisdom. In 1969 this was a big deal; both Wicca and its related pagan religions were, like the rest of the whole world, not friendly to queers, under the guise of a very limited concept of "fertility." But the history of queer liberation is steeped in a love of history: generation after generation looking back to find something of itself amongst the rubble of persecution. Sometimes the past is used to feel less alone, sometimes for political leverage. Nestled within this tradition, Martello initiated me into a line of witches for whom bodily liberation was inextricable from spiritual ecstasy. I was one of them, and I was hooked. Martello's history was mine, and our future would be shared.

And now I was on my way to my second initiation, in a small town outside of London, where a stranger who visited the bookshop had invited me to his house. At the recommendation of several trusted witches who knew him and attested to his benevolent nature—*He's ruled by Jupiter, he's very generous, he takes mentoring young people very seriously*—I overrode my initial skepticism. That, too, felt like the appropriate, emotional rite of passage—the majority of archives are held by institutions I do not trust. This kept me sharp and critical, but it was only one facet of a landscape of emotions that influenced what was possible for me to know at any given time. Initiation requires sacrifice in order to fully surrender to the wisdom it offers, and I was ready to trade up.

*

Throughout the 70s, Martello published a newsletter out of his tiny apartment at 153 West 80th Street in New York: *W.I.C.A.*, an acronym for "Witches International Craft Associates." I had been invited to look at a complete run of the newsletter—an ultra-rarity, as none of the typical institutions held any record of the publication at the time, or word that it had existed, even in New York City where they'd been printed. This second initiation was classic to many traditions of modern witchcraft, an introduction to privileged information that was shrouded in secrets and mystery, thought to have been destroyed or lost with time. I had never met anyone who had heard of or read the newsletter, and yet here they were, 30 issues published from 1970 to 1975, in pristine condition, far from the climate-controlled, secured and sanitized archives of academic institutions.

Every rite has its own procedures and particularities, prayers and preparations. Obviously, I had properly bathed and cleansed myself that morning, and made offerings at my altar as the Moon trined Venus, then Jupiter. Later that day, Venus and Jupiter would be in conjunction—a very, very powerful transit for me, as both were in Sagittarius, my ascendant sign, *and* the moon was in Leo, my Sun sign in the 9th house. I was a Leo with a Leo stellium in search of a man named Leo; it was fitting that I was making pilgrimage to an unknown location in pursuit of spiritual expansion, in keeping with how the stars of my birth related to the stars in the sky that day.

I was taken on a tour of the house in an order that felt initiatory too: the front hallway, a gallery of images and art depicting ancient deities, then up the stairs into an "office" crammed with magical equipment—ceremonial swords and knives on the walls, chalices and rods, a painting made by Aleister Crowley, incense burners, and robes passed down by several generations of witches. A door in the ceiling was tugged to reveal a hidden stairway to an attic the length of the house, filled with meticulously labelled boxes. This treasure trove documented the witchcraft revival of the 20th century, a vast counterculture of weirdos from many walks of life. *The Weird Ways of Witchcraft* laid out a paper trail: letters, pamphlets, newsletters, and magazines, self-published, privately published, secretly published and written, sprawling Europe and North America. From these, a few boxes were selected for me to consult, and we carried them in procession down the staircases to the most important place in any witch's house: the kitchen hearth. At the kitchen table I had as much time as I needed to rummage through the boxes; to keep me company, there were endless cups of tea and a friendly black cat.

Before taking a methodical approach I flicked through and opened a newsletter at random, and the first thing I saw was an advertisement for a record called *Guitar Grimoire*, "a fantastic new stereo record album of transcendental music experiences created specifically by a gifted musician and mystic to be utilized as a tool in *Magickal Practices, the Craft and Psychic Meditation*," by Master Wilburn Burchette. I found the album on my phone and put it on, to influence my research.

Opening up the first issue of the *W.I.C.A. Newsletter* from the spring of 1970, the first thing that caught my eye amidst the abundance of typewritten news, gossip, and sassy opinions was an item for a "WITCH-IN" Martello was planning:

> **WITCH-IN: Saturday October 31, HALLOWEEN, 1 p.m. in Central Park's Sheep Meadow. Bring candles, capes, incense, food to share. FREE STYLE ESBAT.**

Witch-In? Free Style Esbat? Further down on the page, there was another section that gave more context:

> **WITCHES LIBERATION MOVEMENT: Like other minorities witches have only been the dumping depot of other people's garbage. In medieval times the only liberated woman was a witch.**

She slept with whom she pleased. She was a threat to the Church & Establishment. Unlike other religions, male chauvenist, [sic] witchcraft has always held the women in high esteem. Witches have to define themselves; challenge the stereotyped roles forced on them; to throw off the societal & sanctified manure dumped on them. Witches must learn to like themselves and each other; no longer give the Establishment 'the sanction of the victim' and permit the age old tactic of divide and conquer: SAY IT LOUD: I'M A WITCH AND I'M PROUD!

Martello, who co-founded of the Gay Liberation Front in the immediate aftermath of the Stonewall rebellion in June 1969, was importing the language of his activism into the sphere of his spiritual life ("Witches must learn to like themselves and each other"). And it went both ways; Martello wrote articles for *Come Out!*, the newspaper published by the GLF beginning that same year, as well as a regular column, "The Gay Witch," in the first weekly queer newspaper, *Gay*, edited by another witch, Lige Clarke, and his lover Jack Nichols. Here's an excerpt of one of Martello's columns, titled "My Curses for 1970":

I curse all those who have hounded and harassed homosexuals simply as a result of their own sex hangups, with having sons who turn out homosexual. I curse all those who exploit the gay power movement in order to promote other non-gay ideologies to get exactly what they deserve: Contempt . . . I curse all those black robed sexually hungup judges who mete out unjust prison terms to homosexuals with having their hearts literally turn to stone . . .

I wanted to know more about this furious Witch and the Witch-In, and I wanted to know what a "Free Style Esbat" could be. Ritual is about 50% historic re-enactment, and I wanted to consider the Free Style Esbat as a distinctly queer act of magic that prioritized the friendship, frolicking, fucking, and frenzy necessary for the Gay Liberation movement to take shape in the way it did. Issue #2 of *W.I.C.A.* had more details:

WITCH-IN: HALLOWEEN '70: New York, Central Park's Sheep Meadow, Sat. Oct. 31, starts at 1 p.m. This is NOT a Sabbat but a free style ESBAT (a social gathering of witches). Our Sabbat celebrated at night, coven members only. Dress up: Costumes,

capes, candles, incense. Bring food, have fun, meet others, make contacts & friends. This is a spontaneous 'happening' thus athames, ritual swords, and our cauldron will be left at home. "Do your thing."
THIS IS THE WORLD'S FIRST PUBLIC WITCH-IN . . . ALL WELCOME!

Finally, in issue #3 of *W.I.C.A.*, Martello described the Free Style Esbat he held on Halloween with his High Priestess, Witch Hazel:

About 1000 people came, including news media, dozens of photographers, TV, reporters, etc. After Hazel and I answered many questions standing on a rock we all DANCED THE WITCHES REEL and sang [an] old Wiccan tune, London Bridge Is Falling Down with new words composed by Witch Gwen Thompson of North Haven Conn[ecticuit]. Here's the first stanza:
WITCHES MEET IN CENTRAL PARK, CENTRAL PARK, CENTRAL PARK
WITCHES MEET IN CENTRAL PARK, FOR OUR LADY!
All joined hands into an ever expanding MAGIC CIRCLE.
TV cameras were inside!!!

The word *esbat*, any witch will tell you, comes from the old French verb "to frolic." But its use to describe witches' meetings is, as far as I can tell, a totally modern reinvention bearing lyrical compatibility with witches "sabbats." Nowadays, the sabbats refer to the eight holidays of the pagan year: two equinoxes, two solstices, and four midpoint days. Halloween is technically one of the sabbats, falling at the midpoint between the autumn equinox and winter solstice. "Esbats," on the other hand, are a witch-4-witch construction.

Sabbat from "sabbath" are a reclamation of 15th-century descriptions of witches by lawmen and Inquisitors, a term coined by oppressors. In *Origins of the Witches' Sabbath*, Michael D. Bailey puts it this way: witches are most threatening when they're plural, a group, a coven. Especially when they recruit, when they could be anyone, and when they meet in secret to party. Central to the origins of a moral panic that destroyed tens of thousands of people was a *scaling up* of witchcraft, from earlier notions of individual hexers and healers to a conspiracy that there were hundreds, thousands of people living in our midst who met in secret to worship demons, have sex for pleasure, steal from the rich, and kill innocent Christians and their children. The name given to this conspiracy was: the sabbat, from "sabbath."[23] Constrained by its history, its naming by those who persecuted witches, it's impossible to imagine a Free Style Sabbat. The word is too mired in meaning. In naming his "World's First" public action an Esbat, Martello was really onto something: liberating witches from a spirituality predicated on *mere* reclamation; welcoming outsiders to an expansive and playful idea of what it could mean to *frolic* together with the divine.

"Magic and history are truth games in which working in the dark is essential to the spirit of the enterprise," writes Peter Hobbs in his 2010 collaboration with AA Bronson, *Queer Spirits*. "Magic has much in common with archival research. In magic, you visit a botanica and piece together a spell, a potion, a recipe. In the archive, you request a file of newspaper clippings, a book, or a photograph and piece together a story, a possibility, a history."[24] For me it goes deeper; magic is archival research, and vice versa, if you're open to it; a ritual to conjure up the past for the pleasures and urgency of the present, a spell to alter my path into the future, a source of wealth, ornamentation, embellishment, nourishment, kindred spirits, dissenting opinions, strategies to keep, strategies to exhaust and leave behind, to write out and burn up.

The simple act of reading and transcribing the newsletters while listening to songs with titles like "Raising the Pyramid of Power" began to bleed into and warp my reality. I smelled burnt leaves. In the kitchen of a suburban witches' house in England, the W.I.C.A. Newsletter opened up a portal to another place and time. I received clear visions of the Free Style Esbat, hands clasped in the dance, the folds of robes and picnic blankets, laughter, the creepiness of day turning to night in Central Park, the crispness of the air that Halloween in 1970, the kissing and stroking and frolicking and fucking the park was known for after dark. Someone started to say: *We're closer to the dead than ever tonight*—I was sitting on one of the blankets sipping hot coffee out of a thermos looking down at a hand on my leg that wasn't mine. A black cat darted toward me and jumped onto my lap. I blinked and was back in the kitchen, the cat still on my lap purring, looking into my eyes.

---

23   Michael D. Bailey, *Origins of the Witches Sabbath* (The Pennsylvania State University Press, 2021), 3.

24   Peter Hobbs, "The Art of Drifting: 43 Lessons from a Naked Cocktail Party," in AA Bronson & Peter Hobbs, *Queer Spirits* (Creative Time: 2010).

All around me living strangers became activated by the dead witch and came into my life; out-of-the-blue introductions to people who'd known Martello, a chance invitation to the New York Public Library which turned out to have a complete run of Gay so I could read Martello's column. An unplanned tour of a library in North Carolina where a stack of books by Martello awaited shelving. *Okay, but if you want to speak through me,* I'd told Martello on the 20th anniversary of his death, *you need to know the kind of transsexual you're dealing with; I'm not like the boys you normally go for.* Then, a few months later, a bookseller in Salem, Massachusetts put Martello's library up for sale, around my own birthday. *I haven't put it all on ebay,* he wrote after I reached out to him. *You can have a scrapbook he made for $115.* In the prudish way of many straight witches, he had kept offline the gay porn found in Martello's library, but he wanted too much money for it—most people don't know how to value pornography, most straight booksellers will price it at homophobic, high prices. Other books were scattered besides. I couldn't afford them all. I was becoming part of a loose coven of witches I knew, and many more that I didn't, book collectors and librarians who were meant to be custodians of this information. As a historian I believe that the paper trail of a person's life is too much for one person to make sense of (territoriality and the goal of total knowledge are imperialist fantasies); sharing the responsibility of partial knowledge heightens what is possible. As a witch I believe group consciousness produces a stronger magic. And crucially as both historian and witch, dispersing the thrall of looking backward reminds you to live your own life.

The box arrived filled with the scrapbook and other books that were rare and out of print: Martello's self-published *How to Prevent Psychic Blackmail: The Philosophy of Psychoselfism* (1966), then *Black Magic, Satanism & Voodoo* (1973) and *Witchcraft: The Old Religion* (1974). There were scrappy little pamphlets he had made: *Curses in Verses* and *Witches Liberation*. There were books inscribed to him by friends: Don Teal's *The Gay Militants* (1971), Larry Mitchell's *Faggots & Their Friends Between Revolutions* (1977), Arthur Evans's *Witchcraft and the Gay Counterculture* (1978). Everything smelled like burnt patchouli—for a while I barely let myself open the box other than to huff the books. Had the scent come from Martello himself, the books tightly packed up in boxes after leaving his home? Or had another witch imbued them with a protective magic for the past two decades? What occult forces had led to my custodianship of these items? The only way to keep the smell of incense fresh from a substrate as absorptive as paper is to keep it burning continuously. This felt like my elevation into the priestly grade of a magical religious order. I now had tools to work with, material to host my own ritual to perpetuate the lineage.

I took what I had of Martello's paper remains with me to engage with in my history workshops that doubled as Free Style Esbats. We'd have snacks and food, conversation, and introductions, then pass his writings around, take turns reading aloud. Sometimes we'd light candles and write prayers together, to a general assembly of queer spirits. Each person would recite the line they'd written, then we'd repeat it together, a call and response, *I lovingly call into the circle those who have died because their idea of finding god was fucking. I lovingly call into the circle those who have died because their idea of god involved crossdressing for pleasure and for profit. I lovingly call into the circle those who have died feeling alone in their perversions—we are with you! I lovingly call into the circle those who sacrificed all worldly concerns to the truth of their bodies, we are awestruck by your beauty!* Martello had started me down a path in *The Weird Ways of Witchcraft* that began to flourish into many more roads to walk down, a litany of prayers, an abundance of living companions, and a clearer understanding that for over a century, the most outrageous and rambunctious facets of revolutionary energy toward queer liberation was undertaken by dykes, fags, and trannies who were all witches.

I decided to put out a call: *Come to the WITCH-IN!* I was printing a lot at the time, on letterpress with lead, wood, thick inks in matte and metallic on thick, absorptive papers; on risograph with bright, juicy inks based in soy and reproduced at lightning speed. I took some images and text from Martello's description of the Witch-In and made an imaginary poster for it. I used a graphic of Baphomet, the divinely androgynous horned god, posters of whom Martello used to sell via mail order forms from his newsletter. I designed and printed 66 copies of the poster and started to distribute them at zine fairs and a craft fair that happens around every Sabbat in London, called the Satanic Flea Market. I had this idea that, by ritually engaging with the creation and duplication and dispersal of these posters, they would act as spells in the world to continue the "EVER EXPANDING MAGIC CIRCLE" Martello and Witch Hazel had cast in 1970.

*

It's the new moon in Gemini, June 2024, six years after Leo Martello first tapped me, and part of his spirit and personal effects have moved with me to Los Angeles. I've spoken about Martello in London, I've spoken about Martello in New York, I've spoken about Martello in Pasadena. Each utterance has opened up new leads, offered up new names. I'm giving a workshop in a house called the Moon Sanctuary as part of a Spiritual Skills Share, started by Michelle Tea. There are nine of us including me, and it fills the little room—actually the ideal number for a coven—13 is too many, and 9 is the number of the moon. There's a totally new landscape to introduce myself to here, new names to look up and pursue among both the living and the dead. I'm reminded of Martello's "Witches Encounter Bureau" ("W.E.B."), a correspondence service of addresses belonging to witches, shamans, Satanists, and pagans that he published in the *W.I.C.A. Newsletter*, which spanned the USA. There are many queer and trans witches out west, and I'm finding them in this part of the world that gives birth to new spiritual movements in a way that reminds me of footage I've seen of the youngest earth, islands produced by volcanoes at the bottom of the ocean.

The workshop I'm giving is called "Thrifting History," and it's about the items you put on your altar, with a focus on salvaging and thrifting objects and incorporating historic research into ritual. I don't use grave dirt, but I use objects owned by dead people I want to build a relationship with; I don't use a dead criminal's hand for my Hand of Glory used to open All Doors, but I do think it's possible to work with old jewelry, clothes, photo albums, and letters that way. As an initiate of Hekate, I am always careful about keys; there are many ways to open up a path.

Everyone was asked to bring an object they want to work with, but if not, I have things on hand to assign them as I see fit. I pass around the objects with different lessons I've learned from each; about aura, charge, about intuition, about rummaging around thrift stores and eBay, about building relationships with stores and dealers so they will let you know when they have the kind of thing you're into, about loving temporary custodianship. For the second half of the workshop, we get to spend time with our objects; writing detailed descriptions of what they look like, how and where we found them, then prayers and questions to these objects, then automatic writing where they tell us what they want us to know about their histories. It's a beautiful exercise only because people are willing to take it seriously and share their beautiful writing. I have brought the scrapbook of Leo Martello because I am at an impasse with this essay, and I want it to give me direction about what to write next. As the workshop facilitator, it's hard to know if I will experience the magic I'm trying to make for others.

It turns out, I experience it quickly and unmistakeably. It turns out the scrapbook has a lot to say, even though it's an item I thought I knew intimately, page by page of plastic-covered paper containing newspaper clippings and correspondence pasted on black construction paper, many of the images and topics repetitive if not duplicates. The moment I open it, a blue envelope jumps onto my lap, wedged between some loose folded magazine pages. I'd never noticed it before and check out the sender's address: Bakersfield, California, a two hour drive north of here. The postmark was dated June 4, 1970—a few months before the Witch-In. Opening the letteraddressed to Martello from Don Jackson and filled with gossip, an invitation:

> . . . The Advocate let me have it with both barrels in their long nasty editorial about me, and Nasty things about Witch Lady Sylvia Cynthia . . . Lady Sylvia wants to have a curse-in at the Advocate. The Satanist will join in because the Advocate's reporter is sueing Satan's [sic] because he fell and broke his wrist on the floor as he walked in front of the horned goat. I don't think Satan liked the announcement of the disintegration of Gay Lib that the reporter wrote up in the May 27 Advocate.[25]
>
> I will write up a review of the book and submitt [sic] it to another publication.
>
> I enclosed the camp-in notice. It is a possibility for you to consider for the summer. It would be a relief from the large city. Getting back into communion with nature is, I think, quite important for witches.
>
> We shall overcome,
> Don

Enclosed were two typescript copies of the invitation:
YOU ARE INVITED TO A CAMP-IN

> **Come out. Come out of the hot and smoggy city, come out for 9 days of fresh mountain air, clear sunshine, meditation, building**

---

25   The article referenced is "Gay Lib survives bitch fit only slightly shrunken—so far," *The Advocate*, May 27-June 9, 1970, 1.

new friendships, sex in the bushes and building [sic] the Gay counter-culture and feeling of love and commaraderie in the Gay Lib community.

[. . .] The ancient Venerial rites of cunt idolatry and cock worship have appealed to the religious inclinations of many Gays in the Bay area, and church members hope that many Gays will find happiness in the ancient faith at the camp-in.

The letter was the latest clue to another lost ritual, and to understanding the true sprawl of the Witch-In, with fresh insights into Martello's friendships with gay and trans witches on the West Coast. It was through initiation by Martello years ago that I could recognize the names now: Don Jackson, who would go on to found the St. Priapus Church dedicated to cock worship; Sylvia Cynthia, aka Angela Douglas, founder of the Transexual Action Organization, who would go on to hold Curse-Ins against *The Advocate*'s assimilationist politics, Robin Morgan's transphobia, the movie adaptation of Gore Vidal's *Myra Breckinridge*. Complicated people with complicated spiritualities. It was a snapshot of the witchcraft I am already engaging in today, hexing against transphobic and assimilationist gay agendas, a craft I can take part in more consciously now that the ghosts of the past have intervened and saved me from my ignorance.

The ever-expanding Magic Circle gets wider, its power runs deeper. Shocked by this fresh lead from an old source, I ask the book—what must I do next? An the exercise in bibliomancy: I randomly opened to a page in the album with a clipping of an article by Martello titled: "Learning In Your Sleep." Time for more frolicking, time to start a dream journal again, time to use these items as anchors, moving further into the spirit world to see what I might bring back.

Amanda Yates Garcia

Incantations for Navigating the Cardinal Directions of Los Angeles – North

Hail, Guardians!
Spirits of the North
We call you

Spirits of Los Angeles, we call you

Spirits of Elysian Park
Spirits of Echo Park, Edendale, Atwater
Spirits of Los Feliz we call you

Spirits of Silver Lake
Spirits of Dodger Stadium and Chavez Ravine
we call you

Spirits of Mount Washington, Forest Lawn
and Glassell Park, we call you

Spirits of Glendale, Toluca Lake
and Studio City we call you

Spirits of Laurel Canyon and Topanga Canyon

Spirits of Encino
Spirits of Reseda
Spirits of The Valley,

Spirits of Yaangna
Come let us honor and adore you

Hail and welcome!

You will seek to find the true spirit of the North
You will ascend the secret staircase
You will find purpose and strength
You will take the 5 North
Your strength will grow tenfold
Your power will grow by the power of the 110
And you will achieve your heart's desire

Ascend the secret staircase. Do not rest. Even if charged by the ghost of a runaway piano. Keeping moving up. Beyond the fences crackling with aged paint. Do not waver. Climb past the doors to your right, beyond the veil of bougainvillea. Do not be lured into the vacant yards to your left, the sirens in the sprinklers, nor by the tangle of fairy lights. Stop your nose against the tentacles of skunk weed. Keep marching up. Navigate your way through the labyrinth of cul-de-sacs; pass one-way streets and hilltop gated communities. Burst forth into the pink light of Sunset. Beyond the amber festooned hills. Showered by piano song tumbling down between the cracks of the wooden deck. Find the Reservoir: the Northern Spirit of Water. Walk thrice 'round it. Dogs will come, seeking your scent. Smelling your sex. Sensing your nature. They are temple dogs, and they will let you pass.

Go.

Keep going.

See specters from your past, lurking on the earthquake ruptured sidewalk. Distracting you with a mirage of your past weakness. The time you wasted a whole year under the spell of a vampire who could not love you.

See those ghosts?

Ignore them. If they come any closer, run. Ask help of the seagulls—jutting out atop the water in a perfect line. Beg help of the running figures, men and women holding dogs like babes to their breast. They will take you to the kites. A blue dog, a puffy red cat, two rainbow windsocks, three triangles all dangling on one thin string out into the sky. Become the hawk. Follow the line of the kite, propelled by the howl of the temple dogs, their wisdom sends you spiraling up through the vapors of the Northern wind.

You will be a lightning rod for the spirit of love.

Angelenos might tell you that you are in the East, but really you are North. How do you know the North? Start at the center with the morning sun at your right.

Go forward.

How do you know the center?

Start inside yourself, inside your cells, where your cells begin.
Travel forward.

Start inside the city. Start at the Mission. And dig down. Into its center cell. You are on Tongva land. Underneath the Pueblo de Nuestra Señora la Reina de los Angeles. Now, you hear them jingling. Here is an Aztec dancing ceremony. Men in feathered headdresses stomp with rattles on their ankles. Eat a tamale from a cart. Eat a blue ice cone and let the electric dye run down your arm. Buy a Mexican blanket on Olvera Street. Only then can you advance.

Go as the crow flies.
As the pigeon flies.
Go as the hawk.
The parrot.
Cross Figueroa.
Cross Beaudry.
Cross Vermont.

Go with the city inside you.

Toypurina, medicine woman and freedom fighter walked these lands, her daughters still do. The Queen of the Angels watches from the Y of the Hollywood sign. Inside your organs, the city thrums her synergistic pulse. Her blood mingling with your blood. No separation, no distance. Travelling in circadian loops along the highways, through the hills, along Mulholland—where the devastation of

Carmaggedon

is a myth. You travel
the city as a cell driving
the vascular system of

the Interstate.

Find yourself at a secret garden. The one in Griffith Park. The one that was destroyed by fire. Carry in your procession a rock or seeds. Dig in the ground. Find a shoelace. Dig in the ground. Find a moccasin. Rising Spirit of the Old Man arrives to help you, he brings his temple dog. You all dig together. His garden was destroyed by fire. It will grow again. He will help you grow it.

Find yourself
at the Old Zoo.

In the summer, the plays are free.
Shakespeare's ghosts surround you. Learn that

the North is the land of ghosts.

The land of bones and wood and stone. And that if North is 12 o'clock, that's where the day ends. The midnight of your life. Before the new one comes. From the East. Depending on where you are standing. And the players dance around you as people lounge, drinking wine from plastic cups. And pouring the dregs as libations into the grass. And in the Fall you will come again. To huddle with friends on the haunted hayride, while girls in striped tights dangle their miscarriage, and bald men with chainsaws chase after your hay truck as you follow the vehicle with

the celebrity VIPs.

The North is the land of trickery and murder
The North is powered by blood

You're in a strip mall parking lot. "Mani/pedi" poster beckons with white hand and dragon red nails. A bikini wax that will leave you bare as a peach. And fro yo and sushi. Eat the sushi. Even the puffy yellow urchin, slimy as a tongue. Eat clams. Eat oysters. Sit next to a porn star. She wears jean shorts and spiked plastic heels and is a secret goddess. Secret goddess of the North. Hidden in refuse. A wounded and primordial goddess you met on your way out of hell, naked and stripped of all dignity, you both were, but navigating still. She points the way to Las Virgenes. The Virgin is her other incarnation.

You drive past the Mountain Mermaid and the Theatricum Botanicum. Past the Hindu temple, with the gods and goddesses protected behind iron bars and perfumed clouds of saffron, with petals and pistachio skins crunching on the floor. Drive past the cyclist, carefully, in his purple Lycra pants and pointy helmet. Twisting his way along the roads towards

Malibu.

You are hiking through the dry hills of the North. When you get to the top, see the pale aether misting over the ancient Angeles forest into the valley of San Joaquin. Hidden now under a sea of chemical cow pies. Because the North is the place of hidden things. Like gnomes. Like arrowheads. Like the ancient glass ring you found in the dirt beneath Happy's doghouse—that ring can tell your fate. Can show you where to find the perfect burrito or an empty parking space. A tree growing in a bookstore. The winding staircase up to the observatory, where you will hold the hand of your imminent spouse and gaze through the telescope out into the future of the universe.

The script in the Northern coffee shop can also tell fortunes. It can sing of all your fates in the city named, for the time being, Los Angeles.

And your neighbor who has taken a break from writing is only pretending to hustle for an agent on his iPhone, really he is an Angel, speaking to you. Foretelling your success. "You WILL make your living doing what you love," he says. Then he describes a beloved object that you thought you lost but that really you left in the back seat of your friend's car. And when it turns up again, under your seat at the Hollywood Bowl, you know at last that you can quit your day job.

So, go to the concert with your friends. Bring wine. A Lambrusco. Bring fancy snacks from Cook Book and sit under the stars. Families of revelers wear polar bear masks given out for free by the Natural History Museum. Listen to the LA Phil playing *Frozen Planet*, as it blasts its way through a melting ice cap. See a melting glacier. A fighting elk. A gaseous green flash of Northern light. See, from your nosebleed seats at the Hollywood Bowl, see the stars above. See, well, see at least

ONE star through the ambient smoglight.

You only need one star to guide you true north, Ninety degrees adjacent to above. Follow it by the power of the five. By the power of 500. Until the power goes out. And the city collapses under a rolling blackout. And the North collapses under its own weight, like an aged elephant. The earthquake comes. And the Northern fires twist their way down the fault lines, from Santa Barbara through the Angeles wood, burning and twisting, dancing like salamanders or Bond girls. Scorching an ecstasy from the North. Destroying everything.

Laugh.

Laugh, as fireballs spit across the freeway and people stop in their cars on the shoulder, turning their camera phones on the raging demon burning up the hills, defying the notion of the North as a place of ice.

Stand as the tree burns in the dark like an Olympic torch, calling a swarm of helicopters. And condominiums. And unjust sweeps of the unhoused community. Fireballs ignite the tar bubbling up out of the ground on the dusty hiking trail. Where oilrigs suck at the earth like gobbling locusts, and Doritos wrappers get caught in the weeds, flung out the windows of big rigs and family cars.

You've driven these roads before. In the middle of the night. To see your parents. To see your lovers. To get away from the city. With your temple dog's nose poking out from the window, her tongue flapping in the wind. As you drive North, she becomes a wolf. And you fling yourself into the night, speeding past the Rest Stop with the sea wind at your back, to escape the gravitational pull of the city and

all the things that you don't know
all the times you've fucked up
all the things that scare you.

With the window unrolled to keep you awake and the somehow delicious smell of smoke lingering red on the horizon of the most beautiful sunset of your life.

Tell your mother that the fires aren't so bad. They make beautiful sunsets. And the freeway is empty. The semis are banked on the grade getting weighed. And you know you can drive the 5 all the way to Canada. To the wolves and bears and moose. To the only rainforest in the Northern Hemisphere. Through San Simeon, Big Sur, Mt. Shasta, Mt. Saint Helen, to the North Pole. And by the time you get back, you will not be so surprised by the vital reality of your mistakes. You will forget about all the time you have wasted. All the pointless anxiety over things you couldn't control. All the times you failed to meet your expectations.

You will be strong and free of worry.

For that is the promise of the North.
The strength to overcome
your mistakes.

To turn over
the heavy stone
of your history,

and burn

the bones of
your old life

until
all
that's left

is ash.

So, hear me, O! Initiates—

Take strength, the strength of the North!
To ascend the secret staircase and leave your history behind.

Trust the power, the power of the North!
Its burning fires will cleanse you, and light your way forward.

Take strength, the strength of the North!
The humor and humility of the temple dogs will educate your spirit.

Trust the power, the power of the North!
With patience, the glaciers will teach you to carve your own way

Back into the ocean where you will be born again and again and again.

CAConrad

First Light

    go ahead
call me a
child for
asking
  is there
  no war
  somewhere
  instead of this
  daily butterfly   fighting
  suck of
fan blade
you should
   break up is my only   relationship advice
on the
way to
  slaughter
pigs on
truck pass
 deer with broken neck
where love
     is merely an   afterthought
we must banish
   the intrusions or become them

we forget the pledge
of allegiance on the
path to finding No
 a flower widening
  a crack in the rock
  when we excel as   father's least
favorite it's
 time to put
 a foot in
 the poem
  I tell you
   there's
   nothing like
  waking in
   the flu>er   passing
hours of barbed
wire across America
the road beneath
us the only
 public space

when you
win the
lottery
every
dollar is someone
else's dream
  once
in a
mirage   listening
into the
open hole for
the fallen
if I see
him again
questions for the crocodile inside
   my old friend
perfume
 of fiction
 on his
  breath
I'm glad I was
     there to stop   myself from
gnawing
the burnt ends of forgiveness

Séamus Isaac Fey

The Voice

My first conjuring didn't come from a candle, or herbs, like I'd use now. I didn't have a grimoire to work out of, a mentor, or even a website telling me how to use magic. It started with a pencil, wood, and a desperate, striking need.

There is a blanket of honesty that the evening hours throw over us, and under it we are forced to confront our lives for what they are. Even me, ten years old, lying in bed. Begging myself to just go to sleep.

I had no words for it then—all I could do was lie there and hold my chest. Now I'd call it a cocktail of suicidal ideation, misery, and a depleted desire to go on. It was too big of a feeling for a little kid. I would cry and sometimes scream, usually into the pillow. I can't imagine it was quiet, but it's easy not to be heard when no one is listening.

School was, at one point, a reliable place. Or, at least a space where it was unlikely I'd come to any harm. It was 5th grade when that changed. We were in the new house, and while kids at school were never kind, this is when they showed me their worst. I didn't have any friends. Once, a bully asked everyone in class to raise their hand if they hated me. They all did, all except one kid who didn't like me but wasn't cruel.

At the end of each day, I crumpled into bed and the anguish took over. Some days it was immediate; some days it was slow poison. Always it arrived in the hours I was supposed to be sleeping, trying to charge up to survive the next day. Words did not always accompany this weight, but if they did, I would cry and think, "I can't do this anymore" until, eventually, my thoughts were silenced by exhaustion—usually one to three hours before I had to go to school again. I was ten and already too tired. I wanted to die. To this day, I marvel at how such a small creature could wrestle with such a big feeling, my mind calling me to end the pain.

At this time, my mother's routine was as follows: two to three days cemented to her bed, either in a pill-numbed stupor or sleeping; then, for half a day or so, she would come out of her cave, brimming with energy for violence. Sometimes it was dodgeable anger, like an argument. This was the best-case scenario, because even as a child, I never cared about winning. I'd choose to be wrong in order to find something that resembled peace. But there were days she took the more vicious path, and on those days there would be blood, and it would be mine. She'd add another series of scars on my arms and hands. I preferred it this way; I would rather be wounded over any of my siblings. She seemed to prefer me, too.

My stepdad, who was a guiding light and place of relief earlier in my life, had relapsed and was drinking again. I could find him drunk on the couch in the basement, often in a pool of his own pee, or he would be out on the streets somewhere.

Months earlier, a Saturday morning, I overheard him say he was going outside for a walk. I was still in bed, but a walk with him sounded nice, so I leapt out to get dressed. I heard the door close, but knew I could catch up if I ran. I sprinted out and turned my head right, then left, to see which way he'd gone. I started down the sidewalk, thinking I'd find him eventually.

A rustle came from a bush on the side of the house, and I saw his hair and shoes sticking out. Approaching the bush, I discovered him sitting behind it, half lying, swigging back a 5th of vodka. I knew what that clear bottle with a white and red label meant. More than the bottle itself, I knew by how quickly he stood up and shoved it into his pocket. I knew by his red warm cheeks and brush-it-off giggle. He had broken his 15 years of sobriety.

I ran back inside, my heart banging against my ribs, tears running down my cheeks. I heard him calling my name, but I didn't turn around. I ran to my mother and told her. My siblings started to gather around. He didn't come back in right away, but when he did, he was swift to call me a liar. When I told her to check his jacket, she found nothing. Of course, he'd disposed of it. She smelled his breath. Clean. Years later, I'd learn he carried mouthwash for this purpose.

They all believed him, of course. I didn't blame the kids, they needed that hope. They were all so much smaller than me. If one of us had to carry the burden, it should go to the oldest and the strongest.

He told them I was lying to get attention. For the next few months, even my siblings looked at me with disgust. It would take a long time for everyone to find out that I was telling the truth. Still my mother didn't apologize, and even the truth wouldn't make him sober again.

Seeing my mother for who she really is was my first heartbreak. Losing the friendship and support of my stepfather was my second.

I was so new to heartbreak; the task of what to do with it was at its highest level of difficulty. Where now I'd do a cleansing bath, a simmer pot, a cord cutting, a ceremonial burn, what I had then was the kinetic energy of a broken heart. Today, I know the power of heartbreak because I paved that path all those years ago. Now when I am cracked open, I pour myself out and thoroughly examine my contents. Move through spellwork with practiced hands.

At that time in my life, every Friday or Saturday, the oldest three of us had to go stay with our biological father. His violence was a different flavor than my mother's. He hurt me, but not with his hands. I felt so confused about how he could demand to see me every weekend even as he clearly disdained the sight of me. He loved to set question-traps for me, like turning on a song and inquiring if I liked it. If I did like the song, I either did not like it enough or I was wrong to like it. He looked for any reason to call me stupid or ugly. To say I was exactly like my mother. If I wanted more food at dinner, he would comment on my weight. If my siblings argued, somehow I started it. The only benefits to being there were the chips and sweets in the cabinet. They made my stomach hurt, but food was food. At my mother's, even that was becoming a rarity.

My father lived in a one-bedroom apartment. During the day I tried to be in whatever room he wasn't. At night, we all slept with him in the bedroom, which had two full size mattresses placed next to each other on the floor and a TV stacked on top of a broken, chestnut-colored nightstand. The drawer was taken out of it at some point, leaving a hole where it should be. The walls were white and scuffed, and the carpet a dirty, almost-orange brown. There was a window at the end of the bed on the right side of the room, one I fantasized about crawling out of and blazing a path into the night. Each of us kids had to take turns sleeping next to him, where he would force us to sleep in his arms. It made me want to crawl out of my skin. It was disgusting and confusing. I hated the way he smelled, like sour aftershave. Why would he want to be so close, when all day it seemed I was the cause of everything bad in this world? I rarely got any sleep at his house, knowing he was nearby. Even if I was fortunate enough to be three feet away in the other bed. If I had to be next to him, I wouldn't sleep at all. Sometimes, after he fell asleep, it was possible to move away from him and squeeze as close to the wall as I could. Sometimes, my brother would take my turn for me, as a radical act of care. Though it could only provide so much comfort, as I didn't like the idea of my brother or sister having to sleep next to him, either.

I could never figure out what I'd done to earn this profound hatred. I tried to feed him the right answers, to take the path of least resistance. I never talked back or spoke my mind. Still, I was wrong in every way. Everyone in my life seemed to feel this way: the kids at school, my mother, my biological father, and now even my stepdad. I believed it must be true. After spending the weekend suffocated by one parent, I went back to the other. Then school, and home again.

This is the time in my life that I came to conjure. In my mother's home, where no one was coming to save me. The energy of my agony needed somewhere to go. Tears could only release so much, and there was still a bone in me that wanted to survive. It started as a voice. Sturdy and constant, coming from a place I had no access to until I needed it. Now, I'd call it intuition. Then, I just did my best to listen.

At some point, I started sleeping in what was supposed to be my brother and sister's room. My room was in the basement, but the basement had become infested with spiders, so I couldn't sleep down there without getting bitten. My brother preferred sleeping on the couch, and my sister slept on the floor next to him. I don't remember where my two baby sisters slept. There was no order, when our mother left her bed, it was to hurt me or yell, not to see if anyone brushed their teeth or if they were in their respective beds.

My brother and sister's room had a trundle bed. Opening the door unleashed a waft of musty air. It was maybe one of the least dirty rooms, but that wasn't saying much. There was never any laundry done in our house, so the bedding was dirty and made me itch. The trundle bed was a dark auburn color, and each bed was twin-sized. The room was on the side of the house that didn't get any sun, so it was always very dark. There was a small window in the wall that let in a modicum of streetlamp light. I remember feeling tired in my body when I would get into bed, thinking I would sleep, but then become awakened completely by my racing mind.

Staring at the wooden slats on the bed above me, I'd picture the knives in the kitchen. *There will be so much more than this.* The one with the black handle, sleek, pointed, meant for everyday use. The tiny green one, a little rusty, but still sharp. Meant for paring fruit. *You will have everything you could ever want and more.* The pocket knife on my stepfather's keychain. *You will build a family nothing like this one.*

I never considered pills. I'd seen them do enough destruction for at least one lifetime. But I yearned for this to be the last day I had to wake up to my life. *You are destined for great things.* The voice got louder—it had to offer me something more than the peace of ceasing to exist.

Keep going.

So I did.

When I thought there was no way I could take another moment, the voice would strengthen my resolve, compel me into another day of breathing.

Magic practitioners often lament that the manifestations and spells we pour into others are more potent than those we do for ourselves. I think this is because when we pour into a spell for our own life, we are simply manifesting ourselves. It is our energy we call upon, or what is already on its way to us. This is not to say that I don't believe spellwork or manifesting work in our own lives; only that what we are conjuring is our own tenacity and divine will to make what we want or need happen.

Eventually, the voice moved into my hands. I let it move me to pen and paper and I'd write out all the qualities of the person I wanted to be.

I didn't know why my parents were not the kind of people I wanted to be. I just knew they made me feel impossibly hopeless. Like I didn't belong anywhere. Like everything was my fault. There weren't any good examples in my life of people I wanted to be like, not close by, except for those I read about in books.

So I put all of the impossible-to-carry energy into a vision: who I wanted to be on the other side of this. Sometimes a bad example is enough. Sometimes being the opposite is a good start. I knew if I lived through my childhood, I'd want to make the people around me feel the opposite of how my parents made me feel.

In this way, lying in bed, making lists of the qualities I wanted to possess: I was manifesting myself. This voice became a lighthouse, and I followed its light through waves of darkness, where I couldn't see myself as having possibility. When I'd get close to finally ending my life, if the feeling of needing it all to be over washed over me with enough strength, I would receive another dispatch from myself: *keep going.* It came down to one evening at a time, one message at a time.

I'd write near copies of the same list:

Kind. A good listener. Respectful. Hard-working. Honest. Loyal. Loved. Creative. Patient. Responsible. Reliable. Brave. Forgiving. Generous. Humble. Grateful. Safe.

I'd picture a sturdy, tall person, surrounded by loved ones. Who I'd listen to, deeply. I'd picture the books I would write. Having the resources to be able to share. Having what I needed, admiring the world around me with grateful eyes. I poured all the energy I had into this vision. I saw it, I wrote it, I listened to the voice. I conjured myself into being.

Sometimes I would write on the wood above me from the top bunk. That way, whenever I would look up, I'd see the list of every good thing I was building inside myself. This was compelling: to turn despairing energy into something new. A furious and necessary alchemy. I thought that whatever I did or didn't do with my life, if I could build myself into a good person, that would be enough.

Another witch told me a few years ago that because of my Sagittarius Mars placement, when I write down what I'd like to manifest, it will come true. When she said this, I was brought right back to that room, that little trundle bed. Looking over my old list, I am grateful to be able to say it has come to fruition. Grateful for tiny hands and the will to be.

Melissa Chadburn

Rarebit

One late afternoon this past spring, I was driving home down Pearblossom Highway, a dirt rough place dubbed "Blood Alley" for all its fatalities; small crosses with artificial flowers peppered the roadside along with scrub and brush. Jackrabbits. This is dog-breeding desert. The fish fryers at the roadside diners, the cash registers at Dollar General, the dogs, the trucks, the churches, the goats, the trains all screeched one long concerted outcry. As I rambled along, I saw there in the dust, on the side of the road, near a junk car lot and a shuttered motel, three stringy white guys, two of them jumping the third. The guy who was getting hit was all greasy hair and defeat. It ached to watch him get jumped. Memories of being a kid in a park—late nights with guys drinking 40s that always wound up that same way. Two, three, four, sometimes five on one. It was so unfair, but also something else. Something animal, something rageful in our cores, that came alight. Was it our nature?

*

I saw it in my mother's face sometimes when she shook me by the shoulders. The other face she so often showed to the world, the one she wore in church and at work long gone. This one—the angry one, was it her legit face—was she always working to suppress it? Maybe it was true. She was Aswang. A shapeshifting, baby-eating vampire. Secretary by day, soul sucker by night. I could see that. Maybe she was a witch, all these women who live alone, who know longing, they're called witches. It was always there, hovering slightly, an electric hum in her blood. Prey drive. It's like when my dogs see a squirrel running across the telephone line in the

185

backyard. They jump and bark and howl at the sky and then sometimes turn on each other. What if the prey is tiny, like a squirrel? Like one boy against five? Like a child? A social worker?

*

January 16, 2023, a woman with bruises around her eyes, blood around her nose and mouth, telephone cord wrapped around her neck, stumbled, dazed, into the lavish lobby of the Biltmore Hotel and pleaded, "Someone call the police." The Biltmore Hotel in downtown Los Angeles is a kind of glamorous place, an indoor pool in the basement, flashback-thin old service stairways run along the spine of the building.

The woman is a social worker looking after a young boy, a foster kid placed in the hotel. December of 2021, former director of LA County Department of Children and Family Services (DCFS), Bobby Cagle, quietly negotiated with the hotel's operators to shelter foster youth. Foster children were also housed at a Comfort Inn in Pomona and a Holiday Inn in Lancaster.

This deal was struck on the heels of many of California's group homes shuttering because they were found to be unsafe and because of DCFS's push for long-term foster placement or family reunification. Unfortunately, after the group homes were shut down, not enough permanent or long-term foster placements were made available in their place. The arbiters of care became withholders of care.

*

The word *arbiter* is likely derived from the name Gaius Petronius Arbiter, the reputed author of *Satyricon*, a Latin work of fiction believed to have been written in the late 1st century AD. *Satyricon* is an example of early satire. Ironically (or, rather, satirically), the surviving sections of the original text detail the exploits of our narrator, Encolpius, and his 16-year-old slave and intimate companion, Giton.

*

Rarebit is an anagram entombed in the word arbiter. To my understanding, rarebit is a Welsh rabbit stew that does not contain rabbit.

*

Thinking of these kids taken from their homes and placed elsewhere— hotel rooms, group homes, institutions—reminds me of Giambattista Basile's *Petrosinella*. A tale written in 1634 about a woman who craved the parsley of a neighboring garden so badly in her pregnancy, she stole it. Once caught, the witch who the garden belongs to makes her promise to give her child to her. After the child is born, the witch continuously reminds the little girl of her mother's promise. The little girl, Petrosinella, confused by whatever the witch is speaking of, turns to her mother and asks what it's all about; furious and annoyed, the mother relinquishes the girl to the witch: "Oh fine already you can have her." Who knows how Petrosinella behaved in the witch's care? Did she cry for her mother, did she demand all the best crops in the garden? She must've done something to irritate the witch because eventually she takes Petrosinella by her hair and locks her in a tower deep in the woods. A tower with just one window.

The social worker at the Biltmore Hotel was assigned to look after a 16-year-old boy, whom she was given no background information on. She assumed he was no threat to her safety. However, according to an *LA Times* article, "He had been placed under psychiatric holds more than twenty times because authorities deemed him a physical threat to himself or others."

The boy allegedly returned from the MLK parade that day, burst into the social worker's hotel room, and accused her of stealing $600. The social worker reported he began pushing her, disconnected the receiver from the phone, tied it around her neck, and assaulted her physically and sexually. A similar report was made about a social worker supervising a foster kid in the Lancaster hotel.

*

I'm everyone in that hotel room. I imagine the social worker . . . there on the floor, the foster kid, and his rage, and his face . . . the face he revealed to her, grimacing, like when the dentist taps a sore tooth. Both wrestling to get out of the godless place.

*

The witch uses Petrosinella's long ass hair to get in and out of the tower. Inside the tower, she teaches Petrosinella magic arts. One day, a prince catches a glimpse of her long ass luxurious hair in the wind. Petrosinella is overly excited by this—another person, a guy, an age-appropriate guy, one who is ogling her. She blows him a kiss. The prince quietly stalks her, and hears that the witch enters the tower by asking her to let down her hair. Eventually, he does the same. Petrosinella is delighted. They fall in love and continue to do this every night. But a neighbor sees and informs the witch of the romance.

*

I am The Foster Kid. In 1990, I entered foster care. Before that, my mother and I lived in a two-bedroom apartment. Cottage cheese ceiling, thick dark carpeting, fiberglass tub shower combo, we had drawer sets made of cardboard from the Pic N' Save. We had an old fridge, and it was my job to defrost the freezer and chip away at the ice with a butter knife. The building was full of poor people. Junk on their balconies, fried food smells, constant heat and blur, and pluck in the laundry room, the most persistent roaches. Like the others, we were poor. Thin-walled rooms, a vat of arguments, babies crying, my mother yelling, dueling television sets, rabbit ears extended with hangers and aluminum foil twisting everywhichway. We, all of us, were trying for a better life and sometimes giving up. My mother worked long hours, and me sneaking cigarettes on the balcony or out the window. Me swallowing half a bottle of Advil only to discover it'd done nothing. Absolutely nothing.

It's difficult for me to know whether or not this was the right choice for my family, breaking us up, being shipped to the witch's castle. I do know money troubles were much of the core of our problems.

*

I have both lived in and worked in these shelters and institutions. After that apartment building, where I knew the dark scary mouth of Ma's closet—a place I was sent whenever her temper flared, skin, teeth, eyes alive with that feral rage, I lived in a group home called Stepping Stones, across the street from Santa Monica City College. The other kids and I listened to oldies, played gin rummy, and smoked cigarettes.

The Place of Odd Rules; for instance, the staff couldn't give us cigarettes directly, but they could "drop them," and if we came upon them, we could pick them up and smoke them. I remember having a fierce crush on one of the staff members, who eventually slipped me his phone number and asked me out once I left the place. I realized quickly I had a bad case of "group home goggles" wherein all the people from "the outs," those who had access to the outside world, were considerably more attractive inside the group home.

I am The Social Worker. In the early 2000s I worked as a case manager in the Hollywood YMCA, a program that housed women and single mothers. I spent my days at the Y counseling the women, helping them with their resumes, setting them up with burner phones and voice mails, navigating the intricate bureaucratic web of Section 8 housing vouchers. Then, at night and on days off, I was a phone hostess. I worked on a toll number and performed the part of a bodybuilder. *Muscle Chat*, it was called.

I wound up dating one of the residents from the Y. I took her in. We lived together in my rent-controlled apartment that was perpetually dark, shrouded in trees, on a street with permitted parking, where I could not afford the permit, so I circled the neighborhood round and round and once I found a parking space I vowed never to leave it. I was now the witch, this apartment was my vampire den, I'd take my captive there and we'd stay inside, in the dark, sucking one another's blood. And yet I felt I was doing her a favor by bringing her there.

She seemed so troubled. So in need of love. So confused. It was a mistake from the beginning. She had no idea how to be alone. I went to a reading with my cousin, and she drank all my alcohol and blew up my phone, calling me 15 times. When I got home to confront her, she stole away into my bathroom with my dog and tried to cut herself with my razors. In a panic, I pushed the bathroom door open hard, and she let go, and it hit her in the face. Livid about her taking my dog into the bathroom, I got right up in her face, shaking the way my mom used to shake. It was an ancient rage. One that screws my face up ugly and takes me out of that rent-controlled apartment in West Hollywood to some wholly dark unknown place that nothing beloved ever enters. I too was becoming Aswang. I caught myself just in time. "Leave," I said.

*

Before that I worked in a residential treatment center for adolescent boys; they were housed by age unless their charge was sexual assault. If that were the case, they lived on the 3rd floor, the highest level of the tower, where there was a sensor alarm across the threshold of each room. In one scene—a knot of boys fighting and the counselor breaking it up— we were trained in restraints and how to hold a child down. It was called "Nonviolent Crisis Intervention Training."

This technique of restraining a child has continuously been revised due to child deaths. The restraint felt every bit as violent as the fight that was being broken up, all of us smashing the threshold of arms-distance, a misplaced thrill for some, sweat and skin, and fear and rage. The whole event would collapse into chisme later: *Man, you fucked him up.* Or, *Did you see how fast Mama Chula ran to break that shit up?* For the staff, what was once terror became paperwork.

*

As we settle in on the child and the social worker, the mother is wiped clean from the narrative. When I was at Stepping Stones, that group home in Santa Monica, there was a day my mother came bursting through the house, barging from room to room. I hid in the bathroom crying while she screamed and hollered, "I want my daughter!" and, in my teenage perception, made a spectacle of herself. It was what I feared. It was what I wanted.

*

Who knows what brought this child to the Department of Children and Family Services or what attacks his mother suffered? I recently acquired my own case records from the Department of Children and Family Services, and at the very forefront was an unexpected violence—a bill. My mother was given a bill to pay for her representation in the county court system she was subjected to.

*

In another apartment in the early 80s I felt very much that I was in league with my mother—we'd just moved to Los Angeles, and she was attending UCLA and she didn't have a boyfriend, so it was she and me and our little apartment in Westwood Village—calling bill collectors and getting extensions to pay things off, putting the dishes on layaway at Kmart, a SALE, a CONTEST, a PRIZE, a BARGAIN! They were tiny, lovely victories in our struggling life. It was then that I began to seek prizes for my writing, some creative act, some intellectual turn.

*

The arbiter—that invisible hand—crafted the rules and circumstances that have brought us all to the Biltmore, a bloodied social worker, telephone cord wrapped around her neck. In 2018, former President Trump signed landmark child welfare legislation. The US law, known as the Family First Prevention Services Act, ended federal funding for many residential treatment facilities and provided little to no alternative.

In more than a dozen states, children are living in conference rooms, hotels, or in the streets. Last year, for instance, the Illinois Answers Project reported that Illinois's state child welfare agency had more than 2,000 cases since 2018 of foster children being improperly held in inappropriate settings, including offices, shelters, and psychiatric hospitals. The agency's director was held in contempt of court 12 times last year for failing to provide an appropriate placement for foster children.

Which means the chances that this happened—that a homeless kid and a social worker found themselves trapped in a hotel room in an impossible situation, were kind of high. *How did I get here?*, they might've thought, and I can imagine. For me it was mom and her broken picker and her own abusive father who likely had his own abusive father and on and on like that. The military and its corporal punishment, locked in closets, standing on one foot, recitation, late night cleaning frenzies; a fit of anger that ran so deep and dark it brought terror to my young heart— a terror big enough to make me run. I ran toward bad. Forties and cigarettes and boys who sagged their pants too low and two-tone mean streaks we used to write on buses and street signs. This was the time that, at night, I became this other being, hot and alive, not under the scrutiny of Ma. Or the courts. Or the group home staff with their dumb nonsensical rules. My Aswang blood, driving me toward safety.

Meanwhile the arbiters—acting alone, well rested, in suits, signing documents, the ones at the helm, soft hands, no sweat, self-interests secured, not taking flight into the night, not looking back over shoulders like I did, like the other kids, like single mothers in courtrooms, like social workers walking nights to their car doors, keys poised erect between their knuckles, but at home—safe, sound, watching it all in comfort.

*

Petrosinella discovered that a neighbor blabbed to the witch and so she prepared by stealing three magic acorns from the surrounding garden. She used the magic acorns as a distraction by throwing them at the witch as the witch chased the couple. The first acorn turned into a dog. The witch staved off the dog by feeding it a loaf of bread. The second acorn became a lion that the witch fed a donkey from a nearby field. The witch donned the discarded donkey skin as a coat, and so when the third acorn turned into a wolf, he mistook the witch for a donkey and swallowed her whole.

Callie Little

A Thread of Love and Magic

Estrangement suited me. It had been four years since I'd last spoken to my family of origin, two since my mother had died. Somehow, despite everything, I was surprisingly happy. There was grief, of course. It came in waves and oceans and cycled with the wheel of the year and some unknown cosmological mysteries, too. There was the dream I had about her visiting me in a graveyard just to ask if I loved her and when I said yes, she disappeared, and I wondered if it had been a dream or something else. I let it stay unsolved and became more malleable to the wonders of life after the death of the person who made me. My world had shifted, and so did I.

Until then, my career had mostly been in feminist sex shops and community events, and I'd just begun to branch out into the writing career I'd always dreamed of pursuing. I was in my late 20s, living in a bright, cozy, century-old apartment in Capitol Hill, the heart of Seattle's gay community. I'd been married for a couple of years to someone I still refer to, 12 years in, as "the largest love of my life," because I call our eight-pound dog "the littlest love of my life." I had become the kind of person I had aspired to be—someone safe, someone with a romantic love story—and yet, I still couldn't feel it in every part of myself. I yearned for something deeper, down in my bones and blood.

I hadn't started researching my family tree yet but wanted to connect with my roots. Even if I couldn't experience having a living biological family in this lifetime, I thought that perhaps my ancestors could provide some sense of belonging. Since I didn't know much about my great-grandparents and nothing of who came before them, I began researching multicultural folk traditions of European origin. Generalized and non-specific, I figured I might find something that felt approachable. This led me to the tarot: an amalgamation of art, play, and esotericism that has roots in a variety of cultures. It's an open practice, meaning that no one population is entirely responsible for it, it isn't appropriative to partake in it regardless of genetics or culture, and no one is asking anyone to stay out of it. It's something all its own. Like me, it didn't come from anyone who could lay claim to it and how it evolved.

As a child, I had been mesmerized by my mother's tarot cards. She never let me see or touch them—they were kept in a velvet bag and I was told it was inappropriate to share them with anyone—which made me all the more curious. But I'd never satisfied the curiosity, feeling like that old wives' tale that we must be gifted our first tarot deck might be true. At the very least, I wanted someone to gift me a deck. I wished that my mother would have been the one to initiate me, that she'd shared this ritual with me. Even now, I can imagine her pulling cards with her long, cherry-red shellacked nails, fingers stacked with rings she bought at swap meets and the discount gold store down the street, balancing a Virginia Slim Menthol amidst a shuffle. Like many things about my relationship with my mother and the rituals of girlhood and womanhood that we missed, I can imagine a different experience than the one I had. I know, though, there is no point in hoping for a better past. So I chose to shuffle the deck and pull cards for myself.

It began as a morning practice. I'd arrange my kitchen table carefully, laying out a cloth and lighting a candle before beginning, mindful to never touch my phone while in the space. It felt important to me that I behave differently within the confines of this ritual, that I wouldn't treat my cards like just any objects but rather create a sense of reverence and holiness. Perhaps this was some kind of leftover from growing up in a Southern Baptist church, or it could be that I just didn't know what I was doing. When I was ready to begin, I intuitively chose a face-down card from the deck, then journaled about my thoughts and feelings related to the imagery before reading from a very old, battered pulp copy of *Mastering the Tarot* by Eden Gray. I'd bought it for a dollar at a used bookstore in Humboldt County years prior and carried it with me all that time, never using it. I took my time—an hour each morning. I'd take notes, writing down the numerology and correspondences I read about alongside keywords and passages, and then I'd draw my own interpretation of the card on the opposite page. Within a month my readings began to make more sense; some cards would show up days or weeks after I last pulled them, and looking back at my notes I could make connections between current readings and prior experiences that illuminated some of the deeper meanings of the cards. It felt like I was learning to speak the language of the universe. Bashfully, I began to pray before my sessions. Gods, Goddesses, Deities, Entities, Ancestors, all who wish me well, I invite you to share your wisdom with me.

I stored my cards on an altar atop a hip-high bookshelf I'd adorned with an amethyst cluster and a photo of my paternal grandmother. At that time, I didn't have any photos of my mother and no one had sent me her ashes yet, so she was only with me in spirit, but she always has been. Families are like that, no matter the relationship, or even the expiration date. And once she couldn't hurt me anymore—once I couldn't hurt her by staying away—there was peace. She had become an ancestor. And so ever since I've had an altar, she's lived there.

After my 30th birthday, I embarked on my first overseas travel. As it happened, an acquaintance of mine had just moved to Dublin with her husband and children and they had a guest room available. It was also her office; she had crystals lining the windowsill, a wheel of the year calendar, and an altar cloth on her desk. It was everything I could have hoped for on my first trip to my ancestral homeland. By then, I'd done plenty of family tree building and found that I'm a third-generation Irish American on my mother's side. Even if I hadn't done the research, though, I think I might have known; walking around the city along the canals and in dusty old pubs full of laughter, my bones felt at home. Like belonging to something that wasn't mine, due to circumstance, and birthright. Our nervous systems sometimes know things that we don't cognitively have the knowledge to understand, but in that place, I could feel the truth of my DNA.

After a few days in the city, I was tired. I needed a quieter experience, and one a little bit more attached to its history. I took myself to Galway where I bought a silver pendant from the shop that first created the famous Claddagh ring—a design representing love, loyalty, and friendship. The next morning, I went on a day trip through the Irish-speaking Connemara region where I learned about the history of the potato famine and how miraculous it was that my great-grandfather survived. The famine walls that stretch across the countryside tell a story of endurance, each stone placed by someone exhausted, just trying to survive to the next day with no reason to hope for reprieve. I imagined my great-grandfather's life, his departure from everyone and everything he knew to come to America where his strife would have no end. What did he leave behind? In the United States, he'd face employment discrimination, and live and die in poverty. He'd have a son who would become an alcoholic, then have a son of his own, followed by a daughter—my mother. My mother who grew up stealing the neighbor's corn because her parents couldn't feed her, then fed me from food bank boxes, and paid our rent with disability checks. I could feel the curse of trauma trickle down the bloodline and knew that just being there, sober and safe and alive, was something I was doing for more than just myself—I was doing it for them, too. I was bringing us home. And farther back than I can find any record, I came from Pagans. Folk magic and remedies may have been erased from history, or were perhaps "driven out" like snakes, but they are inevitably part of who I am, just like my mother and her father and his. Just like anyone with ancestry stretching back to a time before British colonialism attempted to eradicate it. These pieces of me, my family, and our history, have always existed, but I just didn't know them. All that history and magic was inside me all along, and it took three decades to learn about it.

A few months after my trip, I began a podcast with my best friend, Amber. We've always had so much in common, ever since the 2010s when we met amid the fat acceptance movement's blog era. I knew of her because we both had pictures of ourselves in our underwear floating around the internet, but we also shared a passion for reproductive health and birthwork. She was an avid blogger and I knew she'd gone to midwifery school, and I was just beginning my birth doula training, so I asked if we could chat. Our friendship blossomed immediately. Like so many millennial connections, it was entirely digital for the first stretch, but after a few years, she visited me in Santa Cruz, coming from Seattle. Our partners remarked at how similar we looked: we could be sisters! Our builds were so similar! We traded dresses and went to the ocean, soaked in hot tubs, and spent all the money we had on cabs going between her cabin rental and my place. We bonded over being "pit bulls" who were in love with "golden retrievers": having a reputation for being hurt too much, for being cautionary tales, and loving people who were intrinsically different from us—lovers who grew up well-bred and well-loved by good families. Like me, Amber doesn't have a lot of blood ties, and there is a special kind of comfort in knowing others who've had to live with that kind of longing and hurt.

My spouse, Cee, and I relocated to Seattle two years after Amber's visit. There were many reasons for our move, but a major one was that Cee told me I never looked happier than when I was talking to my friend. Over the years, we continued exploring our own paths, but we've always had surprisingly similar trajectories and interests. As she was learning about the history of witchcraft, I was becoming more invested in tarot. We traded notes. She began taking a divination class, and I started learning about deities. She had started calling herself a witch, so I figured I probably could, too. We'd talk for hours about what we were learning, remarking that "we should just make a podcast already!" One day she asked me if I'd ever seriously consider it. I told her I'd been wanting to ask her the same thing. Amber had just finished graduate school and started working as a licensed therapist, and I'd been working as a peer counselor. In the throes of the pandemic, we thought creating a show about the intersection of magic and mental health was the perfect way to stay connected and perhaps expand our spiritual practice together, as well as give something to the community. We recorded our first episode on Mabon, 2020.

One of the simplest definitions of magic is creating change in accordance with will, and that's exactly what our podcast proved to be—magic.

A few weeks into the show, we made an episode about ancestry which ultimately convinced Amber to get her DNA tested through the same company I had used. I'd sung the praises of this process to her for years, telling her how much I loved knowing more about my history and where I came from. It made me feel more whole and connected, even if I didn't really have any nearby kin to connect to. When her results were emailed to her, she forwarded me her profile so I could see her genetic makeup. I was already logged into my account, and when her profile popped up the website let me know that I was looking at my 5th cousin. This woman I'd met on the internet ten years prior, who was born states away and lived even farther, who looked like me enough that our partners commented on it, whose life experiences have always been different and yet parallel to my own, who I am so magnetized to that I relocated—she has been my family all along. My blood has always known this person. Our blood knows each other. It took a decade before we learned what something inside of us always knew: we belong to each other.

Ancestral veneration was the root of my becoming a witch, and it began as a search for belonging. And what is belonging if not a sense of love, regardless of whether or not it has a place to go? It's fair to say that love was my initiation to witchcraft. Being a witch has given me answers to the mysteries I always felt somewhere below my consciousness. While I've always been loved, and I've always belonged, I didn't know, and I couldn't trust it until I followed the path to the answer.

Because I am a witch, I know I'm not alone. I belong. I am loved. I know who I am.

Edgar Fabián Frías

Maps Are Spells

I take a couple drops of the rue essence Saewon Oh and I made together. My heart suddenly drops down into my stomach. I see my grandmother standing before me. I feel the well of emotion bubbling up within me. A tear cascades down my cheek. She has come with a message. I see her holding a small bundle in her hands. Who knows how far she's traveled to bring this to me? It is such a huge honor to receive this generous gift. As soon as she places it in my outstretched hands, I can feel a warmth envelop me. I feel safe and protected. Surrounded by trees slowly swaying in the wind. By this point the tears are streaming consistently down my face. I look up and I see Saewon crying as well. Our hearts are so open. The plants dance wildly within this space that has opened up between us.

Life can be so hard when you're highly sensitive. When you pick up energies and emotions from all over the place. When people don't talk about energy, dysregulation often leads the way for so many of us. Learning to create boundaries, protection magic; crafting containers for reflection, for clearing, and for energetic hygiene. Not only for those who are highly sensitive, but for everyone.

Maps are not only about surveillance and land ownership, but also about understanding internal and external relationships, making connections, forging pathways and partnerships. Maps as places of integration. Maps as stories and incantations. Maps as Sacred Indigenous Technologies. Maps as celebrating the fragmented, the imaginal, the vulnerable, and the expansive. Maps are reshaping our understanding of technologies and space, influencing how we define and connect with them. Maps as spells.

What does it mean to write in a fragmentary way? To allow memories and emotions to rise to the surface and move through my fingers. To reach you. To find their way into your heart. What am I hiding or exposing when I do this? Who is this for? Why does this feel easier than picking something and sticking to it? What am I trying to find within this?

Fragmentation as a strategy. As a metaphor. As an essence. Fragmentation as a need, as laziness, as RESPITE, as the most concise way we can make it happen. Fragmentation as a symptom, an outcome, a reference point that needs to be addressed and responded to.

Mapping:

I was very much a virgin when I first visited Paris in the beginning of the early 2000s. Having admired the city as a young person from my hometown in rural Southern California, I was shocked to experience what Paris was actually like. At the time I was unaware of Paris Syndrome, which was defined by a Japanese psychiatrist named Hiroaki Ota in 1980 and describes a set of somatic and psychological reactions that happen to tourists who visit Paris for the first time and are shocked to realize that it is completely different than the image they had crafted in their minds about it.

The first thing that happened to me after arriving in Paris was that I was swindled by a person who was pretending to help me in the train station. I had just arrived after a couple of weeks in Berlin, astonished by how friendly and caring the German people had been with me. A couple of days ago I had been lost, looking for an art gallery just south of Mitte, and wandered into an eyeglass shop in a posh part of Berlin. The owner of the shop was kind enough to not only give me directions, they even left their store entirely and enjoyed a leisurely stroll through the neighborhood with me to make sure I did not get lost on my way. I was so struck by this act of kindness and care that it opened me up to getting swindled in Paris by someone offering to "help me" purchase a bus ticket to get to my hostel.

Frustrated and disheartened after having approximately 50 euros stolen from me, and finally figuring out my way to my hostel, I was horrified to find it in disrepair. The hostel was filthy, filled with young people from all over the world crammed in small rooms together, sleeping in bunk beds with see-through glass showers in the very same room, drinking and partying at all hours of the night. These rooms were so tiny, they didn't even attempt to give any semblance of privacy or comfort. They were as bare bones as you could get, and for the most part, tourists accepted this as the harsh reality of a "good deal" while visiting this much sough- after city.

To make matters worse, I was waiting for my friend Lisa to arrive from London and received a scared call from her at midnight, several hours after she was supposed to arrive at the hostel. "Help! I don't speak any French and the cab driver doesn't speak any English!" Her voice sounded frantic and stressed. I tried to reassure her that she just needed to give him the address and that he would bring her here, but she said that he didn't know where it was and that they had been driving around in circles for over an hour. This was before the age of smartphones; all Lisa had was a UK flip-phone that she had topped with just enough minutes to give me a call. It wasn't enough minutes for us to finish our conversation. Halfway through our chat, the call cut off and I received a message saying that the user's phone was no longer active.

*

06/20/2023

Murray Hill comes up and announces Le Tigre . . . and like . . . before this, there was this real drunk dyke girl with a Mohawk who kept talking about how much she loves Kathleen Hanna, and how she is her goddess, and how she loves her and has to see her . . . and suddenly . . . Le Tigre comes on . . . first the two members . . . and they start their music . . . and like EVERYONE pushes forward, and Arturo and I are like: "Eeek," and the first song they play is a cover of "I'm So Excited," . . . AAGH IT WAS GREAT!! But by then everybody is pushing and screaming. And Kathleen comes out right when the lyrics are about to be sung, and EVERYONE goes wild. Everybody is pushing, and I keep feeling like I'm about to fall . . . and I get so hot and sweaty, and realize everyone is sweating and so in the moment . . .

After that, they play another song . . . I don't even remember which one . . . but after a bit, Arturo decides to leave . . . and John comes up next to me . . . and he's real close, and I feel his hand touch mine . . . and I follow John and his friends as they walk out. . .and we go to the back . . . and we're all so hot . . . lol. John introduces me to Giovanny and Manolo . . . and I see Manolo, and John is right . . . that boy is HOT.

I think they play "Deceptacon" next . . . then they also play "What's Yr Take on Cassavetes?" . . . "My Art" . . . "Let's Run" . . . and yeah . . . the last song they play is "The The Empty" . . . which is SOOO great . . . I'm dancing, so is Arturo . . . we're all dancing . . . and so is this little 16-year-old queer boy who was also there with us in the front . . . but supposedly threw up and followed us to the back after not being able to take how hot and wild it was up front . . . and I'm so excited . . . and they played TWO new songs . . . one of which I LOOOOVED! It was totally electro-fast . . . mmm . . . and this other one about dyke visibility. And yeah . . . they leave the stage after their last song and Murray comes out and he's saying that we have to yell for Le Tigre to come out again . . . and he says: "Only one group can bring these people together . . . let me hear it for the feminists . . . (people scream) . . . for the dykes (girls scream). . . for the gay guys (guys scream) . . . for the transgender people (people scream) . . . and for the cool straight kids!! (straighties scream) . . . " Lol . . . why did I scream for every single one . . . lol.

Yeah . . . so, they come back and play this GREAT rendition of "Leep on Livin'!" aagggh! On the screen behind them were pictures of gay battles, of gay triumphs . . . and a story about this transgendered guy who is having trouble being accepted . . . and like so many rainbows and pink triangles . . . "PRIDE!" Everyone is screaming and dancing their @$$es off! I'm so happy . . . feeling accepted . . . among people that don't care . . . that will just leave you alone and LET YOU BE . . . It's utter bliss . . . to feel like I can finally be MYSELF.

Once the song is over we all file out . . . and I'm so happy and tired . . . and we meet up with John, and they're buying stuff at the merch table . . . and all of the sudden I see someone there helping them . . . and realize after a while that it's THAT ACTRESS. . .

The one that I saw the other day when I got the courage from her to go to Kenny's football game . . . the day he smiled at me and my heart sang . . . she's named Clea Duvall and is from the movie: *But I'm a Cheerleader* and SHE WAS THERE IN PERSON! Selling stuff at Le Tigre's merch table! Aaggh! John pointed her out to me. So I just HAD to take a picture with her.

"Keep on Livin'!"

*

03/22/2020

Wow. I don't even know where to begin. It feels as if the entire world has gotten flipped upside down. In the last two weeks, my life has gone from having plans and projects and upcoming trips to a sobering reality that I may need to stay home for the next few months. My worst day was the day I found out about Berkeley. It was the day I had my "corona wake-up call" as I'm calling it.

That moment where your denial and delusion break and you're forced to sit with the disorienting and scary truth that your life is never going to look the same as it did "before." I was scheduled to take a trip to UC

Berkeley to meet the professors and graduate students. Two days before my flight, they announced that they were going to be closing the campus and that all classes would be moving to an online format. I had heard of the virus and knew it was coming our way. But I had also gotten mixed information about what that meant and how much danger we were truly in. In my head, it was still safe for me to fly; the school shutdown was my first taste of everything no longer being "business as usual." I almost had a panic attack accepting this. I am grateful I had Thaddeus to support me. As of now, I've had to cancel/postpone three flights and three major events because of this virus. It's fully altered this year for me and everyone else.

Not everyone has lived through this process gracefully and many are still refusing it. I've been incredibly disappointed by the actions of people, including my younger brother's unwillingness to see this as a real threat, his fucking egotistical desire to keep going out, to even go as far as to make fun of the virus in the insipid "comedy show" he makes with his weird, straight Christian friend. Also—why are my two brothers, who are both in their mid-to-LATE 30s, still living at home with my parents?! Endangering them with their ineptitude and failure to launch?! It's so frustrating to know they could be bringing home this virus since they refuse to mask and stop going out.

As for myself, I'm currently isolating with Thaddeus in Oklahoma, as I am participating in the Tulsa Artist Fellowship and we are in the beginning of our second year here. I feel utterly blessed to be in this situation at this moment in time, as it means I have secure housing and income until at least December 15, 2020. The same cannot be said about millions of others across the earth right now.

In the United States many are waking up to the fact that there is ZERO safety net beneath us; that this government is more concerned about bailing out their business friends than any actual people in America. There have been talks of rent strikes emerging, and, quite honestly, I feel like we should also refuse to pay our taxes. It's at that fucking point—it's been at that point for a loooong time. We're now seeing what kind of dumpster fire the mediocre (at best!) personality cult of white supremacist trash has gotten us. It's created a reality where we have anti-intellectuals in charge of handling one of the worst global pandemics we've seen in over a century.

Capitalism is a broken, myopic, violent system that this virus is allowing us to fully see for the first time in ALL of its evil self-centeredness. The focus on our economy instead of the health and resiliency of those who actually create the profits in the economy is soooo utterly disgusting and ignorant.

I do not respect this government. I do not respect capitalism or white supremacy. I respect my web of witches, queers, and mutants. The oracles that surround me via social media are keeping me sane. Our visions and downloads have been sensing this type of catastrophe. We've all been preparing. Gaia has been asking us to return to our plant allies and our ancestral connections.

Lisa never arrived that night. I stayed up until three in the morning hoping to hear from her. Beat down with exhaustion and a feeling of dread, I was finally able to sleep a couple of hours before waking to the grim reality—Lisa had not made it to our shared room in our dingy hostel. I tried unsuccessfully to call her several times that morning, only receiving the message that her phone was still off. I spoke with the people at the front desk of the hostel and tried to explain the situation. They seemed unfazed and uninterested, and told me I could call the police if I felt like my friend was in danger. That felt, at the time, like a scary thing to do, and I decided that I would go out for a walk, to clear my mind and try not to think about the situation for a moment. I sent a few text messages to Lisa, letting her know that I was worried about her and that I was hoping she was okay. My heart sank when I saw that none of them had been delivered but were just left in limbo.

Lisa is a strong person. She's traveled the world on her own and has the wildest stories to tell. I hoped that she used some of her street smarts to protect herself and that she would have another story to share with me soon. I was worried about the implications of going to the police, especially with both of us being foreign exchange students from California, and with me having little evidence that something had happened to her. I was also tired, felt betrayed and bewildered, in this city that I had been looking forward to visiting for much of my young adult life. To say that I was disoriented and confused is an understatement.

In the midst of that confusion, deep down, I heard a voice say to me, "Just try to enjoy yourself, do something you've always wanted to do here in Paris." I immediately knew what this was. I would go to the Palais de Tokyo, a gallery I had only ever read about, had been obsessed with since high school. Art has always been one of my most precious resources when it comes to regulating my mood, offering possibility, and helping me ground into the experience of witnessing the results of hours of craft, cognitive labor, and care. When I arrived I was greeted by the exhibition *Babydoll* by the Taiwanese-American artist Shu Lea Cheang which featured what looked like the cups from vomit-inducing, spinning fairground teacup rides, with massive pink neonate human-animal hybrid "clone baby" dolls inside, wearing red diapers that resembled something Mickey Mouse would wear. The second exhibition was Interminável by the artist Artur Barrio, who filled a whole room with coffee grounds, loaves of bread, and light bulbs, among other objects and ephemera.

It was in this exhibition where I finally received a text from Lisa, "I'm fine. At the hostel now. See you soon."

Love is a psychic phenomenon. How is it that two people are able to know each other without knowing each other? What are the symbols and sensations that emerge between people when love begins to blossom? How is love felt so deeply yet such an ephemeral force? Love is one of the most powerful energies in our Universe, and yet it is fickle, and emerges and retreats spontaneously, sometimes in milliseconds.

I was half drunk on the dance floor with Lisa. The club was dark and sweaty and the music was loud. Minimal techno mixed with a few top 40s had the crowd dancing wildly, and everyone seemed to be in a good mood. Lisa had warned me before coming that it looked a little "too straight" for our tastes, but that we'd go anyway and hope we'd have a good time. The previous night we wandered the streets and drunkenly asked people if they knew where the gay or lesbian bars were, only to be met with confusion and, at times, disdain. We settled on going out to this club, as we had been told by a group of tourists in our shitty hostel that it got really busy and was a mix of Parisians and travelers from all over the world.

Halfway through the night Lisa had, unsurprisingly, met a boy who was trying so hard to sleep with her. He kept buying her drinks and would sporadically buy me one, too. At some point Lisa disappeared with him into a dark corner of the club, and I was left dancing by myself on the dance floor. A few minutes passed and I noticed a young Parisian boy speaking with his friend and looking in my direction. He kept making eye contact with me and smiling. I saw his friend leave and was left dancing near him.

He looked younger than me, and had short brown hair cut closely in a somewhat quiff fashion. He was wearing a bright white dress shirt and slightly baggy black skinny jeans, casual black boots that looked brand new. We made eye contact a few times while dancing, and I decided to take a risk and move closer to him. It didn't take long before he approached me and whispered something unintelligible into my ear. I asked him to repeat himself and he looked at me confused.

"I am sorry I not speak English," he said in a thick accent, and smiled shyly.

"Je parle un peu de Français," I said to him, attempting to remember as much as I could of my high school French in the semi-drunken state I was in. This seemed to put him at ease, and he smiled and leaned over and kissed me on the cheek.

I told him I was 23-years-old and asked him his age. He said he was 21. I told him I didn't believe him, and he laughed and pulled out his ID to show me. Funny—he was actually 19 and had lied to me about his age. After dancing for a few minutes, I coyly touched his arms and hands. I could see him opening up and getting excited. It didn't take long before we began to embrace, allowing our hands to do the talking and connecting. Mapping, exploring our landscapes and valleys. I was nervous and so excited as it was the first time I had ever kissed someone, and I was in utter disbelief that it was happening in a straight club in Paris, after what had already been such a shitty trip.

Our kisses were passionate, messy, and transgressive. I remember at some point reaching down into his pants to feel his hard-on. Both of us getting lost in the mix of excitement and the sounds of the music blasting all over our bodies, getting lost in and around each other. We made out so hard that at some point one of us started bleeding from our hands and arms rubbing up against the hard metallic walls. Maybe we were throwing each other into the walls or into each other; to be honest it's all kind of a blur. I just remember that both our shirts were left with blood stains by the end of the night. As these kinds of experiences sometimes go, we never saw each other again, but we knew that, if anything, we were going to leave a mark on each other. I don't remember his name and I'm sure he doesn't even remember mine, either. It lives on as a moment of magic that faded as quickly as it emerged; the traces left behind still live within me. Mapped into my being, and in the vast, uncharted neural pathways of my mind. I wonder sometimes if he remembers me, the chance encounter we had decades ago. I wonder if the Universe will chart a path for us to reconnect again someday. Maybe I'll finally know his name.

Myriam Gurba

Feeding Iyami: An Interview with Ever Velasquez

Ever Velasquez is an artist and traditional healer who practices curanderismo, a form of Latin American folk medicine. She also engages in orisha worship, a Yoruba derived religious practice that involves spiritual messengers, orishas, who help humans to communicate with the divine. According to some scholars, thousands of orishas exist. In the Americas, where Ever practices, orishas who are widely venerated include Eleggúa (orisha of the crossroads), Obbatala (sculptor of mankind), Yemayá (orisha of the upper ocean), and Oshun (orisha of freshwater, beauty, love, fertility, prosperity, and wealth). I interviewed Ever about her practices, speaking with her about her spiritual past, present and future. Our conversation has been lightly edited.

MYRIAM GURBA: I'm so excited to be talking to you and to honor you through this interview! Please, tell me about your roots.

EVER VELASQUEZ: I was born in East Los Angeles and grew up all over LA. My mom was a single mom. My dad was in and out of our lives, but when he was there, he was always a good dad. We moved around a lot. The '90s were heavy, and my mom worried about what it would be like for us to grow up in East LA and so she started slowly moving us out towards the inland Empire. During my high school years, I lived in Chino Hills, which was nothing like the Chino Hills of today. Back then, people would get excited about the opening of a new supermarket. They would go to the opening of an Albertsons.

MG: So, you didn't fit in?

EV: No! I grew up with natural gifts that I know now are gifts. At the time, I didn't understand that they were gifts. I had a lot of night terrors and visions of sickness and death. I would vocalize those to my mom in public. This embarrassed her and she would say, "You don't do that. You don't tell people that they're sick. You don't tell people they're going to die soon."

I come from a long line of curanderas on my mom's side, and I started to work herbs as a kid. My mom would get upset because she would wash my clothes and find that the laundry was ruined. I had filled my pockets with leaves and flowers, and she would ask, "Why is this in here?" I would answer, "I needed it." She would ask, "What did you need it for?" I couldn't really explain why so I would just say that I needed it. My mom didn't let me really develop when I was younger, so I started to work on my own, secretly developing. Then, as I got older, I started to experience long periods of vertigo and insomnia. I hardly slept. When I did, it was like for an hour or two. I travelled to Japan and found peace there. When it was time to come back home, I realized that I needed to find peace here.

MG: How did you do that?

EV: I met someone important, my friend Vincent, at the release party for Barrio Queer Zine. He talked to me about his spirituality. There was something about how he spoke that made me feel like I had known him for a long time. We talked about tarot readings, and I told him that I was interested in having one. Then, he said that spirit had a message for me, that spirit wanted me to know that there is a lot of generational trauma in my family, and that I'm the only person who's going to be able to do the work that will restore balance. He said, "You have a large task ahead of you, and the spirits want you to listen. They want you to take this seriously." Next, he said that spirit told him to tell me to bathe with red and white roses.

MG: Did you do it?

EV: I thought about it, and I was like, "What's the worst that could happen to me?"

I took the bath, felt my back crack, and then a lightness. Afterwards, I called Vincent, and he did my first reading. It was the worst reading in the world. Everything was messed up in my life. I was told that I had a lot of work to do.

MG: Is that how you found your godmother?

EV: Not exactly. I started to do the work and things were flowing. Originally, I was taking the Ifá route with a friend. Her priest, though, ended up being creepy, and a situation happened where I felt very unsafe. It triggered past traumas, and I had to make myself invisible to stay safe. Once I escaped, I called Vincent, and told him what happened. I asked him if I could speak to his godmother. This was my second time asking. When I asked the first time, he said, "No, she hates Capricorns. She's a libra, and she doesn't want female godchildren."

Because of what happened with the priest, he said that he would reach out to her and soon after, I met with her at her home. She explained to me that the priest had tried to spiritually rape me and that the spirits who protect me knew that and guarded me. She told me that I could leave that behind and start over with her. She said, "I'll take you as a godchild, but the rule is that you must listen to me." My madrina is very traditional and very non-traditional at the same time. She has a queer ilé (spiritual house), and she's very upfront.

My madrina told me, "Look, your spirits are already talking to me, and they're telling me that you should have begun doing this a long time ago. This is going to move very fast for you. I'm hosting a spiritual mass in two hours if you want to stay." I stayed and received messages but didn't feel that I could vocalize them because I was new. When you're on a spiritual path, but you grow up being told that you're not good at things, that you're not good enough, you question yourself. You ask, "Why am I given these gifts? Why would I have the gift to help people and heal people? I received my elekes (protective necklaces) a month later. For the first time, I also saw someone be mounted.

MG: What was it like seeing someone be mounted? (Note to reader: Those who worship orishas invite these deities to descend and take possession of worshippers. The mounted celebrant becomes possessed and might transmit important messages to those present.)

EV: I was in shock. You see dramatizations of this in movies, stereotypes in horror movies. I watched the elders around me help this person while they were mounted and channeling messages.

MG: How would you explain orishas to those who are entirely unfamiliar with them?

EV: With African spiritual traditions, you're always going to encounter people who will say, "There's only one God and what you're doing is devil worship." But if you get down to the basics, orisha worship is a practice of community are and also of self-care. This is a practice of community healing. If I could change the bad qualities in myself to better myself and the world around me, everybody heals together. I'm crowned Obatala. Obatala is the owner of my head. Some people say that Obatala is like Jesus Christ. He was put here to create the world as we know it. I can talk about the ocean as the place Yemaya and Oshun and Olokun.

MG: How do you fuse curanderismo with orisha worship?

EV: It ties in a lot with the orisha Osayin. He is the keeper of the forest and the herbs. Those are worked to be able to make medicine.

MG: Have you experienced negative consequences or even punishments for your spiritual choices?

EV: Yeah. Some people, once they find out, are like, "Oh, okay, we're not going to talk to you anymore." That's fine. That's energy I don't have to deal with in my life.

MG: You helped to facilitate the "coming out" of Patrisse Cullors, an artist and one of the founders of the Black Lives Matter movement, as an Ifá practitioner. I'm curious about that and other ways in which your career in art intersects and overlaps with spiritual practice.

EV: I had set a date to work with Patrisse and then her cousin was murdered. Charlie, my boss at the gallery, was like, "Oh, my God, what do we do?" I said, "There's nothing we can do other than check on her. So, let's check on her." We had a meeting and offered to reschedule her show. Patrisse said, "No, I need to do this work." Charlie was worried because we still hadn't narrowed down what this show was going to be about." I told him, "Spirit is telling me that this is a time to heal within community. I have complete faith. We just need to back off and give Patrisse space, and it will come together. Spirit will make this come together." Then, the most extraordinary thing happened. After we made the decision to be hands off, I noticed that two crows had begun to make a nest on one of buildings. That's significant because in our tradition, they represent the iyami, ancient mothers and powerful witches. They can shapeshift, and they've been given the strength to do whatever they must because they're here to avenge all the women who have been wronged. Men fear them. I fed these crows just the other day. And so, everything flowed together very magically. Everything was like water. Everything must flow like water.

Ingrid Rojas Contreras

People Who Come to See Autzana, the Curandera

Husbands. Wives. Parents. The desperate. The ill. The lonely. The curious. The afraid. The pregnant. The wanting a pregnancy. The out of work. The sleepwalking. The can't sleep at night. The can't go to the bathroom. The everything is water coming out of them in the bathroom. The addicted to sex. The sex workers. The having a sexual disfunction. The starving. The refuse to eat. The can't breathe very well. The cursed. The ones who put on a curse. The how do I forgive. The I cannot forgive. The ones looking for a lucky break. The ones looking for a woman. The ones looking for a man. The ones with a ghost upending the house. The I have a burial in the backyard. The I have a secret. The I want to know what's being hidden from me. The heartbroken. The I can't feel a thing anymore. The betrayed. The betrayers. The I turned my brother in. The my sister was taken by paramilitary. The how do I protect my son. The in the middle of the night all I hear is my Auntie's screams but she's been gone for a long time, why is she still screaming. The I can't tell nobody who I am, if anybody finds out I'm demobilized, I'll be killed. The I did things, I did horrible things. The Please help me. The I'll do anything. The I want to take it back, show me how to take it back.

Frankie Mirren

The Catte

England 1631

It is autumn when a catte opens her eyes for the first time and finds the world crisp and golden, a bed of orange crackling beneath her, a coldness that pierces her organs, shafts of low bright sun. She struggles to stand, searching for the hot milk flesh of her mother's belly or the warm scrabble of sibling fur. She can find neither. The limp, still things around her are changing in smell, their familiarity turning putrid. All this in a brand new world.

A woman is walking back across an open patch of land, taking the meandering path of the sheep and cattle which graze here and the rabbits which burst from hedgerows then flee back to cover. Her skirts balloon as she crouches to pluck something from the ground before she weaves towards the trees then away again. As she gets closer, she pauses and mouths words to the air, her fingers moving as though she counts birds in the sky.

The kitten mews. The woman looks down. They both feel a new path open before them.

"You poor spirit." The woman picks up the catte, just a scrappy handful of black fur, eyes gummy, tail like a bottlebrush. Below them, the kitten's siblings and mother have grown cold in their nest of fallen leaves. The woman holds the catte in front of her and the kitten observes: a pale long creature, wild black fur on its top which tumbles down its back and needs chasing, small teeth, no smell of milk. Catte is bundled into a scarf and placed in the woman's basket. The smell of wet earth and curdle.

A journey and then, unwrapped, the kitten finds herself in a warm dim space, a single room whose hearth sends smoke spiraling through a hole in the roof; around the ceiling hang herbs and fronds of dried fern. Two pairs of eyes. Woman and catte, catte and woman. An old sock, it turns out, is a good place for a kitten to sleep, and the broth from a stew fine to drink. Fleas may be treated with a paste of catnip and oats. Yarn, unspooled is a thing of mad joy.

So, they live together, Ellen who is human, and Gille who is catte. Gille drinks milk and eats whatever Ellen leaves out for her, but mostly she hunts. To the smaller creatures of fur or wing, she is a green-eyed terror, a wild tearing nemesis whose soft night coat and soundless paws flail in an instant into something demonic. But Gille feels herself part of the blood-pulse of the earth, messenger of an endless thrum so deep and low it is almost imperceptible, and from that first moment of awakening in the dying, gorgeous day, she knows that death can be a beginning, just as life.

Ellen tells her she's a good little catte, the best catte, and Gille flicks her tail and sleeps.

Ellen, who is human, lives on little: water from the well boiled with thyme, bread which she bakes, eggs which she steals, ale brewed herself (wort boiled in copper cauldron, ferment in a wooden vat), meat, occasionally, brought here by a guest. These guests, the men who leave gifts and sometimes coins on the bed after Ellen tugs and slops and sucks and opens her legs, prickle Gille's spine, raising her hackles. She is forced to hiss and spit.

"Don't mind her. She only wants to protect me," Ellen says, and she will pretend to be angry. "Shoo, Gille, mannerless catte!" but Gille knows that, truly, Ellen would follow her if she could, darting out into the wild world, crouching silent in a tree or flying up to the rooftop, until the men were gone.

In the mornings, they set out, woman and catte, across the common where they find berries, mushrooms, nuts, and herbs, and where the woman keeps a goat too old and tough for either milk or meat but who, the woman says, is a shrewd judge of character. They pass a stream (catte sits on human shoulder) and, in the woodland beyond, the woman finds a shimmering gray feather, a fir cone, a malformed acorn, and an empty snail shell of intricate pattern. Tonight, the woman will place these on the floor and lie among them smiling, her eyes closed. She will hear: a rushing that contains the reaching root whisper of trees and the gasp of the wind, the chatter of sunlight, the dark coils of solitude.

Other times they walk past the forge with its sparks and fire and the ring of hammer on anvil. Past the inn with its songs and shouts and its overspill who might fight or laugh as they tumble from its doors. At a house on the far side of the village, Ellen whistles and they go inside. A woman greets them, arms around Ellen, a morsel for Gille. Here, Gille settles on a rag by the hearth, curled into a circular shadow. Here, Ellen smiles and words spill from her lips. In the hearth light, the women's faces flicker with heat and sometimes Gille wakes to find them dancing, stirring up dust as they whirl. Once, when the woman has killed a hen, she makes Gille a plaything, feathers knotted to twine, and this Ellen trails behind her as they walk home.

The other villagers, Gille knows, keep their distance. Ellen knows too. As she grows older her once striking face loses its softness. Nose of a hawk, cheeks of parchment, chin sharp and folding around the hollow of her gums. The loss of her beauty makes people angry, as though it had been some cheap trick all along and now they find themselves vindicated. Her muttering and seclusion, her welcome of village husbands into her bed (oh yes, they knew, only tolerated it as, truth be told, Ellen's ministrations saved many wives the bother) becomes a cause for speculation and gossip. What is it she mouths so frantically into the wind? What words does she cast to the earth as she scrabbles in hedgerows? It is heresy, surely, or something more diabolical still.

That summer, people wake one morning to strange men in their midst, men who measure land in booted strides, hammer a sign to a fencepost declaring this property now the Earl's. Within a week, a field is fenced off and filled with sheep. There is no longer room for Ellen's goat, the parcel of land left to the village shrinking like a puddle in drought.

A pox infects the cattle and someone at the alehouse wonders if the woman's Imp carried out this Deville's work? Another says he saw a Marke on the woman, an unnatural thing, but will not tell how he came about the sight. "Only bide my words," he says. "That catte is fed with the milk of a human teat. That Imp!"

Sometimes, in the evenings, catte and human sit by the window and watch the sun sink beneath the line of trees. Every year there are starlings, moving in one twisting celestial body. Ellen reads their murmuration for signs, taps messages into Gille's fur. Sometimes Ellen laughs, an abrupt, harsh sound, and Gille is forced to leap from her lap and sit sternly on the table until Ellen is rebuked. Other times, water gloams from Ellen's eyes, tasting of underground, falling on Gille's fur.

Ellen talks and Gille listens and what she hears forms part of the endless thrum.

On a bright harsh-lit day in 1645 Gille senses a change in the air before she hears the shouts. It is a frightened, hungry hoard who burst through Ellen's door, demanding retribution which will never be theirs on a body which played no part in their agonies. Ellen is adding garlic to a stew and she turns slowly as though she too has been expecting this. She whispers, "Go, little catte." Catte fur against human skin as Gille brushes beneath Ellen's hand. Now, catte (whose belly, though she doesn't know it yet, is full of kittens) darts through the forest of legs and into the thickening day, into the thrum and heartbeat of it all, still beautiful, still milky, raging.

England 2024

My black cat Cleo, a six-month-old rescue when she came to live with me, sleeps curled into the crook of my right arm. She mews until I wrap my left arm over her to make a pillow for her chin. And we sleep. Even me, a lifelong insomniac, and her, a jumpy, nerve-jangled being who, for no reason I'll ever know, will suddenly leap terrified from wherever she sits as though a predator is near; both of us can sleep.

I swear I see into Cleo's soul, and she into mine. I wonder what millennia of memory is coiled into her DNA, what reflexes passed on from ancestors who, 3000 years ago, ran alongside the horses of Phoenician traders as they travelled from the Levant, who caught mice for farmers as they spread across Europe, were carried by the Romans to this rainy isle, who survived the time when cats were regarded as demonic, named in witchfinders' screeds as witches' Imps, channels for the Deville, capable of killing man and beast alike and who, with their humans, were condemned to death.

But Cleo is here! The result of an unbroken chain of cattes stretching back and out of sight. I create lineages for her, amazed that any creature survives this world, grateful as she watches me with her limpid-green eyes full of tiny veins like rivers of rust. By day, she sits by the window, behind the net curtains she shredded, keeping watch on passers-by. Sometimes she is indeed possessed by the Deville and she will scud wildly up the stairs as though the hounds of hell are behind her. I imagine she finds me ridiculous, my endless blather, my hoarding of stones and feathers and shells, my inability to jump onto doorframes. Still, she tolerates me, deeply trusts me, loves me even. She is always by my side. Like Gille and Ellen, like all the Gilles and Ellens.

I tell her she's a good little cat, the best cat, and she twitches her tail and sleeps.

Fariha Róisín

Excerpted from "Goddess of All Things Tituba"

I am me, I am a thousand things.

The Lord knows, knows how long I've toiled through this dark and treacherous land. They say we pass things down. Yes, I do believe that.

I am told I got my magic from my grandmother, my nanu, *Tilottama*, a great Bengali beauty and seer, a witch of many beings and identities—the first shapeshifter I had known who taught me all that I came to know.

We, the children of Jessore in fecund Bengal, our lands laced with vegetation as high as the hills, greens in many shades and varieties. Here, in these lands, we spoke grandly of her powers, it was evident to us as the wind. Children are keen observers, they see the world with fresh consideration, this at times means seeing with more truth, with more eye-balled, wide-eyed vividness.

In the village, we all knew her to be a sorceress, as pure as they come, a *jadukari*, of many shapes and amalgamations. Everybody had needed her at some point, needed her timely vision, her concoctions of herbal medicines, her pranayama techniques learned through deep yogic discovery coupled with the vibrating power of her chanting *Surah Yas-in* throughout the day in whispers and enchantments, which was known to cure ailments, headaches, and even ease people into the afterlife, spoken by her in soft whispers in their humble final moments. The balmy sounds of *La ilaha il Allah, Muhammadur Rasulullah*, evoking spirited visions of the afterlife, the Prophet (ﷺ) dressed in all white, mysterious, and handsome.

216

Tilottama knew the plants in an intimate way. She knew how tulsi could relieve one's nerves, how it could focus and stabilize a person in one gulp. Methi leaves could lower one's high blood pressure, and drinking soaked methi seeds could relieve constipation, as well as help with inflammation of the gut if food was too spicy or the body was out of balance. As prescribed, I watched nanu drink it herself each morning, especially if she had *mishti* the night before, soaking the seeds extra-long in a milky, frothy tea to drink in small, short gulps. She taught me that salivating on a small piece of ginger was a great remedy for stomach disruption, for fevers and indigestion; crushed mint could cure nausea and was therefore a perfect remedy for a newly pregnant parent. Raspberry leaf tea could support anybody with a uterus, aiding a healthy womb, but you could also induce labor if need be, pressure points on the tender fleshy curve between the heel and the balls of one's feet massaged with warm mustard oil help with the movement of the birth. Everything had a place and a knowing, a remedy of numerous inventions.

If there was ever a case of nazar in the village, she would be the person to instruct its removal. She would tell us of the noble Ibn Abbas, the greatest mufassir, as well as a humble cousin of the Prophet ﷺ, once said, "The evil eye is real. If anything could precede the divine decree, it would be preceded by the evil eye." It was said to bathe the body was of utmost importance, garnishing it in warm water and salts.

Tilottama would guide, cotton sari wrapped around her in tight loops, crooning over a metal basin full with liquid and herbs, chrysanthemums and rose petals. If anyone was struck by the nazar she would ask that person to take a bath and perform ablution, then the request would be granted, and the protection would prevail. I had performed such acts with her, praying surahs as rituals were performed and enunciated, it was a divine orientation to see her ability to clear the very energy that stood abound and around us.

Nanu had this curiosity that was alive, and like her, I was eager and curious of the great mysteries that surrounded. I wanted to know the world like her, one that evoked so much question and challenge, even within a small girl like me. I soon came to understand that a desire to learn, to read, to comprehend eternity was an astonishing feat that most adults rather not engage a child intellectually. Nanu was not this way. She was patient, inquisitive of my instincts, and told me she liked witnessing a child's mind in conversation with itself. I don't think I understood until much older, until she was no longer by my side, how compelling it was to have an elder who believed in your capacity for profundity. Especially as a young girl. Still, that never let her define me. She said she found it illustrious, *intriguing* even, that I wanted to understand the plants like her, and I did. I wanted to understand the planets and the entire world, too.

The Qu'ran means that which is read, recited aloud. Nanu saw my intrigue as a resuscitating example of Allah's mark, a reflection of God's existence and ear. That I had been born was a great miracle. It seems my mother had not been ripe, like some women are, and before me, she would lose births consistently, a child would not stick. I wondered many years later if those premature deaths had been signs of an inopportune match. I had been told that we choose our parents, and perhaps this is true; how necessary it was for me to be born, so this sacred lineage could be passed down.

In many ways, nanu was not like the others. How?

Well, firstly, she was not hell-bent on delaying a husband's collapsing mortality—Tilottama had lost Dadabhai well before I was born. So, unlike other women her age, she had emerged decades prior, a woman unshackled by societal expectations, of all the baggage and grit that men bring. She was unphased and unreformed, lacking interest in a status quo that easily silenced women. She was uninterested in the way things were.

She could deliver the justice of an elder unlike other nanus, and because she was unwilling to marry me off, she decided, instead, to keep me close—both as her granddaughter-companion and also as her apprentice. She had much to teach me, so I knew, well enough, that I was lucky to be taught by a great woman like herself.

Other girls my age would not have been able to handle it; my mother couldn't. She was too lost in her own romantic imagination, but I was primed into precision by my grandmother's vision. She positioned me into a warrior like her, that made others scared of me. I liked it better that way, I enjoyed the silent intimidation that my body gathered. This meant I was also protected from the unwieldy gaze and desires of men, because I was granted her protection of me at all times. They didn't dare tempt themselves so they kept their eyes to the ground. Nanu would joke that this kept men chaste, as the Qu'ran asks men to be, to shield them from the torrent of their own unwieldy lust.

She fostered such intellectual resilience that it taught me many things about myself in the quietness of my mind, space I was given just to be a child, blooming in curiosity. As much as she fostered that intellectual infrastructure within me, she would also call me *amar choto babu*, "my little baby," in an endearing way, not in an infantilizing way, saying it with a care and affection that my own mother had never been able to give me in its entirety. It's not because Amma couldn't emote, or that she was withholding, but it was because her nerves were always present and that made her fearful, cowering, impotent—the fight of an animal caught and captured, a need to please and satiate men. This, I assumed, kept her trapped in place, immobile at times. As a daughter it was hard to watch, to see my father as the sun, and she, a flower depleted from his nurturance.

She had never been brave like Nanu, they were not made of the same cloth. I don't know why really, it was just something I had always known and it lingered in the air. Perhaps she felt the pressure of being the great Tilottama's only daughter and child, perhaps she wanted a simpler life, but my Amma's weakness was abundantly present, the calamity juxtaposed against the disappointment of someone's easily amended incapacity. She was not strong-willed, nor did she have patience for work. She was anxious but misdirected, following a flighty feeling rather than trusting or gathering her own self knowing. She wasn't someone who could surrender and accept. She would putter and sulk, believing she could worry herself into a different kind of disposition.

She wanted to be told what to do, but not by her mother. This made her permanently removed from reality and unwilling to comprehend a different fate for herself.

Observing this from birth, I was loving, but from a distance. If a child can't latch onto the security of her Amma, she will find a caretaker who will. I found Nanu in her stead.

There was something so voluptuous and otherworldly about my grandmother that I didn't understand my mother's refusal. She always knew of things before they would happen, and would often download prophetic dreams that were laced with self-interrogating clues and wisdom from different planes. "The commencement of the Divine Inspiration to Allah's Messenger (ﷺ) was in the form of good dreams which came true like bright daylight, and then the love of seclusion was bestowed upon him." Aunties came to her for romantic advice, for spiritual lessons of the future—she was a huge resource in any given scenario because she was equipped, she knew about Islam, of the plants, the spirits, the jinn, the world outside of this plane. Trained through her own accord, her own self-seeking, precise, and curious mind, she had a guttural knowledge of all things. They called her a healer, and this is something that provoked me into questioning what kind of life did I want to lead, to live? Who did I want to be?

When I would ask her, *Ai nanu, apni atho kichu kemon janen?* "Hey nanu, how do you know so much?" Her answer would always be, Eh atho chalak na, tui por na! "You're not very wise, why don't you read!"

I found her odd and disarming, charming even, not pallid and soft like my mother. Nanu's causticness was an elderly Bengali woman trait; she was powerful like a whip, funny too, brutal with her humor, languishing insults if she were ever in a bad mood. Yet, she was sympathetic mostly, kind, and delicate if she wanted something from you; in that sense, she was manipulative, but it was a dance, an art form, she was never cruel, and abhorred vindictiveness or the petty workings of others. She was constantly creating herself, saw her life as a small act of service, so she taught herself as much as she could contain in this lifetime to serve others with this depth of knowledge.

Her father was an astute man, Saqib Shaib. I had never known him, dead too long before I was born, but Tilottama told me it was her father who had insisted she look for more in the world around her, reminding her a husband would never truly fulfill her. He was a mystic, a man of the Qu'ran, a *hafiz* himself, who had venerable respect for the Prophet (ﷺ) and admired him greatly. At the same time, he was also a medicine man. He believed the surahs were magical verses translated into Arabic for the people, a direct instruction from God and the heavens. So he raised his daughter accordingly. Tilottama was educated on *tafsir*, poems by Jahanara Begum, and the teachings of Jameh ul-Tamseel, *The Collection of Fables* (التمثيل جامع) as Saqib Shaib was fluent in Persian as well as Arabic, and he adored the rambunctious, tantalizing tales and grand poetry of Imru' al-Qais and the allegorical animalistic fables of *Panchatantra*. By his own declaration, Tilottama was raised to believe that she could be anything, as there were many more folds in the universe than just this physical realm. He encouraged her to not lose sight of the ethereal, the unknown, all the currents of the world she could also understand and control, outside of this one. Dreams were important, and she began to read coffee and tea leaves young—as per instruction. She was ardent like this, bold-faced and deliberate as her abba had raised her to be. I guess I was similar enough, like her, a lightning strike, I was marked.

This quelled in my mother a fear that I would be taken into an unseemly life, a life of witchery. Yet, it was through my nanu that I was able to understand what existed out there for someone with my attributes.

Normalcy was not a path made for me, I was ladened with strangeness from infancy, making me seemly and cold to be around. I always wore my emotions on my face, which was unfortunate because I already had such a dramatic face. A recognizable one, too, one that left an imprint on the faculties of one's mind. It was through my face, this aura I had through etchings of my carvings— long aquiline nose, button-shaped at the tip, my mane hair long and crinkled, and through the tectonic shifts of my eyes, almond-shaped and bordered with long, thick lashes, I knew I provoked something in whomever could behold me. Brows thick, *kuch kuch kalo chul*, black, bountiful hair gave me the confidence I needed to disrupt the flow of existence I was lurched into in this lifetime. God made me magnetic, as there was no other way to survive such a plane. So, knowingly, decisively, I had to nurture this part of me—these unseemly qualities of a witch don't do well in such a harebrained society hellbent on reprisal, so I had to learn how to listen to the wind. Through this, I knew young that this society, of toil and of blood, was built on what it can take from you.

Amma, innocent, unseemly in the sense that nothing moved her outside of love. She hated the horrific realities of everyday life and longed to live in a constant mirage. How her mother was my Tilottama I will never know—but there was a sense of denial my mother had that was not passed down onto me, a resilient seeker of truth. She was arranged to wed my father at 15, as girls often were in Jessore, Hindu or Muslim. She was married to a good-learned man from a local mullah's family. My father, Abir Mahmoud, ten years older than she, was a *hafiz* from childhood as well, memorizing the Qu'ran and its united verses, long before I was born. Though his family did not have vast riches, they were educated, as all children of Allah often were, developing their quick minds and deliberation at *madrasas* shaped to engineer conversation, to encourage rigor, *tafsir*. My mother was no doubt enchanted by these residual benefits my father inherited, showcasing an intellectual freedom she longed for herself but was denied— perhaps out of fear, as clearly it was not out of circumstance. To be in the shadow of the eternal student her mother was, I think flattened her own understanding of herself; instead she chose a simpler life.

It is a shame, that even with a blueprint such as Tilottama, the imprint of feminine expectation was so distinct on my mother, that it was hard for her to latch out of the fragmentations. At least I know this now, how I was saved by my own impertinence, by my nursing of wounds and the ability to taste blood without drawing it gave me skills that were unworldly and thus unwanted. But I did not want to be a wanted warrior, I was born to be invisible. Not by time, here I keep my record. I'm livened with purpose here, on the page, speaking to you, but in my own lifetime, I was not seen as I should have been. In the end perhaps this is how I survived. I disappeared through the edges of history so that I could tell my own story through you, when the time was right. I've been waiting for more absolution, for my liberation.

Not all beings are made to be seen. Some are only meant to echo and chant something through the ether. For me, that was how I was best in service to others, and even while I was alive I knew this to be true. I knew this was my gift to the world, a way I could offer something concrete via my body, my legacy—my spirit. Some of us are only meant to be a sacrifice for something more, something else; some of us are only meant to communicate with others after death. There is functionality for us later, in the afterlife.

::Perhaps I am here to instruct, or maybe I am here just so you know my story::

My abilities made it so that if you looked at me for too long, my face's image would eventually disappear, transmuting into sand, blurring into another image elsewhere, shifting translucently. No matter how beautiful or striking I was, if I wanted—I could make you forget me. It was with the many skills taught to me through Tilottama's telepathy that I will now instruct you. Long before we left, and she died, we learned how to communicate together in the dreamtime. This eventually carried on into my waking life. It is now a skill I have, even in death. We are fortunate that we are given such planes to understand ourselves.

Soon after my apprenticeship had begun, I knew details of my Nanu's mind (at least all that she wanted to show) so that when she wanted to communicate with me, she had a direct line right into my soul. I would hear it, however, in my mind's ear, adjudicated to me via the amygdala, into a stream of consciousness that I could understand, like a whistle in my ear, she was so clear. Her thoughts soon became my own, as I absorbed her knowledge, metabolizing it deep into my soul.

I would often think of the story of Al-Harith bin Hisham, a steadfast warrior and companion of the Prophet, who asked Allah's Messenger (ﷺ) "O Allah's Messenger (ﷺ)! How is the Divine Inspiration revealed to you?" The Prophet (ﷺ) replied, "Sometimes it is (revealed) like the ringing of a bell." I did not pretend to be divine, anywhere near the exalted divinity of our Prophet (ﷺ), but I sought his guidance at all times, I sought his word. I wanted to be in a constantly evolved state, absorbing all the material and density around me.

There are some who don't believe that such things could be true, that powers bestowed in us by the sacred elements, by God, could be a mythological fiction rather than fact, tried truer than true. The magic is not for everyone, not all can wield it, like amma. So, instead, we are forced to believe these gifts aren't ours for the taking, but rather a satanic dance—instead of ritual with Allah, *subḥānahu wa-ta'ālā*, ritual with the cosmos and the deen. There was so much I did not understand, but Tilottama taught me to seek the mystery out and turn it around in my hand, to see that all things were possible.

Tilottama was a steely and strong woman, tall—while I was small. She wore her sari elegantly, but swift enough that it, too, could shift alongside her needs. It was a beautiful way to be, to exist mercurially like this, between planes, a constant chimera of changing needs. When you begin to harness magic, you must keep yourself aligned with God's principle so as to not be seduced by Shaytan's whisper. As much as I understood the shadow, I never immersed myself in it, I used an arrow to pull me from one point to the next, to clear myself through any confusion, *wudu* became constant, to be in the genuflection of God. My ability to see through the thick fog, unable to be hoodwinked for very long, *if at all*, was a trick Tilottama taught me through observation. Always carrying a Qu'ran handy, she, like my father, like her father as well, had memorized the Qu'ran—but young girls were not spirited to do such things—they were not nurtured to have their own interpretations of God. We are merely forced to succumb to what men think of Allah's decree, even when we know man is the furthest from divinity. No elegance could hide such an absolute fact. What they see in us as limitation is merely their own faultiness. But how to wrestle with an animal who has no logic? Who spits and steals and calls himself enlightened?

As I said, I was not like my mother in many ways, as amma had not inherited her mother's proverbial pearls, the distinctness of Tilottama's skills had not been passed down to Ferdaws, but instead to me, her only child and daughter. And, unlike my amma, I did not appraise the attention of men, this was my loophole. It's not that I did not desire their attention or glance, but that I had bigger priorities keeping me focused elsewhere. I was the carrier of our lineage's storm, and it would take my entire life to understand what to do with it all, how to harness something so evocative yet disregarded? How to transmute in the way I needed to be and to do in this lifetime?

Sometimes power skips a few generations until it hits the gong that will ding through the centuries, reverberating the cry of power that women have suppressed through a millennia out of fear of being burned as witches. But I am a witch and so was my mother's mother. I have no shame about that at all.

Yet I also knew, like amma knew, and feared, watching her mother live a crueler life. To me, instead, it was a life of dignity, of choice, of a self-command that I never wanted to lose. Yet life was tough for those like us, the self-sufficient types full of resolve. When I lost both abba and amma, becoming an orphan, unwanted and unknown, I realized that my path had taken me to a kind of loneliness I could have done without. I didn't know, but there was nothing that could be done. People can't choose their destiny. I had spent many lifetimes resisting. What I knew in this incarnation was that it was my duty to be in the muck of it all. To face the deluge.

I don't know where I heard it first, that word, *misery*. Like a cool steel punishment, I felt it. Maybe it was passed down to me through my mother's routine nightly oil swishing past my ears and down the nape of my neck, her astute fingers roving the warm oil through my upside-down hair. Though she was a pursuer of love, she spent most of her time lovesick, starved of my father's attention. I absorbed her entirely in those moments, taking on her pain like I was created as sympathy for her hardship. She leaned on me like a mother should not, and I became a vacuum for her sadness, for the losses she counted endlessly.

My amma loved me, I knew this because she told me so. Not everyone had the love of a mother and a devoted nani who wanted to shape you into the clarifying mold of destiny's command. Amma told me she'd passed down her sadness to me, and it was true, she had. She told me she had given me her hurt and I felt it like a torrid and ravaging wind inside of me; but what saved me was that I knew it was hers, all hers.

Nothing was my own, all of it had her misery's stain, and magic for me, perhaps, was a different encounter than this misery. I could choose my way out of it, or at the very least, choose a different path than my mother. It was a way I could work in my favor. Amma wanted to save me from the world, her fright was a way to take heed. She wanted to protect me from all that she had seen, thrust, and tricked into, of losing her freedom to a man. This became her only destiny.

Yet, my father, Abir Mahmoud, was no ordinary man either. He longed to be like the serene Muslim geographer Muhammad al-Idrisi. So he pursued the trail from Bengal to the tip of Africa, right to its center. Amma went with him to meet the Sanhaja Berbers and to find the great Sufi masters, she came with him, camel in tow, using guides and word of mouth to find those they sought, eventually moving up to Al-Andalus to see what it had in store. Abir Mahmoud was a man who longed to see the vast shores and to understand, with deeper knowledge, what stood beyond the edges of our civilization.

He was inspired by the great work *Nuzhat al-mushtāq fī ikhtirāq al-āfāq*, the atlas commissioned by the Norman King Roger II in 1138 and was detailed by al-Idrisi, looking towards Ptolemy's *Geography* and Abu Ma'shar al-Balkhi, the great astrologer of the Abbasid court, as men who carved a path through diligent and methodical documentation of human socialization of a specific time, to teach him more of what he didn't know. Longing to be influential as well, like his biggest hero of all, Ibn Khaldun, Abir Mahmoud wanted to make his concerted mark on literature and being. He was hungry to be in service.

Born and raised in Jessore, his great grandfather, Alauddin Isfahani, also known as Mirza Nathan, came to Bengal with Shaikh Alauddin Chisti, a Mughal who had brought the capital of Bengal from Rajmahal to Dhaka. Serving the Mughal army in Bengal, Isfahani was a historian, and wrote the *Baharistan-i-Ghaibi*, a text that chronicled the history from Bengal all the way to Cooch Behar to Assam and Bihar under the reign of Jahangir, the 4th Mughal emperor. Perhaps Abir Mahmood was living under the shadow of his ancestral lineage, as well, feeling ashamed of what he had not achieved, though having his ancestor's template. Abir Mahmoud's father, Sami-ul, was just a simple man, a man of God in the humblest sense. But not his son. There was an ambition in him to be something *more* that had always astounded me. In some ways, it reminded me of nanu, but it was misdirected, pushed away from self-discovery, and instead was something more external.

Baba was a mystic, a seeker, as well as a geographer, and astrologer—a man who wanted to understand himself amidst the sun and the stars— as well as the land, searching for that ethereal serenity that knowledge and discovery brought him. In that way, he was like his ancestors, in constant searching, and thus, inevitable documentation. Ferdaws wanted enlightenment as well, but more than anything she wanted love. Her naivety led to following a man with limited direction and an overgrown sense of self and responsibility, mixed in with an incessant obsession for meaning, but only what was outside of himself. With a child in tow, it is my father's unbridled curiosity which is what cost us our freedom.

It was there, in what is now called Senegal, that we were all captured, and taken to what they are now calling the Americas.

It is how an entire trajectory can change in a mere moment.

Being a traveler's daughter, it was normal that the world felt expanded and protracted. I had never known a boundary. It not was like what it's like now. Military checkpoints, border patrol officers—I observe this modern world of yours in horror, knowing how the ease of one's territorial existence, outside of warmongering, was once a state of being—you could just be, multifaceted with no territorial obligation.

I was young, but I will never forget what I witnessed on those ships.

Held on a terrifying island before being put on those ungodly vehicles, chained like animals, and whipped with no concern, it was there that my mother was punctured first with regret, sadness for the life she left behind her. The riches of her mother's garden, the chirrup sounds of the birds of Bengal, like the common yellow beaked *myna*, otherwise known as *shalik pakhi* or the *charai*, with its orange flame feathers. I knew she would miss the smell of *haleem* stewing, the shredded ginger melting from the heat, turning into a paste as it blended with the mutton and dhal in the midday heat. She would never again feel the fine silks on her skin, never feel the breadth of a sari across her belly again, that life was over.

So she wept those merciless months across the waters, a chorus of daily weeping, agony incarnate for the loss of life, everything stolen. He was not cruel, but I imagine he was an absent husband, leaving my mother to embody quarrels on her own. Tilottama told her not to go, *Ak kotha shoonish, eh chelake cheredish*, "I have one word, release your hold of this boy." She didn't listen, instead she threw herself at this lacuna of a man, believing love was possible, that all he needed was her love.

Witches

Michelle Tea is the publisher of DOPAMINE Books, and the author of the books *Modern Tarot* and *Modern Magic*, among others.

Yumi Sakugawa is a second-generation Japanese Okinawan inter-disciplinary artist based in Tongva land and the author of several books including *I Think I Am In Friend-Love With You, There Is No Right Way to Meditate,* and *Your Illustrated Guide to Becoming One With the Universe.* She is also the creator of *Cosmic Comfort*, an affirmation deck for caring for your soft and tender self as well as the well-being of the collective. Sagittarius sun, Aquarius rising, Virgo moon. @yumisakugawa

Kathe Izzo (she/they) is a conceptual poet, guide, & matriarch, raising her daughters & grandaughters on the Outer Cape for the past 35 years. Izzo is the originator of many social engagement communities, including The True Love Project, The Aliveness, & The MA Platform, a chain of continuous femme prayer circling the globe with love.

Emilia Richeson-Valiente is a performer, dancer, writer, and aerobics-witch! She's the founder of Pony Sweat, a dance aerobics project inspired by feminist-punk ethos. She lives in the San Gabriel Valley with her wife and pup.

Molly Larkey is a multidisciplinary artist and writer based in Los Angeles. Grounded in a vision of utopian possibility, their work explores word, image, and material to provoke radical shifts in perception. They have exhibited widely with museums and galleries internationally and their writing has been published with *Los Angeles Review of Books*, *Contemporary Art Review Los Angeles (CARLA)*, and *Haunt Journal of Art*. In 2019, they founded People's Pottery Project, a nonprofit ceramics initiative run by and for formerly incarcerated women, trans, and nonbinary people.

Ashley Molesso (she/her) is a queer artist who writes for fun. She is the other half of Ash + Chess, a queer and trans-owned stationery company, and is the co-author of *Queer Tarot: An Inclusive Deck & Guidebook* and has been published in *Erato Literary Mag*. She lives in the Hudson Valley.

Dori Midnight is a community care worker and healer, ritual artist, and writer re-enchanting traditions from her sephardic and ashkenazi lineages towards collective healing and liberation. Dori has maintained a psychic/intuitive healing practice for over twenty years, makes potions, teaches on magic as a liberatory practice, writes radical liturgy, weaves community ritual spaces, and makes good trouble for Palestinian liberation, prison abolition, and queer/trans liberation. dorimidnight.com

kai cheng thom is the author of six award-winning books in various genres, including the novel *Fierce Femmes and Notorious Liars: A Dangerous Trans Girl's Confabulous Memoir* and the poetry collection *Falling Back In Love With Being Human*. Kai Cheng is a recipient of the Stonewall Honor Book Award, the Publishing Triangle Award, and the Dayne Ogilvie Prize, among others. For four years, she wrote the advice column *Ask Kai: Advice for the Apocalypse* for *Xtra* magazine. In addition to her literary work, Kai Cheng has been widely recognized for work as a theorist, practitioner, and teacher of somatic trauma healing, conflict transformation, and Transformative Justice

TJ Payne is a writer, investigator, and behavioral analyst whose Substack, *Personally Curious*, unpacks the intricacies of human behavior and societal issues. His experience in investigative journalism and true crime writing informs his creative endeavors, including a suspenseful book project that weaves layered narratives with psychological depth.

Carolyn Pennypacker Riggs is an interdisciplinary artist and composer making solo and collective site-responsive performance, installation, and sculpture. She has presented work at High Desert Test Sites, the Getty Center, the Broad, Hammer Museum, REDCAT, MOCA LA, Anchorage Museum, and LA Public Works Triennial.

Shelley Marlow is a queer feminist American novelist, playwright, essayist, and artist. Marlow's work deals with gender, transformation, and magic. Marlow adapted the play, *Isobel, A Witch's Life,* from their manuscript, *The Wind Blew Through Like A Chorus of Ghosts.*

Ariel Gore is the author of *Rehearsals for Dying: Digressions on Love and Cancer* and other books.

Mya Spalter is a poet, an editor, a ghostwriter and the author of *Enchantments: A Modern Witch's Guide to Self Possession* (Random House, 2018/The Dial Press, 2022). She is a Cave Canem fellow and a member of the Sister Spit 25th anniversary tour. She's mostly a poet, but she's writing a novel anyway.

Emily Carr is a beach witch, love poet, Tarot reader, author of four collections of poetry, inventor of the poetry crossword, fitness coach, and recovering professor. She founded the MFA in Creative Writing at Oregon State University - Cascades and the BA in Creative Writing at the New College of Florida. These days she works as a Learning Design consultant for nectar, inc. and as the Progam Manager for Project PRIDE SRQ. Make Magic with Emily in person in Gulf Coast Florida or online via her Soul Floss Substack and her @dr_mle YouTube channel.

Rachel Yoder is the author of *Nightbitch*. She lives in Iowa City.

Kirk Read is the author of How *I Learned to Snap*. His analog collage has been featured in *Khora* and *Contemporary Collage Magazine*. He is a public health nurse in Portland and coleads the Pacific Northwest Collage Collective.

Mia Arias Tsang is a writer with a cat. Her first book, *Fragments of Wasted Devotion*, is out with Quilted Press in Feb 2025. She's a Sagittarius stellium —you can find her anywhere.

Cat Tyc is an interdisciplinary writer/artist. She lives in Hudson, NY.

Natalie Lima is a Cuban-Puerto Rican writer and a Professor of English at Butler University in Indianapolis. She is currently working on a coming of age memoir and an essay collection. Follow her happenings at natalielima09 and at <u>NatalieLima.com</u>.

Sophia Le Fraga is an interdisciplinary artist and the author of four books. Her work has been featured in *Best American Experimental Writing*, *BOMB*, *The Cut*, *Texte zur Kunst*, and *Dazed* and has been exhibited or performed at MOCA, United Artists Theatre, Greater NY, and Performa.

Adriana Rizzolo is an artist, teacher, and writer. She is the founder of Body Temple Church and the creator of Body Temple Dance. Adriana is a Taurus sun. She is a Gemini moon and Aquarius rising doing her sacred work liberating others to share their authentic creative and wild expressions as a spiritual mentor, somatic healer, adult sex educator, and movement ritualist.

Saskia Wilson-Brown is a Cuban-British-American artist based in Los Angeles. In 2012, she created The Institute for Art and Olfaction (IAO), a social art practice devoted to access and experimentation in perfumery. In addition to running the IAO, Saskia produces and hosts a radio show /podcast called *Perfume on the Radio*, is writing a book (released in Spring, 2026), and is working on her PhD exploring power relations and accessibility in the fragrance industry at University College Dublin's SmartLab.

Sarah Shin is weaving stories and practices engaging with dreams, myth, cosmic speculation, and transformation. Her collaborations include: *Bodies of Sound: Becoming a Feminist Ear* co-edited with Irene Revell; with artist Sammy Lee, *Mirror*, a video game that journeys through a mythical world of correspondences; and *Concrete Poetry* with architect Mark Lowe. She is a founder of Silver Press, the feminist publisher, and Spiral House, a new imprint for art, poetry, and ways of knowing; Ignota, the creative publishing and curatorial house that closed in 2024; and New Suns literary festival at the Barbican Centre.

Sarah Yanni's writing has appeared in the *Los Angeles Review of Books*, *Mizna*, *Wildness Journal*, *Autostraddle*, and others. She holds an MFA from CalArts.

Veronica Gonzalez Peña is a Mexican-born writer and filmmaker. She's the author of *twin time: or how death befell me*, *The Sad Passions*, and a book on the Mexican drug war, *So Far From God*, all published by semiotext(e). Her forthcoming memoir, *Notes on Disappearing: A Life in Fragments,* will be out next year.

Lily Burana is the author of four books, most recently *Grace For Amateurs: Field Notes on a Journey Back to Faith*. She holds a Master's Degree in Social Justice from Union Theological Seminary, and was awarded the school's Frederick Buechner Prize for Excellent in Writing. The great-great granddaughter of a Norwegian folk healer and herbalist, she is low-key witchy in New York's Hudson Valley.

Brooke Palmieri is a writer and artist based in Joshua Tree. His writing considers the past as a supernatural encounter, spanning hundreds of years of queer and trans history, and the magic, mystery, and erotics of working in archives. In October 2025 his first book, *Bargain Witch: Essays on Self-Initiation*, will be published by Dopamine. bspalmieri.com

Amanda Yates Garcia is a writer and public witch currently attaining a PhD at UCLA. Her work has been featured in *The New York Times*, *The LA Times*, *The SF Chronicle*, *The London Times*, *CNN*, *BRAVO*, as well as a viral appearance on *FOX*. Amanda hosts monthly moon rituals online, and the popular *Between the Worlds* podcast, which looks at the Western mystery traditions through a mythopoetic lens. Her book, *Initiated: Memoir of a Witch*, received a starred review from Kirkus and Publisher's Weekly and has been translated into six languages. To find out more visit *Mystery Cult with Amanda Yates Garcia*: www.amandayatesgarcia.substack.com

CAConrad has worked with the ancient technologies of poetry and ritual since 1975. They are the author of *Listen to the Golden Boomerang Return*, *Amanda Paradise*, and many other collections of poetry, teachings, and exercises and rituals.

Séamus Isaac Fey is a Trans writer from Chicago. Currently, he is the poetry editor at *Hooligan Magazine* and co creative director at Rock Pocket Productions. His debut poetry collection, *decompose*, is out with Not a Cult Media. You can find him on socials @sfeycreates.

Melissa Chadburn's debut novel, *A Tiny Upward Shove*, was published with Farrar, Straus, & Giroux in April 2022 and was longlisted for the PEN/Hemingway Debut Novel Award. Melissa is a worker lover and through her own work and literary citizenship strives to upend economic violence. Her mother taught her how to sharpen a pencil with a knife and she's basically been doing that ever since.

Callie Little (she/they) is a multidisciplinary human who travels and makes as much art as possible. Get her book and tarot deck, *Every Little Thing You Do Is Magic*, wherever books are sold. www.callielittle.com

Edgar Fabián Frías is a boundary-breaking multidisciplinary artist based in Los Angeles with degrees in Psychology, Studio Art, and an MFA in Art Practice from UC Berkeley. Their immersive works blend diverse artistic disciplines, challenging conventional categories. Frías explores resiliency and radical imagination through Indigenous Futurism, spirituality, and queer aesthetics.

Myriam Gurba is a writer and activist. Her first book, the short story collection *Dahlia Season*, won the Edmund White Award for debut fiction. O, the Oprah Magazine, ranked her true crime memoir *Mean* as one of the best LGBTQ books of all time. *Creep*, her most recent book, was a finalist for a National Book Critics' Circle award in criticism, and won the Lambda Literary Award for Bisexual Nonfiction. She is a co-founder of Dignidad Literaria, a grassroots organization committed to combatting racism in the book world. She is active in the anti-rape movement.

Ingrid Rojas Contreras is the author of *The Man Who Could Move Clouds*, a 2023 finalist for the Pulitzer Prize, National Book Award, and National Book Critics Circle Award. Her debut novel, *Fruit of the Drunken Tree*, was the silver medal winner in First Fiction from the California Book Awards.

Frankie Miren is a witch, a writer, and a long-time hooker. She is the author of *The Service* and *Morbid Obsessions* and she lives with her cat in a house full of fir cones and feathers by the sea in England.

Fariha Róisín is a writer, culture worker, and educator. She is the author of *Survival Takes a Wild Imagination*; *Who is Wellness For?* and other works of poetry, fiction, and creative non-fiction.